I can satisfy them. I have met a number of my old pals in here who knew me years ago. I still have my perpetual grouch and I don't believe it will ever wear off until I pass out completely. That time can't come too quick to suit me. Just at present I pass my time in sleeping, eating, working, reading and thinking. And the last is not the least.

I have wondered about you a number of times and since reading your letter, the thought has occured to me that you may be keeping house or getting ready to. The name sounds English. Kind of musical too. I had hopes that you would by this time have found yourself in a better job with more congenial surroundings and a cleaner atmosphere. Take my tip and drop that job like you would poison. Thats no kind of a job for you. Your built for better things than that. How is your literary lady friend and yourself getting along in your writing the Biography of the meanest man you ever knew. I have been passing my time away by scribbling a bit now and then. So far I have written about 30 or 40 thousand words. Should you ever come to this place and if you cared for it I would gladly make you a present of my little contribution to the worlds worst literature. You owe me nothing but I consider myself under some obligation to you.

Well, I'll wind up this tale of woe, by saying So Long and best wishes.

I am very truly

Carl Panzram #31614.
Box 7.
Leavenworth.
Kansas.

A letter from Carl Panzram, "the meanest man you ever knew,"
Henry Lesser ("Henry James").
This letter was written seventeen months before Panzram's exec
hanging on September 5, 1930.

KILLER
A JOURNAL OF MURDER

KILLER

KILLER
A JOURNAL OF MURDER

THOMAS E. GADDIS & JAMES O. LONG

THE MACMILLAN COMPANY

The Macmillan Company
866 Third Avenue, New York, N.Y. 10022
Collier-Macmillan Canada Ltd., Toronto, Ontario

Library of Congress Catalog Card Number: 74-129749

FIRST PRINTING

Printed in the United States of America

ACKNOWLEDGMENTS

The authors owe a special debt to many who helped in this project. We thank the late Harry Elmer Barnes, Helen Bilkie, Patricia Byrd, Stanley A. Furman, Martha Gaddis, Tom Garrity, the late Warden Clarence T. Gladden, Jerome P. Harkins, Catherine Howatt, William Kennedy, Arthur Lerner, Sidney Lezak, Ruby Long, Austin MacCormick, Richard Marek, Robert Markel, C. Dudley Martin, Karl Menninger, J. S. Murray, Patrick O'Rafferty, Orville B. Pung, Negley K. Teeters, Leonard Thompson, James Welch and Donald P. Wilson.

Thanks also are accorded to those who must remain unnamed, and also to the many authorities and sources who responded to our inquiries.

T. E. G.
J. O. L.

Distrust all in whom the impulse to punish is powerful.

—Nietzsche

PROLOGUE

I started doing time when I was eleven years old and have been doing practically nothing else since then. What time I haven't been in jail I have spent either getting out or getting in again.

What you have done and are doing to me, you are also doing to others. What I have done to you, many others also do to you. Thus, we do each other as we are done by.

I have done as I was taught to do. I am no different from any other. You taught me how to live my life, and I have lived as you taught me. If you continue teaching others as you taught me, then you as well as they must pay the price, and the price is very expensive. You lose your all, even life.

Now, you who do not know me or my wishes, you decide without consulting me in any way; you start to try to revoke the judgment of a legally constituted court and the sentence that was pronounced on me. I tell you now that the only thanks you or your kind will ever get from me for your efforts on my behalf is that I wish you all had one neck and that I had my hands on it.

I have no desire whatever to reform myself. My only desire is to reform people who try to reform me. And I believe that the only way to reform people is to kill 'em.

I may leave here at any time for some big house, mad house or death house, but I don't give a damn where they put me. They won't keep me long because no power on earth can keep me alive and in jail for very much longer. I would kind of like to finish writing this whole business in detail before I kick off so that I can explain my side of it even though no one ever hears or reads of it except one man. But one man or a million makes no difference to me. When I am through I am all through, and that settles it with me.

In my lifetime I have murdered 21 human beings, I have committed thousands of burglaries, robberies, larcenies, arsons and last but not least I have committed sodomy on more than 1,000 male human beings. For all of these things I am not the least bit sorry. I have no conscience so that does not worry me. I don't believe in man, God nor Devil. I hate the whole damned human race including myself.

If you or anyone else will take the trouble and have the intelligence or patience to follow and examine every one of my crimes, you will find that I have consistently followed one idea through all of my life. I preyed upon the weak, the harmless and the unsuspecting.

This lesson I was taught by others: might makes right.[1]

Carl Panzram #31614.

From a letter written by Karl Menninger to James Long:

YOU HAVE been so patient and persistent in trying to get something from me about the Panzram case that I have chosen this dark day, June 6, 1968 (Robert Kennedy having died this morning), to tell you about a man who felt that he was too evil to live.

I saw him at the request of a federal official. He sat in the anteroom of the federal court on a cold spring day in Topeka—his arms and legs in irons and five policemen standing around him. He was bald and burly, and in the impressionistic photo gallery of my memory, the skin of his scalp was mottled. I remember how brawny he was and how fiercely he talked.

At one point I told him that in spite of how bad, terrible, vicious, ruthless and cruel he might be he really didn't frighten me: I didn't believe he would hurt me since I had done nothing to hurt him.

His answer was characteristic of our interview. He leaped forward as far as his chains would allow him, he shook them and startled the police officers and me, too. "Take these off of me for three minutes," he said "and I'll show you. I'll kill you right before their eyes, before they can stop me. You wouldn't have time to be scared. Take them off me and see."

Without hesitation he told me of murder after murder that he had committed. Then he went on in further diatribe about the incurable evilness of mankind, justifying complete extinction, including himself.

> No one can read [Panzram's] manuscript in its entirety without an emotional thrill. On the one hand, there was

> the terrific hate, bitterness and incredibly sadistic cruelty of the man; on the other hand, his clear evaluation of himself, his wistful faith in and affection for one federal official . . . [and] his curious interest in bettering the world in spite of his feeling that nearly all human beings were so bad that it would be better if they were all killed. It was an incongruous picture of stark reality which produced an effect comparable to that of gazing into the interior of a human body torn open in some horrible accident, with all the vital organs laid bare, the person retaining consciousness with a superhuman ability to endure pain so that he could calmly discuss the accident and his approaching death.[2]

I carried away a vivid image of this earnest, very intense, very profane, very ugly, but obviously thoughtful individual faced with the problem of evil in himself and in the rest of us. He was a remarkable man in his fierceness, in his restless mental activity and his great embitteredness. I have always carried him in my mind as the logical product of our prison system.

Karl Menninger, M.D.

I

CARL PANZRAM scrawled out his life on lined paper with a pencil stub in the Washington, D. C., jail during the fall of 1928. He pushed it a few pages at a time through the bars of an Isolation cell, late at night, into the hands of a fledgling guard, Henry Lesser.

Panzram had been caught loosening the window bars of the cell. For this offense he was tortured. When Panzram was returned to his cell, Lesser, on a friendly impulse, gave the half-conscious prisoner pocket money.

"You are one of the very few people I do not wish to harm," he wrote to Lesser, after their acquaintance deepened, and he continued with a full confession.

Carl Panzram was thirty-six then, a bearlike man with smoky gray eyes and a noticeable limp. He was awaiting trial for housebreaking and the theft of a radio. He revealed that although he had never been arrested for murder, he had killed more people than he could remember.

Panzram and Lesser must have resonated something deep in one another, because Henry Lesser, for the next forty years, became a kind of Ancient Mariner of penology, stopping any who would heed in his effort to get Panzram's curious chronicle before the world. Many well-known writers and penologists have felt the urgent buttonholing of Lesser and his burden.

Henry Lesser stopped me in 1956. He was then a clothing salesman in Los Angeles, a well-preserved man with iron-gray, curly hair. His strangely troubled eyes, the whites showing around gray irises, were magnified by heavy glasses. I read Panzram's confession and wrote a summary version for a national magazine.[3] At that time, no publisher would consider the gross detail of this saga of punishment and hate. Then the assassination of President Kennedy followed by the death of Oswald, the mass murders by Whitman and Speck and the serial horror of the Boston Strangler fixed the eye of the country upon the man who acts out hate. Other murders and assassinations followed. At the same time, our language grew untrammeled and more direct, even as the multiplying young looked at our world and began to turn away.

Henry Lesser persisted, and now in our crowded crimson room of overkill and eroticized violence, Panzram's account will sit as an early portrait. It describes the subculture of sadism and punishment which was stitched into the underbelly of an earlier America. For the young, this account may tell something of how it was to be alive in an earlier setting of violence.

Panzram is able to explain what it is like to kill and why he came to do it. There is in him something of the unbreakable personality who is unendingly punished. It is not hard to think of him lying restless in his unnamed grave until "his side of it" is told. Perhaps this telling will put a quietus on him, and will bring the long journey of Henry Lesser to its end.

The reader should note that the passages set in distinctive type are Panzram's own words; we have corrected some of his spellings and punctuated some of his clauses. The unadorned impact of his account can be had by reading his confession, but we have written around it in order to portray Carl Panzram's world as he lived in it. We have added more detail of the major turning points of his career and have continued his story after his own narrative has ended. Although his formal confession closes in 1928, he was still writing about American prisons during the time that was left for him. To this date, no major statement in his confession has been disproved.

Some of the names have been changed. Notes in considerable detail are provided, which will be found in the back of the book. We have tried to feel free and unrestricted in these notes, citing research and dealing with various questions dredged up by this venture. It is a setting known to few.

II

This is a true statement of my actions, including the time and places and my reasons for so doing these things, written by me of my own free will at the District Jail, Washington, D. C., November 4, 1928.

I was born June 28, 1891, on a small farm in Minnesota. My parents were of German descent. Hardworking, ignorant and poor. The rest of the family consisted of five brothers and one sister, all of whom are dead except three of us brothers and our sister.

All of my family are as the average human beings are. They are honest and hardworking people. All except myself. I have been a human animal ever since I was born. When I was very young at five or six years of age I was a thief and a liar. The older I got the meaner I got.

My father and mother split up when I was about seven or eight years old. The old man pulled out one day and disappeared. This left my mother with a family of six on a small worked-out farm. As fast as the older boys grew up, they also pulled out. One died. This left me, my sister, one older brother, and my mother. My sister and I were sent to school during the days, and as soon as we came home in the evenings, we were put to work in the fields where my older brother and mother were always at work, from daylight until long after dark sometimes. My portion of pay consisted of plenty of work and a sound beating every time I looked cock-eyed or done anything that displeased anyone who was older and stronger and able to catch me and kick me around whenever they felt like it, and it seemed to me and still does now that everything was always right for the one who was the strongest and every single thing that I done was wrong. Everybody said so anyway. But right or wrong I used to get plenty of abuse. Everybody thought it was all right to deceive me, lie to me and kick me around whenever they felt like it, and they felt like it pretty regular. That is the way my life was lived until I was about eleven years old.

At about that time I began to suspect that there was something wrong about the treatment I was getting from the rest of the human race. When I was about eleven years old, I began to hear and see that there were other places in this world besides my own little corner of it. I began to realize that there were other people who lived nice, easy lives, and who were not kicked around and worked to death.

I decided that I wanted to leave my miserable home. Before I left I looked around and figured that one of our neighbors who was rich and had a nice home full of nice things, he had too much and I had too little. So one night I broke into his home and stole everything that to my eyes had the most value.

Those things were some apples, some cake, and a great big pistol. Eating the apples and cake and carrying the pistol under my coat, I walked to the railroad yards where I caught a freight train going to the West where I intended to be a cowboy and shoot Indians. But I must have had my wires crossed because I missed my connections somewhere. Instead of going out and seeing the world, I was caught, brought back home and beaten half to death, then sent to jail and from there to the Minnesota State Training School at Red Wing, Minnesota. Right there and then I began to learn about man's inhumanity to man.

The hearing that ended in young Carl's quick commitment was held in the Municipal Court of East Grand Forks, a tough sawmill town on the Red River, less than a hundred miles from Canada. E. J. Sullivan, the part-time town judge, may have been influenced in his disposition of the case by recalling Carl's previous appearance at the age of eight on a charge of being drunk.[4]

Carl had not yet been born when his parents and four older brothers arrived in the small Minnesota community in 1888. The Panzrams were immigrants rather than pioneers, the first in a new class of European poor whose increasing numbers aroused fear in native Americans. The prejudice that the new arrivals faced would strain a marriage already beset by troubles.

John Panzram, Carl's father, was a tall, violent-tempered man who wore a walrus moustache of the type popular in his native East Prussia. He had fought through the Franco-Prussian war, mustered out as a sergeant and shipped for

America to make his fortune on the frontier, where he found that homesteading opportunities had all but vanished. Foreigners were eagerly sought after only for the mines, tenement factories and railroad construction.

Deeply resentful, John Panzram escaped the teeming ghettos of the East and worked his way to the upper Midwest. He joined the German community at Sauk Centre, Minnesota, where he took a job as a farm laborer, renewed his dreams and married a young German-born girl named Mathilde Elizabeth Bolden. Lizzie, as she called herself, was to be Carl's mother.

Lizzie had spent her early years in Berlin and came to America with her parents at the age of thirteen. She was reared in a strict German Lutheran household, and she matured into a self-reliant, industrious woman. She centered her life around the Lutheran church, reinforcing her piety with an iron disposition that was to bode ill for her marriage.

The newlyweds moved two hundred miles northwest to Marshall County, where they made a down payment on a farm. John's enthusiasm lasted through the first drought. Soon he was leaving his young wife alone to tend chores on the lonesome spread as he visited nearby Warren to hear gossip about homesteading opportunities in Canada. Lizzie claimed later that John was more prone to dream than to face the hard realities of the farm. There were noisy quarrels as John made plans for a new move.

This was not to be, however, for Lizzie announced she was expecting their first child. John reluctantly set his hand to the plow as Lizzie's pregnancy advanced and she gave birth to a son.

Their new son, Paul, was a handsome boy with blue

eyes and a cleft chin like his father's. Quiet and reserved, Paul would little resemble Carl, the strange brother yet to be born, whose restlessness would mirror his father's and whose unmet demands for attention would win him annoyance in the harsh setting of a disintegrating family. Paul was followed quickly by a second son, Albert, and then by Louis, a taciturn, pious boy who was to be Lizzie's favorite.

John Panzram, meanwhile, grew moodier and still more restless as he saw his dreams buried under growing responsibilities and a job in the sawmill. There were hard times when on two occasions the mill burned down.

Lizzie was expecting their fourth child, Louise, when they decided to move to a farm in order to help make ends meet. On October 25, 1888, the Panzrams took a seven-percent mortgage on a small house and two and a half acres along the Red River, south of town.

The move, however, did little to relieve the family's deepening poverty. There were more ugly scenes as John Panzram drank away his mill wages and fell behind in his payments on the farm. On August 16, 1890, with Carl's birth less than a year away, the farm was sold at auction on the courthouse steps in Crookston, the county seat. John scraped together $218.10 and redeemed the farm on July 23, 1891, a month after Carl was born.

Carl was the last child. Lizzie was in her forties, now having high blood pressure and dizzy spells, facing a change of life, but toiling with her children every day in the tired soil of the truck farm. Young Carl must have screamed pink-fisted for the attention no one could give him, and from his earliest years he saw only trouble as the family began to fall apart under the economic blight of increasing hardship.

Beginning in 1892, the country moved into the worst financial depression thus far in its history. Wage cuts, strikes, lockouts and violent repression marked the era. Prices were low, equipment high. In this harsh-weathered land, a man could be hired for twenty dollars a month plus board. Horses were sent to the woods during the winter, where loggers rented them to snake timber into the Red Lake River. Farmers used axes, scythes and shovels. Everything was done by hand.

East Grand Forks, however, had fifty-three saloons and a red-light district to slake the thirst of visitors from North Dakota, the dry state across the river. Lumber was cut and freighted over the Great Northern to Minneapolis. The consequences of the rape of the forests were beginning to be felt. By 1900, when Carl Panzram was nine, four-fifths of the standing forests of the United States had been cut down.

When John Panzram disappeared, his sons Albert, Paul and Louis were left to help Lizzie with the farm and care for Louise and Carl. The Panzram boys were like their father—big, rough, rawboned, hotheaded and roving. Paul and Louis left the farm. Albert quit school to help, but he was unable to keep away from the lively poolrooms and night life of the town. He stood six feet four inches and later became a policeman.

Carl's toys were a shovel and a hoe, and he looked up to a phalanx of strong brothers and a desperate struggle to live with his sister in the fatherless household. Carl was ill often. He went to school and managed to learn to read. He became a holy terror and was beaten for it. He faced reform school at twelve.

Now, on the trip to Red Wing, young Carl rode topside on the railroad as a legitimate passenger and ward of the state; this was his last official trip for many years. He watched the autumn countryside blaze with dying leaves, oak, willow and sumac, and stared with disbelief as the train rolled through Minneapolis and thence along the young Mississippi to the outskirts of Red Wing. There he saw, spread out on a bluff overlooking the river, surrounded by huge well-clipped lawns, great churchlike stone buildings with tall, narrow windows. He was brought into the administration building, which was marked by a spired tower with a round porthole.

The entrance records for the twelve-year-old Carl in 1903 list him as without infirmity, forty-seven and one-half inches tall, ninety-five pounds, unmarked except for a mastoid operation scar behind his left ear.[5] Father, living; address, unknown; character, poor; religion, blank. Mother, gardener; character, good; education, poor. Conjugal relation of parents, quarrelsome; previous environment, bad; character of associates, bad; habits, bad; education, fifth grade; moral susceptibility, blank.

These were hardly the details he would remember twenty-five years later in writing his impressions of the time he spent in the not-untypical state training school in Red Wing.

When I first went to the Minnesota State Training School, I was about twelve years old, lively, healthy and very mischievous, innocent and ignorant. The law immediately proceeded to educate me to be a good, clean, upright citizen and a credit to the human race.

They trained me all right in that training school. There during my two years I was trained by two different sets of people to have two different sets of morals. The good people tried to train me to be good and the bad people did train me to be bad. The method that the good people used in training me was to beat goodness into me and all the badness out of me. They done their best but their best wasn't good enough to accomplish what they set out to do. The more they beat me and whipped me, the more I hated them and their damn religion.

In that school there were about 250 boys ranging in age from seven or eight years old up to twenty-one. These boys were divided up into five companies or cottages. Each company was in charge of a manager and a matron. I was first put in Cottage No. 2. The manager's name was John Moore. The matron's name was Miss Martin. And a fine pair of Christians they were to have in charge of a lot of young boys to train. My first reception at the school was to be met by Mr. John Moore who told me the rules. Next he called me into his room to take my pedigree for an oral and physical examination to be put on the records of the institution. He began the oral examination by asking me my name, parents, habits, schooling, home life and history of my associations. He asked me if my father was insane, was he a drunkard, was he lazy or industrious. He asked me if my mother was a prostitute or a drunkard, was she educated or ignorant. After asking me all these questions and explaining in detail just what each question meant and all about it, he then stripped me naked and began my physical examination, looking to see if I was lousy or had any kind of sickness or disease. He examined my penis and my rectum, asking me if I had ever committed fornication or sodomy or had ever had sodomy committed on me or if I had ever masturbated. He explained in detail and very thoroughly just what he meant by these things. That began my education. I have learned a little more since.

This Mr. Moore was a Christian, very much so. I was taught to pray when I got out of bed in the mornings, to say grace at each meal and give thanks to the Lord after it. We sang a hymn at each meal. A Bible lesson every evening before bedtime, and then just before bedtime to say another prayer. On Sundays we were sent to Sunday school in the morning and church in the afternoon. Oh, yes, we had plenty of church and religion all right. I used to be pretty ignorant and not able to read very well so I always had a hard job learning my Sunday school lessons. For failure to learn these lessons I was given a whipping. During the first year I was there I used to get a beating every Saturday night and sometimes three or four more during the week for doing something I wasn't supposed to do or for not doing something that I was supposed to do. Oh, yes, I had plenty of abuse. They had various methods of punishing us for doing wrong and for teaching us to do right. The most popular with them was to take us to the "Paint Shop," so called because there they used to paint our bodies black and blue.

The Paint Shop was a very ingenious contrivance for inflicting the worst punishment where it would do the least harm and the most good. They used to have a large wooden block which we were bent over and tied face downward after first being stripped naked. Then a large towel was soaked in salt water and spread on our backs from the shoulders to the knees. Then the man who was to do the whipping took a large strap about ¼ of an inch thick by 4 inches and about two feet long. This strap had a lot of little round holes punched through it. Every time that whip came down on the body the skin would come up through these little holes in the strap and after 25 or 30 times of this, little blisters would form and then burst, and right there and then hell began. The salt water would do the rest. About a week or two later a boy might be able to sit down. Maybe, if he didn't sit down on anything harder than a feather pillow. I used to get this racket regularly, and when I was too ill to be given that sort of medicine, they used to take a smaller strap and beat me on the open palms of my hands. While the other boys were playing ball, skating or swimming, I used to be given a Sunday school lesson and made to stand at attention with my arms folded and my back to the field where the boys were all playing and enjoying themselves. Sometimes a dozen of us at a time would be lined up like that. We were all supposed to go to school a half a day and work half a day and the rest of the time learn how to love Jesus and be good boys. Naturally, I now love Jesus very much. Yes, I love him so damn much that I would like to crucify him all over again.

At that time I was just learning to think for myself. Everything I seemed to do was wrong. I first began to think that I was being unjustly imposed upon. Then I began to hate those who abused me. Then I began to think that I would have my revenge just as soon and as often as I could injure someone else. Anyone at all would do. If I couldn't injure those who injured me, then I would injure someone else.

The boys in Cottage No. 2 became accustomed to seeing Carl led away for "spankings."[6] The school's officers carried around pads of disciplinary report forms, which made it easy to report infractions. Carl's hostility made the staff aware and anxious. Each offense caused him to lose credits (spelled "loose" by the alert Mr. Moore). His first offense was failure to fold a napkin properly, but this soon escalated under punishment to "bad work," calling another boy a "snitch," "kicking another boy," "filling his hat with sugar from the dining room," "not telling that he was short of cups in the dining room but letting the officers wait without them," using "impudent and bad language," "breaking two dishes," "whistling and amusing himself instead of practicing his music lessons," and (later) for "attempted escape."

Panzram as a young miscreant invariably admitted his offenses, took beatings and became angrier as his muscles toughened under punishment. Thus began the fateful equation of Panzram's life which he expresses above. Few have translated this dark wager into the literal terms that Panzram did. The significance of this was lost upon the overworked, morally indignant staff, which consisted mainly of local native "corncobbers," who gravitate to such work. Two-thirds of the boys in the training school in 1904 were immigrant children, many of whom spoke English poorly or not at all. The antiforeign feeling of the native staff found a ready outlet in punishment of the ruffian-like, unappreciative children of "foreigners." Misconduct was viewed as evidence of ingratitude.

It was under the secure cover of "moral duty" that the secret pleasures of inflicting physical pain were enjoyed by bored and hungry members of the institutional staff.[7]

One bit of staff creativity in Red Wing was a paddling machine. A mechanically inclined custodian rigged up a kind of spinning jenny, outfitted with paddles which swung when a crank was turned. There is no evidence that the machine really worked well enough to make use of it.

I was too dumb to learn anything in school so they took me out and put me to work all day washing dishes and waiting on table in the officer's dining room. Right here I began to get a little revenge on those who abused me. When I served the food to some of the officers, I used to urinate in their soup, coffee or tea and masturbate into their ice cream or dessert and then stand right beside them and watch them eat it. They enjoyed it too because they told me so. I wish they could read this now.

Once each week I used to be sent to the laundry to get the clean linen for the dining room. One [cold winter] day I went there and didn't come back—not right away. I attempted to escape, but got caught, brought back and damn near beaten to death. But they put me back to work in the officer's dining room. The next thing I tried to do was to poison that Mr. John Moore by putting rat poison in his rice pudding. But they caught me, beat me and put me out of the dining room and into the band. There, the first day I learned to play one note and never learned one since.

About that time I began to try to figure out some way to punish those who punished me. The only thing I could figure out was to burn down the building in which the Paint Shop was located. This I did. I got a long, thick piece of heavy cotton string, wrapped it around and around a long, round stick, lit one end of it and hid it in the laundry near some oil-soaked rags. That night the whole place burned down at a cost of over $100,000.[8] Nice, eh?

Some of the boys who were cleverer than I finally put me wise to how I should perform if I ever wanted to get out of that joint. They told me to act like I was a very good boy, tell everybody I met how much I loved Jesus, and how I wanted to go home and be a good boy, go to school and learn to be a preacher. I done just as they suggested and I am damned if it didn't work out just as slick as hot grease through a tin horn. I was called before the parole board one day, and there I told them all the lies and hot air I could and they gave me a parole and let me go home. In that way I first found out how to use religion as a cloak of hypocrisy to cover up my rascalities. One of the boys who showed me how to fool the law was a boy by the name of Ogilvie. He became the Chief or Captain of Police in either Minneapolis or St. Paul.

That Mr. John Moore was dishonorably discharged from his job as Company Commander of Second Company, M.S.T.S., by the then head superintendent, a Mr. Lowell, who fired him for committing some kind of immoral act on some of the boys under his care. This same Mr. Lowell was himself later dishonorably discharged for the brutal and inhuman treatment of the boys under his charge. All of these things are on file among the records of the M.S.T.S. at Red Wing and can be verified by anyone who cares to look the facts up.

After serving about two years there, I was pronounced by the parole board to be a nice, clean boy of good morals, as pure as a lily and a credit to those in authority in the institution where I had been sent to be reformed. Yes, sure, I was reformed all right, damn good and reformed too. When I got out of there I knew all about Jesus and the Bible—so much so that I knew it was all a lot of hot air. But that wasn't all I knew. I had been taught by Christians how to be a hypocrite and I had learned more about stealing, lying, hating, burning and killing. I had learned that a boy's penis could be used for something besides to urinate with and that a rectum could be used for other purposes than crepitating. Oh yes, I had learned a hell of a lot from my expert instructors furnished to me free of charge by society in general and the State of Minnesota in particular. From the treatment I received while there and the lessons I learned from it, I had fully decided when I left there just how I would live my life. I made up my mind that I would rob, burn, destroy, and kill everywhere I went and everybody I could as long as I lived. That's the way

I was reformed in the Minnesota State Training School. That's the reason why. What others may have learned by the same sort of treatment in other and similar institutions, I don't know, but this I do know, that in later years I have met thousands of graduates of those kinds of institutions and they were either in, going into or just leaving jails, prisons, mad houses, or the rope and electric chair was yawning for them as for me.

What school authorities thought was a change in the fourteen-year-old Panzram boy took place late in 1905. His last of the twenty-seven formally reported misconduct reports—whispering in school—was logged October 2. In January, the board released him to the care of his mother. She had sold their farm and rented a small house and truck garden within walking distance of the Immanuel Lutheran Church, across the river in Grand Forks, North Dakota. Sorrowing over the loss of her favorite son, Louis, in a drowning accident, she was joined by her first-born, Albert, now a full-grown, hard-living man, six feet four inches tall and soon to become one of the town police. He would be the last "father" to the strange delinquent returning on the train from Red Wing.

IV

When I was discharged from the school I was given a suit of clothes, five dollars in money, a ticket to my home and a million dollars' worth of good advice.[9] This advice I threw in the first ash can with my Bible and Sunday school lessons and report cards. The five dollars I spent on the train for candy, fruit and a bellyache. The ticket I used to ride as far as my home. The suit was taken away from me as soon as I got home. In exchange I was given a pair of overalls and a hoe, taken to the field, told to earn my keep by work and the sweat of my brow. That didn't sound good to me so I told my folks that I wanted to go to school and study to be a preacher and save souls. I put up such a hot line of talk that it was decided to send me to a German Lutheran school[10] where the minister taught German to kids in the basement on weekdays and saved souls on Sunday in the same church.

This scheme worked fine for about a couple of months and then the kids began to point their finger at me and yell "reform school" every time I passed by. Then I started knocking their blocks off every time I could catch one alone. They told their parents who told mine who in turn told the German preacher to do his duty by me. He did. He started whipping me fairly regular, but I was a pretty big boy and very strong, and one day when he started beating me, I came back at him and gave him a good scrap, but he was too much for me so he won that time. But I had learned a thing or two by then. One of them was a little piece of poetry about a Colonel Colt:

> *Be a man either great or small in size,*
> *Colonel Colt will equalize.*

With that idea in my mind I looked around until I found a kid who had a big, old-fashioned, heavy caliber Colt pistol. I got it. The next day at daylight I stole one of my brother's vests, put the big pistol in the inside pocket, and went to school, and the first crack out of the box after school opened up I gave the preacher-teacher warning to lay off of me or I would fix him. I guess he took it for granted that I was bluffing or incapable of carrying out my threats, so instead of leaving me alone he immediately got his whip and ordered me to the front for punishment. I refused to leave my seat. He came down and tried to pull me out but I held on with both hands and feet. Then he started beating me over the head and shoulders with the whip, and at the same time yanking at my coat and vest collar to pull me out. The buttons on the vest gave out before I did. The preacher gave a yank. The buttons on the vest tore loose, and the pistol fell on the ground and the preacher with it. He fell on his big, fat caboose with his mouth wide open and his eyes as big as saucers. He was paralyzed with surprise and fear. All he could say was, "*Mein Gott,* a gun, a gun." I was not surprised or afraid. I was mad as hell. I jumped out of my seat, grabbed the gun and pointed it at him right between his horns and pulled the trigger two or three times but it wouldn't go off. The school was in an uproar, and during the excitement I figured it was a good time for me to go somewhere else. I did. I went home. I thought I was a hero and I figured they would kill the fatted calf for me as I told my story. Instead of killing the fatted calf, they damn near killed me. They had heard the other side of the story first, and before I had a chance to tell my end of it, I got a wallop alongside of the coco that floored me, and the next I knew was that my older brother had me by the throat choking me to make me tell where I had hidden the gun. I told him and he went out of the back door to look for it I went out of the front door to look for another one to shoot him with. I have never seen him since except once for a very short time. That night I resumed my journey to the West that had been cut short two years before. I didn't want to be a preacher any more. I wanted to be a cowboy and shoot me a few wild Indians and tame preachers. That's more than twenty years ago but I have been a cowboy since. I never shot any wild Indians but I did shoot a tame preacher once, but this happened many years later. At my second attempt to run away from home to go out and see the world, I was a little more successful. Since then I have been all over the world. I have seen it all, and I don't like what I have seen of it. Now I want to get out of this damned world altogether.

I was about 13 or 14 years old at the time I left. In theory if not in actual practice, I already knew how to get by in the world. What I didn't know I soon learned. I started out a hobo and soon learned to ride freight trains and passenger trains, inside and out, without paying fare. For the first three or four months after I left home, I hoboed my way to the Pacific Coast and all over the West, sleeping in box cars, barns, sheds, haystacks or most anywhere at all. My eating I got by begging and telling people lies and hard-luck stories about how I was a poor orphan and how much I loved Jesus, how I wanted to go this place or that place, whichever way I happened to be going at that time. That's where my rich uncle lived who wanted me to come to him—a lot of bunk without any truth whatever in it. But people used to fall for it and feed me and help me on my way. Sometimes, but not always so. I done a little stealing whenever I could. Sometimes I worked for a day or two. One experience I had during that time I never forgot and it had a direct bearing on a lot of my actions later in life.

Carl Panzram was fourteen when he headed for the freight yards of East Grand Forks on the cold afternoon of March 29, 1906. He caught a freight headed west and joined the unique world of the "Great American Road." *Road* at that time meant *railroad;* the automobile was still an open car, rarely seen and unreliable. Henry Ford was yet to mass-produce the Model T. This was an America without freeways or even numbered highways. Hitchhiking existed–for wagon or buggy rides. Air travel was scarcely a concept. Speed limits in towns were six to ten miles per hour. In order to go somewhere at any pace at all, people rode the trains. With money, they "rode the cushions"; without money, they rode the freights in one of several ways, all involving risk–the risk of being thrown off moving trains by tough shacks (brakemen) or being placed in jail by yard dicks (railroad police) when the train stopped at division points. Having accomplished this, the more daring traveler learned to wing aboard passenger trains between the coal tender of the locomotive and the baggage car or between two locked baggage cars, a practice known as riding the blinds. The dangers and delights of riding the blinds were described by Jack London in a classic narrative.[11] The railroad was the swiftest transportation Americans of any economic class could enjoy in 1906. There was equality of travel—money and courage arrived at the same time. Carl Panzram learned to ride both the rods (underneath the freight cars) and the blinds between 1904 and 1906.

Over two generations the railroads had become the great highway of the impecunious. The life of the "Great American Bum" had its own argot, its songs, survival lore and legends of accomplishment. Details of this life survive in many sources, notably in accounts of participant observers, such as Jim Tully, Box-Car Bertha and Robert Stroud,[12] as well as London.

Among the tramps, bindlestiffs, hoboes, mushfakers and roustabouts who formed the migratory underworld of the road, there were more sharply defined criminal elements generally know as "yeggs." The yegg was an itinerant burglar who moved from town to town, often in the company of his "boy," disdaining female company and acquiring a system of values through association with others of the name who passed down a tradition.

Another minority of the road who exercised sexual control and some semblance of inner-directed order were the

Industrial Workers of the World or "Wobblies."[13] These men generally disdained the gang-rapes and degenerate practices of the lowest elements of the road travelers. Unfortunately, Carl Panzram's next encounter was with the latter.

V

I was riding in a box car one night in the West. I was alone and feeling that I would like some one to talk to. I walked over the train until I came to an open lumber car. There were four big, burly bums in it. When I saw them, I told them about the nice warm box car I had just left. It was clean and full of straw. They all immediately got interested and friendly and told me to lead them to it. I did, but I very soon wished that I hadn't because just as soon as we all got into the car and shut the door and the train pulled out, they all began to tell me what a nice boy I was and how they would make me rich. They were going to buy me all the silk underwear in the world and I would soon be wearing diamonds as big as baseballs. In fact, they promised me everything in the whole world, but first they wanted me to do a little something for them.

When they told me what they wanted from me, I very

soon began to figure that that was no place for me. I didn't want any of that for mine. I told them no. But my wishes didn't make any difference to them. What they couldn't get by moral persuasion they proceeded to get by force. I cried, begged and pleaded for mercy, pity and sympathy, but nothing I could say or do could sway them from their purpose. I left that box car a sadder, sicker but wiser boy than I was when I entered it. After that I always went alone whenever and wherever possible.[14]

I had one other similar experience with men. I was in a small town in the West on a Sunday afternoon. I was just a poor, young, ignorant, friendless and nearly harmless young kid. I was broke and hungry and I went into a livery stable where a bunch of town loafers were sitting around rushing the can and hitting the bottle. When I approached them and begged for a bit to eat and told my hard-luck story about how I loved Jesus and what a good boy I was and how far I had traveled and how old I was, they all became deeply interested and very sympathetic toward me. They didn't promise me any silk underwear or jewelry but they had a better scheme than that. They told me how good the beer was and how much better the whiskey was. They first offered me a little drink and then a bigger one, and it wasn't long until I was so drunk that I didn't know my own name and soon after I didn't know anything at all. But I sure knew something when I woke up.

These two experiences taught me several lessons. Lessons that I never forgot. I did not want to learn these lessons but I found out that it isn't what one wants in this world that one gets. Force and might make right. Perhaps things shouldn't be that way but that's the way they are. I learned to look with suspicion and hatred on everybody. As the years went on that idea persisted in my mind above all others. I figured that if I was strong enough and clever enough to impose my will on others, I was right. I still believe that to this day.

Another lesson I learned at that time was that there were a lot of very nice things in this world. Among them were whiskey and sodomy.[15] But it depended on who and how they were used. I have used plenty of both since then but I have received more pleasure from them than I did those first times. Those were the days when I was learning the lessons that life teaches us all, and they made me what I am today. It wasn't my fault that the teachers who gave me my instructions were the wrong kind or that the lessons they taught were the wrong kind. Men made me what I am today, and if men don't like what they have made of me, they must put the blame where it belongs.

After I had hoboed around the country for a few months, I was finally caught in a small petty-larceny burglary at Butte, Montana. I was held in the county jail where there were 50 or 100 older men put in there for all the kinds of crimes and meannesses there are that men could do on each other. I was there a month or two under the name of Carl Panzram. Then I was tried and sent to the Montana State Reform School at Miles City, Montana. There I stayed nearly one year. While there I spent my time either working in the shoe shop or in the fields and garden. When I wasn't doing that, I was trying to escape or being punished for trying it.

I was a pretty big boy at that time—very stubborn and contrary, deceitful and treacherous. I had been in a few small scrapes and all of the officers had orders to watch me closely. That didn't worry me much, but there was one officer there by the name of Bushart, an ex-prize fighter from Boston, who made it his special duty to make life miserable for me. He done a pretty thorough job of it. He kept on nagging at me until finally I decided to murder him.

Every evening in the school room, he used to sit up on top of one of the front seats while he had one of the boys black his boots. He was doing that one evening, and I got a board about 2 feet long and 18 inches wide by one inch thick. This board was made of hard oak wood and had about three or four pounds of iron on one end of it. I took this and sneaked up behind him and whacked him on top of his head. It didn't kill him but it made him pretty sick, and he quit monkeying with me any more. For this I got several beatings and was locked up and watched closer than before. They were going to indict me and send me to the State Prison at Deer Lodge for that, but I was too young. As the law would not permit them to send a 14- or 15-year-old boy to State Prison, they done their damnedest to make life miserable for me. They worked me hard and beat me harder. You see they were trying to make a good boy of me. They took me in the hospital and operated on me by clipping my foreskin off to stop me from the habit of masturbation. So they said anyway. But how the hell they figured that would stop me is more than I could see. I can't yet.

At that time a Mr. Wilson was superintendent. His method of teaching us boys religion was to hammer it into us morning, noon and night, just the same as they done to me at Red Wing. But seems as though we were not getting enough religion yet.

Wilson got fired for stealing the funds of the State, for that money and for the mishandling of boys under his charge.

The next man to take up his job was a devil-chasing soul saver, a preacher by the name of Mr. Price. His method was to pat us all on the prat and tell us what good boys we were. He lasted quick. We all began to leave his happy home as soon as we could get around a corner and then run.

VI

After I was there nearly a year, I began to be good pals with a boy by the name of Jimmie Benson whose home was in Butte and who was a pretty smart little boy. Between the two of us we concocted a scheme that we could both escape the same day. He was trusted but I wasn't, so he was to run away first and while he was gone and all of the screws [guards] were out chasing him, then I was to blow. We had prearranged a place to hide until the hunt was over and then we were to meet at another place about 40 miles away.

We each done our part and the scheme worked like a charm. Our plans called for a meeting place about 40 miles away at the first water tank east of Terry, Montana. The first to arrive was to wait for the other. I arrived there first, on the third night after our escape. I looked around and saw no one, so I took my iron bar which I had carried all the way from the school, then I walked around behind the tank and lay down to sleep, cold, hungry and tired but free and happy.

I was awakened at daylight by hearing someone rattling tin cans and smelling food.

I didn't know who it might be so I peeked around the corner where I saw a man dressed in a nice blue suit with a big Stetson hat on. On one side of him lay a big sack full of clothes and food, while on the other was a belt full of shells and a scabbard of pistol. The man was eating and drinking with his back turned towards me. I was hungry and wanted the grub, clothes and the pistol, so I took my iron bar and sneaked up on him and was just about to bounce it off his head when he heard me, grabbed the gun and turned around so I could see that it was my partner Jimmie Benson.

He laid his gun down and I dropped my iron bar and we began to celebrate. In the sack he had food and clothes for me, which he had stolen a few miles down the line the day before by breaking into a surveyor's and homesteader's shack.

After we ate and I dressed up, he gave me the gun as I was the biggest of us two and probably the meanest. Then we were all organized and ready to do battle with anybody. We didn't get back looking for the screws who were looking for us but we were in hopes that we might meet one of them. We were both pretty damn hostile and we felt that if we couldn't meet any of them, then someone else would do to have our revenge on. It didn't take long for the pair of us to raise plenty of hell with a lot of different people. I stayed with him about a month, hoboing our way east, stealing and burning everything we could.

He showed me how to work the stickup racket and how to rob the poor boxes in churches. I in turn taught him how to set fire to a church after we robbed it. We got very busy on that, robbing and burning a church regular every chance we got. When we got tired of riding a train, we used to open up the journal boxes, take out the greasy waste packing and throw some sand or gravel into it. They wouldn't get far with that car until they had a hotbox.

At that time the wheat harvest was going on in North Dakota and whole train loads of wheat would be shipped, sometimes loose in cars. Every time we saw a car or train loaded like that, we would crawl underneath on the rods and cut or bore holes through the floor so that the wheat would pour out through the holes and go to waste on the tracks as the train was rolling along.

By the time we got as far east as Fargo, North Dakota, we had between us two good six-shooters, each had a good suit and about $150 in cash besides various assortments of watches, rings and other slum that we got by the burglary route and by harvesting the harvesters.

At Fargo we split. Jimmie went back to Butte and it was only a short time later that he got caught in a holdup and sent to the big house at Deer Lodge, Montana, for ten years. I met him there years later when I myself was sent there for burglary.

After Jimmie and I split up, I went to my home where I stayed only a day or two and then I headed west again.

VII

THREE DAYS after Christmas of 1906, sixteen-year-old Carl Panzram rode a boxcar over the frozen Rockies, ditching it in Helena, Montana, to find a meal. Helena was a bleak outpost in this snowy season. The town offered little hospitality to a wandering adolescent with no cash or family connections.

In a saloon, Panzram stood on the fringes of a drinking crowd, listening to the sales pitch of an army recruiter from nearby Fort Harrison. The boy's imagination was stirred by the soldier's fancy military attire, which included sergeant's stripes and a jaunty campaign hat. Panzram stepped forward and lied about his age.

The same day, Panzram was hauled out of Helena with a wagonload of whooping young recruits bound, they thought, for adventure in the Sixth Infantry Regiment. Their laughter soon faded as they peered over the steaming backs of the mules at the "fort"—a grim collection of long, low military buildings strung out on the level snow.

Like Panzram, many army recruits at this time were well under twenty-one, the legal age for enlisting. Panzram was to meet other youthful runaways and reform school escapees who had sought refuge in the army, permanently or temporarily. The attractions of peacetime soldiering in America's rural outback were so few in 1907 that recruiters seldom looked closely at the unshaven cheeks of those who signed the enlistment papers. Hard military discipline would make up the difference.

Panzram was outfitted in a uniform with tan leggings, a pair of stiff boots, a lumpy army overcoat which smelled of camphor, and a wide-brimmed campaign hat which slid down to his ears over a new army haircut.

The sergeant in A Company showed the recruits gruffly where to get buckets and brushes and then pointed to a row of privies behind the barracks. Within an hour, Panzram was up before the company commander for refusing to work.

First Lieutenant George England was a spit-and-polish career officer whose bristling moustache originated at West Point. Crisply he told the new private what was expected and where he might go if he disobeyed orders. He handed Panzram a copy of the Articles of War, a list of rules and punishments governing military conduct.

An hour later, for what Panzram did with the Articles of War, Lieutenant England ordered the recruit locked in the guardhouse for a week.

Two days later, Panzram was reported by the guardhouse commander for fighting and impertinence. His sentence was extended to thirty days on bread and water.

When Panzram finally was remanded to A Company, Lieutenant England was pleased with the private's fervent promise to become an obedient soldier.

On April 8, 1907, with a twenty-four-hour pass tucked in his trousers, Panzram was hailed by sentries as he tried to walk off the post with two stolen army overcoats, a civilian suit and a pocketful of gold collar buttons. Private Auggie Hill, another Fort Harrison soldier, who had run away from the Montana State Reform School, had told Panzram it was easy to sell these articles in Helena.

Panzram's general court-martial was held on April 20 before a grim-faced tribunal of five officers, headed by Captain Dwight W. Ryther. There were several cases to be considered, and Panzram's was disposed of in minutes.

I was only in the Army a month or two when I got three years in the U. S. Military Prison at Fort Leavenworth, Kansas. My General Court-Martial or trial was held at Fort William Henry Harrison, Helena, Montana, and my court proceedings were reviewed by the then Secretary of War, Mr. William Howard Taft. He recommended me for three years and he signed 'em.[16] Thirteen years later I had the very good fortune to rob him out of about $40,000 worth of jewelry and Liberty Bonds. This happened at his home in New Haven, Connecticut, in the summer of 1920.

On May 20, 1907, the motley band of Fort Harrison prisoners were shackled for the trip to Kansas. Panzram watched a private lock iron rings on his ankles. A long chain was passed through loops in the rings on the prisoners' right ankles, forcing them to keep step on the long march to the railroad. Five guards with loaded rifles on safety paced along with them.

Thus "ironed," sixteen-year-old Panzram must have regretted the traditional lie about his age. His army life had been brief.

The humid railroad car was rank with the smell of bodies as it rolled into eastern Kansas and slowed down on the outskirts of Fort Leavenworth. The prisoners saw lilacs beginning to bloom against the cheerful green of wheat fields. Soon they eyed a low, irregular stone wall surrounding some old-looking building, and they felt their car lurch off the main track to slide along a groaning spur into the United States Military Prison. On the chain with Panzram was the flotsam of peacetime army posts of the West: men sentenced to hard labor for army crimes ranging from petty insubordination to desertion, sodomy and murder.

Club-carrying soldiers stared through the prisoners as they marched stiffly off the train. Two sergeants with blackjacks ordered the new arrivals to toe a painted line on the concrete; resisters were quickly broken.

Fort Leavenworth Military Prison had been built ten years after the Civil War. In 1895, it was turned over temporarily to the Justice Department to house civilian convicts during construction of a new federal prison two and one-half miles away. Older military prisoners whispered stories about the building of the huge Leavenworth wall; and even now, red stone was delivered steadily to the other prison for the construction which continued inside.

The newcomers were quick-timed through a bath,

issued denim uniforms and handed small, blue-covered booklets spelling out a long list of prison rules, including mandatory silence, and listing official punishments.

Panzram had arrived at Fort Leavenworth less than eighteen months after its return to army jurisdiction.[17] The commandant, Major George S. Young, had protested to Washington that the buildings were aged, airless firetraps held together in many instances by iron braces and blocks of wood. He requested that no more prisoners be sent until repairs could be made. The army did not share his concern.[18]

Panzram, meanwhile, learned the prison routine. Each morning he learned to fall out and stand at attention by his bunk before the bugler finished reveille. He took his turn marching out with the iron soilpot provided in the eight-man cell.

He learned to stand up for counts and to keep his shirt buttoned at the collar as he marched to meals with his company, paced by a private carrying a club.

In the military prison, convicts sat in silence at long tables holding sixteen men shoulder to shoulder and all facing the same way. New men came into Fort Leavenworth as second-grade convicts and could work themselves up to first grade, with extra privileges, by staying in line. Those who rebelled were sent down to third grade, where they did "hard time." Panzram was to learn, soon enough, that the word of any guard was enough to put a man down in grade. This meant extra confinement, a total-silence system and man-breaking "exercises" at the whim of third-grade guards.

If a man in the third-grade company broke a minor rule, the whole company was sometimes forced to stand at attention throughout the night. Other punishments included common beatings, running drills and use of a straitjacket cinched tight enough to cause unconsciousness. Escape, or an attempt, brought an additional penalty: the offender was forced to "carry the baby"—a heavy iron ball chained to his ankle.

This was Panzram's first experience as an adult prisoner.

I wasn't there long before I tried to escape but luck was against me. The next thing I done there was to burn up the prison shops. That time I used a candle inside of a one-gallon can. In the bottom of the can was a lot of oil-soaked rags. When the candle burned down to the rags, that set the whole works ablaze. She sure made a fine little blaze, a clean sweep. Another hundred thousand dollars to my credit, and the best part of it was that no one ever found it out until now.[19] I was in stripes as a third-class prisoner nearly all the while I was there. I was always in trouble of some sort. I had a job of swinging an 18-pound hammer in the rock quarry most of my bit.[20] My number was 1874 and my name was Carl Panzram. There I done 37 months. I done plenty of work, and I had plenty of punishment, and the only good part of it was that they didn't try to hammer any more religion into me.

At this time of my life I was about 20 years old, 6 foot tall and weighed about 190 pounds of concentrated hell-fired, man-inspired meanness. I was as strong as two or three average men. I had to be to be able to stand some of the punishments and labor that I went thru during my 3 years in the U.S.M.P. One of my tasks and punishments while there was to be shackled to a 50-pound iron ball for 6 months.

During that time I wore that ball and chain day and night, slept with it and worked with it on. My work was in the rock quarry and that was 3 miles from the prison. The gang of about 300 convicts and 40 screws used to march out in the morning and back at night. The other men had nothing to carry except themselves but my part was to load my iron ball, an 18-pound hammer, a pick and shovel and a 6-foot iron crow-bar all into a wheel barrow and march behind the line of cons, out to the rock quarry and there work for 8½ hours in the hot Kansas sun, busting big rocks, and after that was all over, to pack my little iron pill and my tools into the Irish buggy and wheel it all back to the prison. There eat my supper of stinking codfish, greasy stew or mouldy and wormy rice or beans. But all of that treatment did one good thing for me. The worse the food was and the harder they worked me, the stronger I got. I quit my old habit of masturbating because I couldn't do that and the hard work and punishment at the same time.

I was discharged from that prison in 1910. I was the spirit of meanness personified. I had not at this time got so that I hated myself. I only hated everybody else. Before I left there I sung 'em the same old song and gave 'em the same line about how I sure loved Jesus and what a good, nice young man I was and how much good it had done me to be sent to that prison. I don't know if they believed me or not, but they all said they did anyway. They all declared that I was as pure as a lily and free from all sin. They told me to go and sin no more. I agreed with everything they said. They gave me $5.00, a suit of clothes, and a ticket to Denver, Colorado. Well, I was a pretty rotten egg before I went there, but when I left there, all the good that may have been in me had been kicked and beaten out of me long before. All that I had in my mind at that time was a strong determination to raise plenty of hell with anyone and everybody in every way I could and every time and every place I could.

VIII

When I left there and went to Denver I was busted, and to get a start with a few bucks I took a job in a R.R. mule-skinner's camp. I was there only a few weeks but I licked every one in it and was getting all set to go to work on the boss-man when he fired me, pulled a gun on me and drove me out of the camp. I took my pay, went to town and bought me a gun, the biggest I could find in Denver, and they have some big ones there. With the balance of my money I went to the red-light district figuring on getting good and drunk and then taking charge of that section of Denver. But something went wrong because the next afternoon I awoke to find myself laying in an alley feeling pretty sick. I had no gun, no money, my coat, hat and shoes were gone, but I had a few lumps on top of my head that weren't there before. And the worst was yet to come.

About a week later I found my that my collection also included a fine first-class case of gonorrhea. I began to suspect that the ladies were very good things to leave alone. I have followed that policy pretty closely ever since. Once in a while since then one would get her claws into me, but not while I was sober or in the daytime where I could see 'em first.

After leaving Denver I hoboed around, stealing as I went and not forgetting to take over all the churches I could, until I hit Hutchison where the State Fair of Kansas was being held at the time. There I joined up as a rider for Col. Dickey's Circle D Wild West Show which was playing with Klien's Carnival Company at that time. I lasted about a week but during that time I fought and I licked everybody around there including the horses and steers. Then they got tired of me being on the prod all the time, so they canned me. Then I went over to where the Kansas State Militia soldiers were camped and stole one of their tents and was carrying away some sacks of oats and grain when the sentry caught me, but he was only a tin soldier and a kid at that so I took his rifle and threw it in the horse trough and was going to throw him in after it when about nine thousand more came running to his rescue. It was about time for me to leave there and go somewhere else. I did.

I went to Sedalia, Missouri, where they were holding their State Fair. In a day or so the carnival company with the Circle D showed up to play, but they had had bad luck. The first night's stand they had the misfortune to lose their horse tent and cook tent by some scoundrel touching a match to them. I left there right away quick.

I went to St. Louis where I got a job with the I.C.R.R. [Illinois Central Railroad] as a guard and strike breaker. They first sent me to the yards at Centralia, Illinois, where I started in to lick every union striker I saw. I didn't see many so I started to lick the scabs and guards and I succeeded so well that the Company sent me to Cairo which was a hard town with plenty of trouble there.

When I got off of the train a union picket stopped me to ask me my business. I licked him. A copper stopped us from fighting and I licked him. Anyway, he stopped fighting me long enough to blow his whistle for help and while he was doing that I figured it was a good time for me to go and report to my new boss. When I reported to him, I gave him a letter that my former boss at Centralia had given me to give to him. He read it, got up and patted me on the back, told me what a fine fellow I was and then told me to go out in the railroad yards and, if I saw anyone there who had no business to be there, to knock their blocks off and run 'em ragged. I told him I would, and I did—so much so that the whole town of Cairo was out to scalp me. The next Saturday night being my payday and me having a few bucks in my pocket and feeling pretty good, I decided to go uptown, get a few drinks and then go and see what the girls in the red-light district had to offer.

In the first saloon I struck I met a very nice and accommodating fellow who offered to show me a good time and a nice girl, but first he had to call her on the phone. He did as he promised me. He showed me the town. Something else too. He took me around the corner and showed me about a dozen big, husky male union strikers. They at once proceeded to see if I was such a hell of a fighter as I thought I was.

I wasn't. They cleaned me up in great shape and then the cops came and finished the job by throwing me in the can. My boss got me out of there and gave me a ticket to East St. Louis and another letter to another boss-man there, but when I got on the train I tore open and read that letter. After reading it I decided that St. Louis could try to get along without me. I went to Chicago, looked at the Loop and the lakefront and started out for Mexico where there was a war on at the time. I figured that a Mexican was easier to lick than a lot of hardboiled railroaders. Besides, I had heard that all of the churches in Old Mexico were full of gold and silver. Maybe I could get my share. All the American churches I had robbed wouldn't keep me in cigarette money. I left Chicago, hoboing, stealing any way I could, and by the time I hit Jacksonville, Texas, I had collected two heavy-calibered pistols, some money, not much though, and a curly-haired, blue-eyed, rosy-cheeked, fat boy.

At Jacksonville, Texas, we were pinched. The cops took my gun belt but left me my boy. We were both sent to the county road gang at Rusk, Texas. When we got to the road gang, they gave me a chain to wear on my leg and took my boy away from me. The boss-man's name was Mr. Tate. He took my boy to sleep in his tent. I guess he wanted to save the boy's soul or something. Anyway, about three weeks after I was there, this Mr. Tate and one of his officers by the name of Awkwaite or Hawknight or some such a name got into a hell of a battle and were going to shoot each other. Mr. Tate fired Mr. Awkwaite or Hawknight or whatever his name was. Awk went to town and complained to the county officials and they in turn came out to the camp, investigated the conditions and fired Mr. Tate. Then my boy was chased out of the officer's tent and put back into the prisoner's tent where I was. Then he told me tales about Mr. Tate and Mr. Hawbright and what a queer pair of Christian degenerates they were—both married men with families, too. At the time of our arrest and confinement there, I gave the name of Jeff Davis, and the boy gave the name of Joe M. Hall. This was in the winter of 1910 and 1911.

These things are all on the records and can be verified by anyone.

My sentence on that road gang called for 40 days or $19.70 at $.50 per day. I finished my 40 days and asked the boss-man to cut my chain off and turn me loose, but he left the chain on and knocked my block off instead. The next day I ran away, got caught, brought back and whipped at the Snorting Pole.[21] Then I worked 20 days more and asked the same question of the same man. He gave me the same answer as he had before. The next day I tried again to move out with the same result. Again in five days I tried but that time I was successful in my attempt.

I walked to Palestine, Texas, caught the trucks of a fast mail train and that night I got into Houston, Texas. When I got there, the train couldn't get in because the whole town was on fire,[22] so I got off and walked through the town, enjoying the sights of all the burning buildings and listening to the tales of woe, the moans and sighs of those whose homes and property were burning. I enjoyed it all. Several times people asked me to help them save their valuables. Sure I helped 'em save their stuff but not for them. I wore some of the clothing for months after that. The stuff I stole there kept me in funds and living high until I hit El Paso, Texas.

There I crossed the Mexican border to Juarez in Mexico where I tried to join the Mexican Army, but the Federals were in control there and they wouldn't accept me. I left El Paso on the El Paso and South Western Railroad going towards Del Rio. At that time I was with a young quarter-breed Indian whose home was in Klamath Falls, Oregon. He also told me that he had just got out of the pen at Yuma, Arizona. We palled together for a week or two.

After leaving El Paso we rode our way to some small town about 50 or 75 miles away. There we met a fellow who told us he was about 35 years old, that he had been working in some railroad camp near by and that he had $35 on him. I and the Indian got interested right away. We told him a lot of bull and conned him into walking with us on the wagon road beside the tracks to the next town. We started and got a few miles, then we came to a stretch of road with tall mesquite brush and greasewood on both sides of the road. No houses in sight and no signs of any other people. There I put the arm on him and we dragged him through the fence on the left hand side of the road. We walked into the brush for about ¼ mile away from the road. There we stopped and robbed him of his 35 bucks. I tied him up and we walked away.

We hadn't gone far before the Indian said to me that he had better go back and do a better job of tying him up as I hadn't done a very good job. Lucky we did because when we got back where we had left him he was just about loose. This time the Indian tied him up. First he took his belt off, pulled his pants down to below his knees and tied his legs together, then he tied his hands behind his back. Then he tied his hands to his feet pulled up together. Then he stuffed a sock in his mouth and tied a handkerchief tight over that and then tied him to a tree. He was then ready to leave him and walk away, but I wasn't through yet. I figured that while I had such a good chance as that, I would commit a little sodomy on him. This I proceeded to do. Then I invited the Indian to take a ride but that damn fool was only an Indian. He hadn't received the full benefits of civilization yet like I had, so he declined the honor. We left that guy right there in that shape. He is still there unless the buzzards and coyotes have finished the last of him long ago. This was in the year of 1911, and the town and place was somewhere between El Paso and a railroad division point where we went that night and there bought a ticket to Del Rio, Texas. There we split. Where he went I don't know and don't care.

IX

I crossed the border at Del Rio to Agua Prieta, Mexico, where I enlisted in the Foreign Legion of the Constitutional Army of Northern Mexico. Our commander was General Stanley Williams and the Commander-in-Chief was General Orosco. I was with that outfit for about a month or so but all the churches I ever saw had all been robbed before I got there. All that any of those *cholos* had was a few beans and some pepper—damn few beans but lots of pepper. I didn't care much for their beans and much less for their pepper.

As I couldn't do much business in my line there, I deserted, but first I stole my horse and everything that wasn't tied down. I rode my horse to death before I hit the border, there I left everything I had stolen and then damn near run myself to death before I got back to the land of the free and the home of the brave. I immediately got busy on the S. P. [Southern Pacific] line from Yuma, Arizona, to Fresno, California. During this time I was busy robbing chicken coops and then touching a match to them. I burned down old barns, sheds, fences, snowsheds or anything I could, and when I couldn't burn anything else I would set fire to the grass on the prairies, or the woods, anything and everything. I had a pistol and I would spend all my spare change for bullets. I would take potshots at farmers' houses, at the windows. If I saw cows or horses in the fields I would cut loose at them.

At night while I was riding the freight trains I was always on the lookout for something to shoot at or trying to stick up the hobos that I met on the trains. I looked 'em all over and whenever I met one who wasn't too rusty looking I would make him raise his hands and drop his pants. I wasn't very particular either. I rode them old and young, tall and short, white and black. It made no difference to me at all except that they were human beings. During this time, all along that S. P. line, things were pretty warm. The sheriffs, coppers and railroad bulls were all hostile. I got pinched a couple of times but it was in the daytime and during that time I would have my gun and sap and other plunder planted. But in my pockets I always carried a well-thumbed Bible and a prayer book and a little account book where I had written down a lot of crap about where I had worked on different jobs, how many hours, days, what I earned and a lot of bull like that. So every time a cop grabbed me, I would pull the old innocent and injured racket. Tell 'em how much I loved Jesus and what a good hardworking, honest fellow I was. That nearly always worked fine, but sometimes not.

When I hit Fresno, California, I got 120 days in the can for stealing a bicycle. I done 30 days and then escaped. When I got out of there, I went and dug up my plant where I had left my gun and other stuff and then started north on the S. P. line.

I had not gone far before I met Mr. Trouble. He took the form of a R. R. brakeman. I was riding in an iron open coal car at the time with two other bums. They knew nothing about me except the lies I had told 'em. I was sizing up the youngest and best looking one of the two and figuring when to pull out my hog-leg and heist 'em up. But a shack [brakeman] comes over the top and bounces down into my car and begins bawling us all out and telling us to dig up or unload. He asked us all who we were and what we were.

I don't know what the other two told him but I pulled out my cannon and told him that I was the fellow who went around the world doing people good and asked him if there was anything that I had that he wanted. He said no, that he was a good fellow and never put anybody off of his trains, and to prove that he was a good fellow he offered to buy us all a feed and offered to give us a piece of change. He gave me a piece of change, all he had, and then he gave me his watch and chain and then he was so kind as to pull his pants down while I rode him around the floor of the freight car. When I was through riding him, I told the other two bums to mount him but they declined to indulge in that form of pleasure. But by using a little moral persuasion and much waving around of my pistol, they also rode Mr. Brakemen around.

After our very pleasant and profitable, for me anyway, little trip was all over, the other three got off to walk. They didn't want to but they did anyway. The freight was rolling along at about 15 or 20 miles an hour so I guess they didn't hurt themselves very much. It didn't hurt me any. I have been unloaded from trains going much faster than we were then quite a few times and I am still alive to remember it. After they got off, I kept rolling along into and out of Sacramento, through Oregon, up to Seattle. There I got the can for 30 days.

All this time since I left the prison at Fort Leavenworth, I had been going under the name of Jeff Davis. Now I changed my name to Jack Allen. Under that name I was pinched for highway robbery, assault and sodomy at The Dalles, Oregon.[23] I was in jail there, held for the action of the grand jury. I was there about 2 or 3 months and then broke jail there. I haven't been there since. Before I left there, one day they put an old safe blower in that can. I immediately asked him to teach me how to blow safes. He didn't stay there long enough to teach me but he showed me how I could break out of there. He was taken to Moscow, Idaho, to stand trial for a post office robbery. He got five years in Leavenworth. Later on he got another and bigger hit. His name was Cal Jordan or Doctor Jordan. He also done a bit in the hoosegow at Salem, Oregon, under the name of Hopkins. A few days after he left The Dalles, I broke jail. This was in 1912. From there I went to Spokane. Among my loot there was two of the coppers' pistols. Then I bought six hack saws and tied three on each leg under my sock and underwear. I then went to Moscow, Idaho, to try to get the old safe-blower out. When I got there I hid the two guns, some clothes and food and then walked up to the jail, broke in to it but got caught doing so and got 30 days myself. The thanks I got from old Cal was that he thought I was in love with him and he tried to mount me, but I wasn't broke to ride and he was, so I rode him. At that time he was about 50 years old and I was 20 or 21 but I was strong and he was weak.

When I got out of jail, I got as far as Harrison, Idaho, where I got pinched, and put in the can. I at once tried to break out by setting fire to the jail, but I got caught and a day or so later I was in the jail at Wallace, Idaho, under the name of Jeff Davis.

Some months later I was pinched at Chinook, Montana, for burglary. I quick took a plea of guilty and got one year at the state prison at Deer Lodge, Montana.[24] When I got there I met my old partner, Jimmie Benson, who was doing 10 years for robbery. I stayed there about eight months and escaped. A week later I was arrested at Three Forks, Montana, for burglary under the name of Jeff Rhoades. I pleaded guilty and got a year and was sent back to Deer Lodge, where I was at once brought to court and given one year for my escape under the name of Jeff Davis. Out of these three sentences I served 23 months.[25] In that prison there was work for only a few men and I wasn't one of those. All of the cells were for two men in each cell. Each man could choose his own cellmates and get a new one anytime he wanted one. I used to want a new one pretty regular.

At that place and time I got to be an experienced wolf. I knew more about sodomy than old boy Oscar Wilde ever thought of knowing. I would start the morning with sodomy, work as hard at it as I could all day and sometimes half of the night. I was so busy committing sodomy that I didn't have any time left for to serve Jesus as I had been taught to do in those reform schools. The warden there was a big wolf by the name of Frank Conley. He was the warden of that prison and mayor of the town of Deer Lodge for over 30 years. He wound up his career by blowing out his own brains because he was due for a bit in one of his own cells for charges of stealing the state funds and for a host of other crimes.[26]

When I left there, he told me that I was as pure as a lily

and free of all sin, to go and sin no more. He gave me $5, a suit of clothes, and a ticket to the next town six miles away. I headed back to the West and about two weeks later I was pinched for burglary at Astoria, Oregon.

X

Panzram had chosen one of the toughest ports in the Northwest. Founded at the mouth of the Columbia River by John Jacob Astor's fur traders, by 1915 Astoria had shifted its hospitality to an army of loggers and merchant seamen. When the river overflowed, as it was doing when Panzram stepped off a freight car in mid-April, whooping crowds pried boards off the sidewalks and fished through the holes for salmon.

Panzram now was twenty-three, with the look of the road in his clothes. Prison, violence and roustabouting had hardened him into a silent, strange-eyed man with broad, muscled shoulders and a hairline that was already beginning to recede. His sullen good looks attracted women, but he had avoided them since his experience with a social disease in Denver.

At night, the crowd made its way to Commercial Street and some of the choicest dives north of San Francisco. In the barnlike Louvre, named for its fantastic collection of nude oils and claiming the world's longest bar, gaming tables clattered on the first floor while easy ladies were rented out on the second. But this was hardly a choice for Panzram. He had few coins and needed money to buy seaman's discharges and a sailor's passport.

A few days later, Panzram was arrested in the Louvre as he tried to peddle a silver watch. It fit the description on a list of items taken from the residence of C. R. Higgins, president of the Bank of Astoria. Sheriff J. V. Burns snapped the cuffs shut on his wrists and booked him into the county jail, where he gave his name as Jeff Baldwin. That name was to become vividly know to Oregon lawmen.

Sheriff Burns and District Attorney C. W. Mullins wanted to locate the rest of the stolen articles and to arrange a plea in order to avoid trial. They offered to go easy on the sentence; it would be a token delay on the county road gang. Panzram directed them to a blanket under the docks containing $130 in loose bills, gold shirt studs and tie pins, a box of silverware, a silver pepper shaker and two pairs of gloves.

Mullins drew up two indictments, one for the silver watch and one for the other items. At the jail, Panzram signed a plea of guilty to the five-dollar watch theft while Mullins wrote a notice of dismissal on the larger indictment. From the jail, the attorney walked straight to the office of Judge E. V. Eakin, a somberly pious circuit judge whose daughters sewed doll hats for church benefits. Eakin was a close friend of the Higginses and the burglary vexed him. He received the guilty plea from Mullins, however. Then he firmly signed another order appointing a court guard for safety at the hearing and sentence of Jeff Baldwin, né Carl Panzram.

I kept my word and the judge and district attorney didn't.[27] Instead they gave me the limit of seven years. When I got back to the jail, the coppers laughed at me, locked the door and went away. When they were gone, I got out of my cell and locked all of the other prisoners in their cells. I plugged all the locks so no one could get in or out. Then I went to work and wrecked their damn jail. I tore loose all the radiators and steam pipes, smashed all the electric wiring, took the cook stove, all the dishes, all the food, all the blankets, mattresses and clothing, all the furniture, benches, tables, chairs, books and everything that was loose or could be torn loose and that would burn. Then I piled it all up and set fire to it.[28] The coppers finally broke through the door, put the fire out and locked me up after first knocking my block off. Then I tried to play crazy but I couldn't fool the doctors. They took me to the state prison at Salem, Oregon. This was in 1914 and my name there was Jefferson Baldwin, 7390. I swore I would never do that 7 years.

In June 1915, the surly prisoner was shackled inside a baggage coach on the Oregon Electric Railway and hauled to the state penitentiary at Salem. Panzram was delivered through a tall, iron-pike outer fence and then through a fifteen-foot brick wall topped with eight tiers of barbed wire.

Picturesque in its shady fir grove, Oregon State Penitentiary was actually rated one of the worst in the North.[29] Completed in 1871 and poorly maintained in a damp climate, OSP punished its inmates physically as well as psychologically. Although whipping and firehosing had been abolished by law in 1912, the reforms begun by Governor Oswald West were abbreviated by his Republican successor, Governor James Withycombe. The spade-bearded new governor shared the impatient view of his electorate concerning criminals and looked around for a warden who wouldn't mollycoddle them. His choice was a large, gruff former sheriff named Harry Minto.

As soon as I got to Oregon State Prison I was in more trouble. I swore I would never do that 7 years and defied the warden and all of his officers to make me. The warden swore I would do every damn day of those 7 years or he would kill me. I haven't done it yet and I am not dead, but he is.

Under Minto's regime, more than 400 prisoners were jammed into three overcrowded, weatherbeaten cellhouses radiating from a central administration building.

Silence was enforced. Inmates moved through the prison in lock-step, one hand on the shoulder of the man in front, eyes cast down, marching in a slow shuffle. Talking—or even appearing to talk—or getting out of line could bring a beating from guards who swung steel-tipped canes.

The prison tightened up further under the new warden. On Withycombe's orders, Minto reduced prison industries which had annoyed local businessmen, cutting the pay of working inmates from one dollar to twenty-five cents a day. Money which formerly went to the needy families of prisoners was placed in an "institution betterment fund," which helped buy machinery to earn a profit for the state.

By the time Panzram arrived, unrest in the prison had mounted to the point where Minto was encouraged to rehire several old-line guards, including former deputy warden Jim "Vinegar" Cooper, known among older prisoners as the "Man of Flogs." He was a man of middle height, pale-eyed and regular featured, a lover of roses and religious hymns. Cooper's favorite way to break a rebel was to hoist him on a pillar and lash him with a cat-o'-nine-tails.[30]

Word of Panzram's one-man riot in Astoria had preceded him. Cane-wielding guards hustled him through registration and locked him in the last cell on the bottom tier of B Block. The next morning Panzram doused an officer with the contents of his soilpot. After a beating, the screaming prisoner was handcuffed to the door of a dark cell where he remained for thirty days.

There are coolers and Coolers. Some are bad and some are worse. None are good. Some are cold and wet. Some are hot and dry. In some you freeze and in others you roast and sweat. In all you are hungry and thirsty, filthy and dirty. In some you stay a day, others a week, and there have been times when I have been in the cooler a month or more. Bread and water isn't very nourishing and neither does it generate clean thinking in a person's mind. The milk of human kindness generally curdles and turns sour under such conditions. The more cooler you get, the more heat and hate there is in your heart. In every joint I was ever in, there is always some form of torture that was on tap. I usually got my share of every kind there was. I have had them all at one time or another.

The stock tortures of Oregon prison in Panzram's time were not unique nor would they vanish from penal practice in the supposed enlightenment of the next five decades. A catalogue of prison cruelty, compiled later by Panzram, was fattened in this prison, and it would be echoed and affirmed by others, years later, who served time in Tucker Prison Farm and the Camp Pendleton brig.

The Jacket. Different places and different people have different kinds of torture they use to reform people. The jacket was used on me by jailguards sometime in 1912. It is a form of straitjacket. It's only a piece of very heavy canvas about 4 foot long by 2½ foot wide, with eye-holes on both sides thru which a rope is pulled tight. First the canvas is laid on the floor, the man is laid or sometimes knocked down upon that, facing downwards. Then the ropes are pulled thru the eyeholes and a big burly screw slaps his No. 10 in the middle of your back and hauls with all his strength on the ropes until you're as tight as you can get. I only got one hour of that but it was plenty. I have heard of cases where other men got 6 to 8 hours in the Jacket. After my one hour my blood had stopped circulating and I was numb all over. When I was taken out I couldn't walk hardly at all and not very good for a week. It took more than a month for the effects to wear off. That's your damn Jacket.

The Snorting Pole. This is a very common form of punishment that is used in the southern states. A large post about 12 foot long by one foot in diameter is sunk into the ground. Near the top is a pair of handcuffs to which a rope is made fast. When a man is whipped at the Snorting Pole, he is whipped with the Red Heifer—a black snake whip about 8 foot long running from a lead-loaded butt and tapering down to a fine lash.

The man to be whipped is first handcuffed to the post and then the rope is pulled up tight until the man is on his toes, barely touching the ground. Then his shirt is pulled either off or up over his head, usually the latter, and his trousers are dropped to his feet. He stands in that position and the whipping boss steps off 9 or 10 feet and starts popping the bud to the poor sucker that is being reformed. When the lash begins to take away little bits of hide and the blood begins to run, then the sucker begins to jerk and yelp, jump and snort. That's why it is called the Snorting Pole.

All of the prisoners are lined up to witness the efforts of one man to put the fear of God into another. When a man is let down after being whipped, he has blood on his back and murder in his heart.

A Dose of Salts. This may be a fine remedy for anyone who is constipated and is looking for relief. This is a sure remedy for that ailment. Believe me, I know. If you don't think so, just try it. This punishment is usually tried out right on the job while the men are working.

When the boss-man decides that some one is in need of a physic, he calls another screw who pulls his gun to back up the other boss. The first one will take his No. 4 strap from his saddle or kit, and then call 3 or 4 of the other prisoners to grab the sucker that is to be whipped. I never saw any of them ever hesitate.

They grab the chump, throw him down on his belly, pull his pants down and his shirt up. One will hold one leg, and one the other. A couple will hold his arms and sit on his head. Then the boss man does his stuff. After about 15 whacks with his No. 4, there is no one around there that is constipated any more.

These things were done to me at the Cherokee County road gang at Rusk, Texas, in 1911.

The Bat or the Paddle. This was given to me by the super and 3 screws of the Montana State Training School in 1905 when I was about 15 years old.

The bat or paddle is an ash stick about 3 foot long by 2 inches wide and a half an inch thick, with a handle about 4 or 5 inches long. I was stripped naked and laid face downwards on a bed, feet tied with a rope on one end and hands tied to the other end of the bed. In that position I got the bat laid to my back 50 times, put into a cell for 50 days, then taken out and given 20 more and then put back into the cell for 20 days more. The first 10 days on bread and water, the last 20 on 2 meals a day, and damned small meals they were too.

The Restraint Machine. This I got several times during 1907-10 in the U. S. Military Prison at Fort Leavenworth, Kansas. The punishments were ordered by Captains Clark and Wolfe. The actual punishments were given me by various screws, privates and noncoms. The privates were too numerous to mention but I'll know them in hell when we meet there.

The Restraint Machine—barefooted, standing on a cold, damp concrete floor, backed up to an iron-barred door, hands behind cuffed to the door. A large belt under my arms around my chest pulled tight to the door. Standing in that position for 4 hours, then let down for one hour to eat my bread and water, then 4 hours more. Then to bed which was a board, no blankets. In the morning bread and water and then 4 hours more and so on for a stretch of anywhere from 5 to 14 days. That was the limit. That's your Restraint Machine.

The Humming Bird. This bird is not a bird and yet this bird is a bird. This isn't the kind of a bird that has feathers and flys thru the air enjoying life and freedom as nature made it and intended that it should.

This bird is a bird that was conceived in the mind of another bird. That one was a human bird. A buzzard of the human species. He sure must have been, to figure out a device that would inflict the maximum of corporal punishment with the minimum of harm to himself and the most exquisite anguish on the victim of the Humming Bird.

This bird was made of steel, water, wire, a sponge and a little electricity. Yet it was alive. That doesn't sound as tho it held such a hell of torture as it did.

First an ordinary steel bathtub in which was 4 or 5 inches of ice cold water. The victim is layed down in that and there chained hand and foot. Then the chief torturer enters the scene. He is dressed in his ordinary clothes and has only a rubber slicker and a pair of rubber gloves on his hands. In his hands he holds a common sponge. This sponge is connected to an electric battery by wires. The switch is turned on and the torturer advances on his victim. He first begins on the soles of the feet by gently rubbing the charged sponge there, and then gradually working his way up the body to the head. The sensations of the victim are that there seems to be millions of red hot needles sticking into him. The agony is intense. Two or three minutes and the victim is ready for the grave or the mad house. Yet there is not a single mark or bruise on his whole body.

A physician stands beside the victim and every few seconds feels the pulse and examines him. When he judges that the victim is exactly on the verge of madness or death, he gives the signal to switch off the current.Then the victim is thrown into a cell where he is left for a few days or weeks.

This torture was born in Ohio and practiced for many years, and all that time there were a lot of people who heard of it and investigated and tried to stop it. They were met at the gate by a big, fine, benevolent-looking gentleman who at once told them what a fine prison he had. On the surface everything looked rosy. The food the committee saw was very good. The prisoners made no complaints.

It is the nature to be deceived very easily by those who wish and have the power and the intelligence to do so. People believe what they want to believe. Truth isn't liked.

Torquemada, chief inquisitor of the Spanish Inquisition, was known as the world's greatest torturer. The methods and all of the instruments that he used to inflict torture on other human beings were all very ingenious, but they were crude compared to those in use today.

I have been to Spain and while there I have visited their museums and big cathedrals where some of those old-time implements were on view. I looked 'em all over. I have read many books which told of the methods then in use. The rack, the wheel, red hot irons to burn out the eyes, pinchers to pull off parts of the body, fire to burn and water to drown.

Everything I have ever seen or read on this subject makes me convinced that, though time and methods have changed, men are the same and the actual results are the same.

Torture, pain and agony is a relative thing. When pain reaches a certain point, then it has reached the limit and can be no worse.

The history of mankind goes back for only a few thousand years, but men lived and died on this earth for uncounted thousands of years before the dawn of history as we know it today. Yet in all these thousands of years men have learned little. The men of the world today are doing the same things that their ancestors did ages ago. Men have always had intelligence which never has increased. Only knowledge has kept advancing.

XI

Oregon's prison was on "hard time," and every inmate and guard felt tension in the routine. Reveille was at 6 A.M. The whirring bell was followed within minutes by a din of crashing and clanging as four tiers of cell doors grated open. Prisoners were required to dress quickly, step outside their cells and stand silently with their arms folded for the 6:10 count. As in most prisons then and now, the tiers were like stacks of cages, each with its own narrow walkway, connected by ladder-like stairs.

A vast shuffling sound filled the cellhouses as the men marched down to breakfast, which was always the same: mush, brown beans, bread and coffee. Inmates filed into small jumpseats at long tables, reaching into open boxes for a pinch of salt. There was no talking. A guard strode up and down the aisle, swinging a cane. In a steel cage high on the rear wall, another guard sat on a stool cradling a rifle. Meals were heavy on starches—potatoes, hominy, mush.

The diet had created an illusion: prisoners who looked plump to the casual visitor frequently were suffering from vitamin deficiency. Skin diseases, rheumy eyes and bad teeth were common. Dental treatment consisted of pulling teeth. Since Oregon did not pay for dentures, nutritional problems worsened. The state refused to buy glasses.[31]

The prison was "invisible" in the staid community, silent and apart. Prisoners were allowed one censored letter a month. Complaints were punishable.

Released from the Hole, Panzram was sent back to his cellblock where he put through a request for work. Instead, he was sent to "the island"—where the prison's idle men shuffled in a corner of the yard that was cut off by a mill race which flowed through barred openings in the wall. Panzram mingled little with the other prisoners. Regarded as a "ding" ("crazy," mentally unstable convict) he was left alone.

Several weeks later, Vinegar Cooper, who was having a haircut in the prison barber chair, happened to glance up and see Panzram at work in the crawl space over the uppermost tier, chopping a hole in the roof.

The bellowing prisoner was stripped, flogged and thrown in the Hole once more.

Meanwhile, the tightly capped tensions of prison were beginning to blow loose. Other inmates copied Panzram's escape plan. Trouble flared in the yard, and a committee of guards told the warden they would no longer patrol except in pairs.

Faced by eroding discipline, the big, bewildered warden accepted Vinegar Cooper's suggestion that troublesome prisoners be required to wear red and black stripes.

This turned out to be a mistake. The "hornet suits" became a badge of honor, and whoever wore one was accepted by other cons as a hero.

Panzram wore his hornet suit with swaggering pride and toiled vengefully in his troublemaker role. Beatings became less frequent, as uneasy guards turned their backs on rulebreaking and insubordination. Tougher cons openly lorded it over weaker ones.

I used to go around in the prison all the time scheming and planning how to escape and causing all the trouble I could. If I couldn't escape, I would help everybody else that I could. I was always agitating and egging the other cons on to try to escape or raise hell in some way.

I finally met a big, tough, half-simple Hoosier kid in there and I steamed him up to escape. He done everything I told him to and some more that I didn't. He went to the warden and he asked for a job on the farm. He got it. As soon as he did he attempted to escape right under the warden's eye.

The youth was Otto Hooker, a twenty-one-year-old orphan whose face was marred by a crooked nose that had been broken by a guard's club when he was nineteen.

Hooker eluded the farm guards one foggy morning and broke away into the autumnal woods south of the prison. In the drowsy hamlet of Jefferson nearby, City Marshal J. J. Denson had been notified of the escape and the usual fifty-dollar reward. In midafternoon he drew his gun on

Hooker as he attempted to cross the South Santiam bridge. There was a struggle. Denson fell, badly wounded. Hooker vanished into the brush with Denson's .38.

The tight prison throbbed with news of the escape-shooting. Warden Minto loaded his shotgun and joined the hunt personally. Late that night, Minto and a guard named Walter Johnson were stationed in the brush alongside a stretch of track. When they heard footsteps crunching into the ballast, the warden commanded a halt. Then his shotgun and a pistol exploded together. Warden Minto fell dead with a bullet in his brain. Johnson emptied his own revolver at a fleeing figure.[32]

The death of Minto shocked the state. At the prison, Cooper locked the convicts in their cells and posted more armed guards. Outside, armed men and yelping dogs combed the area. The back roads of three counties were traversed by dusty, open motor cars filled with solemn men clutching rifles between their knees.

The fugitive Hooker was located hiding beneath a house. He was dragged out by two prison guards and was killed by a carbine fired point-blank by an impassive, trigger-happy Portland patrolman who had killed another suspect in Portland three weeks before.[33] The coroner decided that an inquest was unnecessary.

The death of Warden Minto hardened Governor Withycombe's already tough regime. Withycombe began looking for a new warden and found one immediately. His decision started a train of events that escalated the seething hatred in Carl Panzram and toppled an administration.

XII

When that warden got killed, they sent his brother, a John Minto, to take his place. As soon as the new warden got on the job he began to look me up and make life miserable for me, and I in turn done the same for him. I tried to escape but no luck—caught and severely punished. Next I robbed the storeroom and stole a few dozen bottles of lemon extract which I took out to the gang and got 'em all drunk and steamed 'em all up to raise hell and battle the screws. They did just as I suggested. They run all of the yard screws ragged. I didn't drink at all. Next I set fire to the prison shops and I figured that I would go over the wall during the excitement, but it didn't work worth a cent. The fire went good and burned the whole works down, and that was another hundred thousand dollars to my credit.[34] But I got caught that time. They kicked the hell out of me and put me in the cooler for 61 days on bread and water and then carried me out to a new place that they had just built especially for me and a few more like me.

The bullpen—a prison within a prison—was to be remembered as a symbol of John Minto's administration. Minto, a former police chief, was as tall as his late brother and even stockier. As he lunged into the prison, his gray eyes blazing, he announced that every inmate would remember his brother's death. He found a competent assistant in his deputy warden, Cooper.

The bullpen was built with forced labor under Cooper's direction. Inmates watched from the island as new red walls of brick and mortar rose slowly from the center of the prison. Within these walls, eight new Isolation cells were constructed. Their grated doors each opened directly into the tiny yard inside the pen.

"Jeez, friend," one inmate whispered to Panzram, "these houses is gonna be a cold mother, come winter. It'll rain right on your ass."

"Yours," Panzram muttered, scowling at the new structures.

Panzram was dragged from the dungeon and assigned to Cell No. 128 in the bullpen. Under the stare of armed guards, he fell into line with a half-dozen other rebellious prisoners who were forced to walk constantly around a circular path during all daylight hours. Stopping was forbidden. Wandering from the path was considered an attempt to escape; the guards were authorized to shoot. Talking or looking around was forbidden. Walking too slowly or too quickly was a violation and could result in severe punishment. Panzram counted 102 steps around the circle. Once a day a trusty brought in bread and water.

The bullring was not new to old-timers in the prison.

Many had walked it, and stories were passed down over the years of the ceaseless circular walking. But the renaissance of pain which had rebuilt the bullpen did not neglect the rest of the prison. Practices long abandoned were introduced again.

Supper for prisoners became a time of anxiety as Jack "Jack of Clubs" Benson, the beak-nosed captain of the guards, reintroduced a method of discipline know as "standing out." During the meal, a guard would call out the name of a prisoner to stand out as the other men returned to their cells. In the privacy of the empty dining room, Benson and his men would belabor the unlucky standout with clubs to correct some offense against the rules. There were no explanations and no backtalk.

Panzram had seen other changes taking place in the prison before he was placed in isolation. Minto had vowed there would be no mollycoddling of prisoners, and Cooper carried out the edict.

A prisoner whose rheumatic ankle had swelled to a huge size under the steel clamp of an Oregon boot[35] was ordered to carry a slop bucket down a flight of stairs on crutches. When the man fell, another prisoner stepped out of line to pick him up and was reported for breaking a rule.

Confusion over conflicting orders from guards was generally looked upon as evidence of rebellion. One case recited by an inmate concerned the severe punishment meted out to a young prisoner who had been given contradictory orders by two guards. When the first guard returned to find him carrying out the other's orders, the youth was written up as insubordinate and given thirty lashes at the post.

Later, when the youth went berserk in a dark cell and began screaming and chewing on a blanket, a guard fractured his skull with a brass lock.

Panzram's hatred of the new warden deepened when he was refused a job in the prison's flax mill. He had earned such refusal, but nonetheless it deepened his rage.

The mill was the only place in the prison where inmates could earn money. It paid a quarter a day. Since only fifty jobs were available year round, more than three hundred other inmates worked at nonpaying prison chores or were kept in idleness. Many prisoners were unable to buy chewing tobacco, an apple or other small luxuries which made prison life less unendurable. To earn a few nickels a month, some men sold themselves into peonage to other prisoners with mill jobs. Unscrupulous prisoners lucky enough to get a young cellmate could barter him away to a "wolf" for a fancy price.

On the island, idle men complained bitterly and exchanged grapevine rumors about the mill. They said that mill jobs were used to reward "snitches." The rumor about informers gained currency, and restless inmates watched as the administration shifted workers in and out of jobs. Minto and Cooper, in actual fact, regarded the flax industry as a threat to their own discipline.

On May 26, 1916, the flax mill erupted into a sudden blaze. Guards and prisoners seized the firehose, only to discover that it had been cut. Firemen put out the flames only after more than twenty thousand dollars worth of damage had been done. Panzram was identified as the man who tossed a torch into the storage bin. No one was seen cutting the firehose. Panzram was sent to his old abode, the Hole, where his intermittent roar frayed the nerves of Warden Minto and his deputy, Cooper.

The ashes of the mill had hardly cooled when new trouble hit the prison. Governor Withycombe had gotten wind of the brutal treatment of prisoners under Minto. He appointed a three-man commission to study the prison and quickly obtained evidence that illegal whips and clubs were being used. The governor warned Minto that such practices were not to continue.

At the prison, however, the increasing momentum of punishment was not so easily stopped. A prisoner in the bullpen who allegedly threw a rock at a guard was shot to death. The reeling administration tried hard to put on the brakes. When Panzram sensed the letup, he banged his bucket all night long on his cell door and shouted curses at the guards. When the other inmates realized that retaliation was not forthcoming, they joined him. The noise could be heard all over the prison.

Minto, now acutely aware of Panzram's effect on the entire inmate population, had him locked in a dark cell on reduced rations. A few days later, he gambled on a new strategy. Panzram was released and given a job in the kitchen carrying stovewood. Other inmates watched uneasily as the strange prisoner glowered, talked to himself, and grew angrier. Suddenly Panzram dropped a load of wood and went on a rampage with an axe. As the kitchen help fled, Panzram smashed the locks on a row of unused cells. He was clubbed down by guards and thrown back in the bullring.

Panzram made friends with a thin, intense fellow-prisoner named Jim Curtiss, a hitherto unobtrusive convict who was expecting a transfer to the McNeil Island prison. They celled together and made plans. Their alliance was to write the final chapter for the careers of Minto and Cooper. The two prisoners schemed escapes for others because Panzram was contantly watched.

Escapes became a new scandal. Desperate men, suddenly finding a channel for their anger, risked anything to flee. Minto was beside himself. He vowed that he would have the hide of any guard who permitted another inmate to break out.

In addition to patrolling the cellblocks at night, guards began turning on tier lights once each hour and prodding inmates with a long pole of bamboo to make them move. Inmates became more irritable with loss of sleep.

By early November, the prison was so tense that guards refused to venture into the yard. Governor Withycombe told the Board of Control that the penitentiary was in a state of insurrection. He began to think about his program.

Meanwhile Panzram wrested a metal hasp off his cell door and proceeded to batter the walls and the door. He kept up the howling and battering all night. In the morning, the goon squad went to work again and he was thrown into another cell.

The squad found Panzram's hacksaw, with which he had intended to work an escape with Curtiss. Another hacksaw blade went unnoticed, and on the night of November 11, two inmates named Cocky O'Brien and Step-and-a-Half Smith sawed the locks off their cell doors. Using strips of blankets tied to grapples made from bucket handles, they scaled the main wall and disappeared.

When daylight came and the screws opened our doors to feed us, they found two missing. Wow! There was hell to pay for sure. As they couldn't punish the two who got away, they took their spite out on the rest of us. Two of us, me and Curtiss, they stripped naked and chained us up to a door and then turned the fire hose on us until we were black and blue and half blind.

Word about the hosing reached the statehouse. Governor Withycombe sent for Minto. Minto expected support and praise, but the governor was curt in his questions. The warden at first denied that a hosing had taken place; then he admitted that two men "were wet down a little."

Withycombe was furious. He hurried to make his own investigation and read the results at a Board of Control meeting four days later:

> Yesterday, to determine matters to my own satisfaction, and to get absolutely first-hand information, I went to the pententiary and interviewed Deputy Warden Cooper, the four guards who participated in the hosing, the two convicts who were hosed, and two other convicts who witnessed at least some of the proceedings. The total result, in a most conservative form, is as follows: Each man in turn was handcuffed to a cell door, facing it; his clothing was left on him, the fire hose with full water pressure was then played on him from a distance of approximately twenty-

seven feet, and from a point approximately ten feet higher than the position in which he stood; the stream struck him on the left side but he was fastened in such a way that he could receive practically all of it on his back. One man was thus hosed from probably one to three minutes. The other man was hosed from five to twelve minutes. Higher estimates were given by the prisoners. During the hosing Warden Minto and Deputy Warden Cooper were present.

The force of the water at such a distance, as admitted by the penitentiary engineer, would be sufficient to knock a strong man down unless he had something to back against. He states further that the application of such a stream would be painful, even through clothing, and certainly upon the neck and head. Each prisoner testified that his side and back was made black and blue by the punishment. One prisoner exhibited the cuts on his wrists made by the handcuffs when his weight fell upon them. After the hosing the men were left in their cells with the soaking wet clothing on them for probably an hour.

Why this direct and premeditated violation of my instruction and of the law itself was indulged in, I am at a loss to understand. Granting even that the men were bad troublemakers, a prison administration which cannot handle the problems except by employing such antedated methods admits its own incompetence.

John Minto turned in his resignation.

The story of the hosing made headlines. The embarrassed administration, under scathing attack from the influential Portland *Oregon Journal,* began searching for a new warden. Meanwhile, Deputy Warden Cooper was left in charge of the prison.

A new sensation erupted when it was discovered that inmates, plotting a mass escape, had put rat poison in the food of the guards on the night shift. Reprisals were followed by a noisy riot. Cooper's men forced the howling cons back into their cells.

The armed guard was doubled. Inmates continued their defiance by drumming the walls and cell doors with every object they could find.

Outside, the majestic Portland *Oregonian* printed a lengthy interview in which ex-warden Minto told of his long-suffering trial at the hands of Jeff Baldwin—that is, Carl Panzram.

> We kept him in a cage for incorrigibles in the yard. His pals gave him a saw and he sawed two bars off the door and gained the top of the fourth tier. He was trying to dig a hole in the roof when we caught him. We had to put him in the dungeon.
>
> When the incorrigible cells were finished we put him in there. The first thing he did was tear a bunkpipe out of the cement floor and batter the floors and walls, howling.
>
> When we tried to talk to him, all we got were curses and vile language. Bread and water seemed to make no impression. He made so much noise that he disturbed the hospital. Other inmates watched what he did, and they started swearing, too. There was a discipline problem.

The *Oregonian* published an editorial that voiced exasperation and asked old and hard questions.

> In every large prison there is a percentage of men of violent and evil passions and desperate character. Jefferson Baldwin [Panzram] is a bad man. He is a prodigy of physical

strength. He is a confirmed criminal, who is lawless, unruly, revengeful and treacherous, always. He wantonly violated prison rules and defied and affronted prison authority. Time after time he was punished by solitary confinement or in other usual ways. He had a special malevolence against the warden which took the form of noisy and repeated epithets, filthy threats and attempted violence. He wantonly set fire to a storehouse of flax. He was joined in his insolent and outrageous conduct by another prisoner, and he was altogether a constant and intolerable menace to the peace and order in the penitentiary.

The *Oregonian* will not say that it approves of "hosing" or any other primitive and cruel form of punishment; but it is obliged to confess, frankly, if asked to say what it would have done otherwise with Panzram, that it does not know. It passes the question on to humanitarians. . . . What form of chastisement or reproof would reach a desperate man like Panzram? Force is the law of his elemental being, and it is the only thing he respects and fears. Confinement in a dark cell makes no impression on him, and a meager diet merely weakens his body without softening his ugly and murderous spirit.

Isolation—ah, that's it. Isolate him. If he were to be put in a separate cell, removed from the companionship of his fellows, he would tear his lungs out with his futile yellings and disturb nobody but himself. He could curse his keeper to his wicked heart's content, and, watching his chance, empty his slops upon him, and no one would be there to watch, or hear, or encourage him. That would no doubt subdue him, if it did not cure him. But where at Salem is this fine scheme of isolation to be carried out? And what is to be accomplished by it except insuring quiet in the main corridors and cells, and feeding and fattening an unregenerate animal in his sodden and ugly bestiality.[36]

The question left dangling by the *Oregonian* must have been in Governor Withycombe's mind as he pored over applications for the warden's job. He looked at one, and a shrewd compromise formed in his mind. He wanted neither a policeman nor a civilian. What about a former military man? He thought about it a long time.

Meanwhile, deep in the revolt-ridden prison, Carl Panzram felt escalating hatred throb unchecked by the death of one warden and the resignation of his brother, the death of an inmate who followed his advice, or by his third destructively successful arson.

Still reeling from the firehosing, he rubbed his water-hammered back and gathered the thoughts he was to write about years later.

Once again, time, place and men change. The punishment also. The only thing that remained the same was the result. I was given the hose by Mr. Cooper and Mr. Minton with the help of Nancy Fisher, Cherokee Bill, Lilley, Johnson and another screw by the name something like Mitzer or Mitzger. Anyway he was the one who spat upon me and cursed me. I would know him if I ever saw him even if I don't know his name. At the end I was out and hanging by my arms. When I came to, I was nearly blind, all swelled up, from head to foot, ears on the bum for months afterwards, black and blue all over the front of my body, my privates were as big as those of a jackass. The full effects of this didn't ever wear off completely. This is more than 10 years ago but still every time I catch an Oregonian and get him in a corner, I give him hell. Many a man has paid for what those men done to me that Sunday morning. Maybe that hose did wash a lot of dirt off the outside of me, but it also washed a hell of a lot of dirt inside me too. That's your damned Hose.

XIII

A new warden came then. An ex-army captain by the name of Murphy, and a pretty good old scout he was too. The new warden's method of running that prison was a radical change from the old system. I had never seen anything like he was doing. There was no religion about him and no brutality. Those who wanted religion could have it. There was no punishment of any kind except one and that was to be locked in a cell, given a bed to sleep on, three meals a day, plenty of books to read and exercise twice each day. When I first heard that I thought he was crazy. That was wrong. Then I thought he was a fool. That was wrong. Then I thought he must be a bit queer sexually. I thought he must be a punk or some kind of fruit. But damned if that wasn't wrong too.

Old-time guards developed misgivings the first time they laid eyes on Charles A. Murphy. Their mental image of a bristling martinet vanished like an Oregon mist as they watched Murphy's mud-spattered Oakland Eight lurch to a stop in front of the administration building.

He gripped the extended hand of his chief clerk, J. S. Murray, in a big paw covered with sandy hair. When his blue eyes crinkled in a smile, he looked younger than his forty-nine years. Murphy was an engineer with a passion for machinery and a liking for people. He spent hours tinkering expertly with the engines in his four cars of varying age. Years before, Murphy had risen quickly to a captaincy in the Spanish-American War. A hospital engineer in eastern Oregon, he had accepted the warden's post on certain conditions, including the immediate dismissal of Deputy Warden Cooper and nine of the tougher guards.

Murphy abolished the worst of the dark cells in the Hole, ordered the bullpen emptied and established KP—potato peeling in the kitchen—as the worst punishment a rule-breaker could receive. So many prisoners were set to peeling potatoes that the warden won the inevitable nickname of "Spud" Murphy.

Morale climbed as the new warden termed the prison food "horse manure" after trying a sample. A new steward was hired. Murphy repaired the prison telephone system and tramped ankle-deep in mud around the flax mill, watching listless inmates and studying operations. He wanted to increase the number of jobs to reduce idleness. Even at twenty-five cents a day, this put a strain on the skimpy prison work budget.

Compared to the glacial pace of prison change, Murphy was moving very fast. Prison tension went down, and little was heard from the "hardcores" and incorrigibles, including

Panzram, during the cold, wet winter. But inmates and staff both knew that there would be incidents and tests. Old-timers on the staff were sufficiently awed by Murphy not to cross him. They solaced themselves with the observation that "there would come a time." Murphy, however, had been studying the incorrigibles as closely as they were studying him. He lacked the reptilian survival qualities of the bureaucrat. He wanted to effect change and he was trying to understand a strange occupation. He was not without courage. He was making a daring foray into an approach far ahead of his time.

Heavy spring rain was falling when, on March 25, Deputy Warden Charley Burns reported to Murphy that Panzram had been caught cutting the bars on his cell and wanted to know how long Panzram should be placed in a strip cell. Murphy asked how many times Panzram had tried to escape and whether he had received punishment in the Hole. Burns reported that he had been punished every time, eight times. Murphy observed dryly that experience wasn't teaching much. He surprised Burns by ordering extra rations and, assuming that Panzram could read, some books as well as magazines.

Deep in the prison, Panzram read, ate the improved fare and grew stronger in his sworn intent to escape. On March 30, Burns was back in the warden's office with a complacent expression, reporting that Panzram had been caught sawing the cell door hinges with a hacksaw somebody had dropped into his cell. The warden sent for Panzram. What ensued, in the vivid words of Panzram's confession, written a decade later, forms one of the classics of penology.

He told me himself just what his ideas were. He was an idealist. A lot of his theories were way over my head, and I was too dumb to understand all he told me, but one thing he did tell me that I did understand was this. He told me that he had looked up my record and it was just as bad as it had been told to him. The first officers and the former warden told him that I was the worst man in the prison and that they thought I was the meanest and most cowardly degenerate that they had ever seen or heard of. I agreed with what they told him. Then he told me that he didn't believe them at all and he told me I was not the worst man in the prison. I told him to show me a worse one. Then he told me the biggest surprise of my life. He told me that if I would give my word of honor that I wouldn't escape or try to that he would open the gates and let me outside of the prison to go any damn place I wanted to go but to be back for the count at suppertime. I thought for a few minutes and then I gave him my word of honor that he would see me there for suppertime and that I would not try to escape. Even when I told him that, I had not the least intentions of keeping my word of honor. I fully intended to escape at the first chance. But something went wrong somehow. Old Boy Spud was as good as his word. He opened the gates and I was free to go any damn place I wanted to. I just stood there dumbfounded and so surprised at what I couldn't understand that I didn't try to escape at all. I just walked around a little while to see if any screws were watching me but I didn't see any so I sat down and tried to dope out what it was all about.

Of one thing I was sure. I could have gone if I had cared to. And another thing I was sure of was that there wasn't any more honor about me than the stone I was sitting on. I just thought as I couldn't understand what it was all about that I would stick around a while and see what would happen and then I would sure beat it after a few days. That evening I walked up to the gate of the prison and demanded to be let in. Spud Murphy was waiting for me. He asked me why I didn't beat it. I told him I didn't know. He asked me if I wanted a job on the farm as a trusty. I told him no. I went back into the prison and all the cons told me I was nuts. I thought so myself so I asked the doctor to examine me to see if I was crazy or not. He said I was sane. The warden gave me a job inside of the prison. I worked for him where I would never do anything right for any other wardens in other prisons. In other jails if they made me work, something always went wrong and damn quick too. If they put me to work around any machinery, it soon went on the bum, either the bearings burnt out or something else was sure to happen. But I worked for Spud all right.

He soon got a baseball team organized, and a band. He told me to learn to play ball and some kind of musical instrument. The tailors made me a band uniform and a baseball uniform. But I had never had any chance to learn to play baseball when I was a boy, and I was too dumb to learn music. Then he told me to learn how to be a drum major and lead the band but I was too dumb to learn even that, so finally he asked me if I was too dumb to carry a flag in front of the band. I could do that fine. Every week after that the whole band of 30 or 40 men and the baseball team of 10 or 12 men would load onto trucks or on the train with only one guard with us, and we would go to towns all over the state of Oregon.[37] That outfit of cons had every kind of a mongrel crook and murderer there was in the prison, some doing life, some 99 years, some 50, some 20 and so on down to 1 or 2 years. The state was in an uproar. The papers all over the country had their eyes on Spud Murphy and everybody was watching his experiment with interest.

This game went on all summer and during that time I was put to work outside the walls as a trusty. A few fellows escaped but not very many. I stuck it out, that was for about 7 or 8 months, and made no attempt to escape in any way. I was allowed to stay out in the evenings till after dark, just walking around or passing the time away talking, smoking and enjoying life.[38]

The sheer audacity of Warden Murphy's decision checked the onrushing pattern of Panzram's life and afforded him a curious choice and pause. His changed attitude was followed by a drop in disciplinary offenses throughout the prison.

Murphy went ahead with his refurbishing of the prison. He opened up an unused cellblock, furnished it and housed men one to a cell instead of two. The arrangement was unpopular with some determined "jockers,"[39] but most of the men preferred privacy, ironically the need that was most difficult to satisfy for most prisoners.

Shortly after this, Warden Murphy received a severe letter from a policewoman in Portland complaining about the activities of Jefferson Baldwin (Carl Panzram). She sternly admonished the warden about letting Panzram send hair chains to the daughter of a friend, a small girl who had infantile paralysis. He had asked her to sell them to her friends as curios and thus help him get transportation to South America.

She wrote, "I think Baldwin [Panzram] got her name through her picture being in the newspaper. . . . I would also request that you do not mention me to the man as I happen to bear the same name although I know nothing of him."

Her name was Lola Baldwin; the girl's address was Baldwin Street; Panzram's alias was Jefferson Baldwin. The coincidence was odd. Warden Murphy acknowledged the letter with a curt one-line answer. The sending out of hair chains was stopped.

Two weeks after Panzram was brought to the warden's office, the United States entered the First World War. Liberty Bond drives and patriotic displays blossomed in Oregon. People had no time for gossip about the prison.

In April, the warden had sent an embarrassed guard to purchase a flat of red petunias to adorn the base of the flagpole in the prison yard. Murphy's flagpole was a new landmark at the prison and quickly became the pride of the inmates. Prisoners saluted Old Glory in passing, and any convict who skylarked during raising or lowering ceremonies invited trouble. There is some evidence that Warden Murphy then tried to get prisoners to salute the guards also, but the plan quickly backfired. Failure to salute became a mark of esteem. Murphy quietly dropped the whole idea and moved on to other things.

He revived the honor system initiated by Governor West and amplified the idea by having inmates guard each other on work details outside the walls. The "Murphy Honor Lodge" of prisoners put on Red Cross benefits and excited patriotic admiration in the town. The arrangement prospered until twenty-six members of an "honor gang" chased down three runaways who were also German aliens. The gang members felt they had practically won the war. They expected pardons and were outraged when the governor refused to grant them. Rules were broken and the honor system slowly faded into disrepute.

With a small appropriation wheedled out of the state, Murphy established a school in one corner of the prison dining room. Inmate volunteers installed blackboards, distributed writing slates and sorted out a collection of donated textbooks. The annual book and textbook drive became a tradition in Oregon State Penitentiary and was later called "Prose for Cons." During the afternoons and early evenings, the corner was usually occupied by a small number of burglars, stickup men and murderers who worked on subjects ranging from grade-school grammar to secondary-school mathematics and verse.

"The men did not respond to the efforts in their behalf with avidity and zeal which might be expected," Warden Murphy confessed to the State Board of Control. "Yet the general effect was good. All who attended regularly were noticeably advanced, while those who did not attend were also stimulated to read and study."

In July, Warden Murphy received a letter[40] about Panzram from an unexpected source. An Elizabeth Novell, whose address was given as the Arctic Club, Seattle, wrote:

> I have been in correspondence with Mr. Baldwin [Panzram] for some time. I cannot tell what a change has shown in him since your taking the helm. He appears a man of some hope, his better nature is coming to the front. His former cellmate who was transferred to McNeil's Island told me that Jeff was not guilty of the burning of the buildings. There was no reason for him to tell me an untruth for Jeff had stopped writing to me and I did not know if I

would hear again. I have since learned he spent ten months in solitary confinement, that is why I did not hear.

I have been in prison work about five years in different prisons—Deer Lodge, Walla Walla, Huntsville, and others. Some of the boys have kept in correspondence with me for years after their release, and I try to understand them. No matter how bad, I find something good in them after all. What is your opinion of Mr. Baldwin in securing a parole? He requested me to write to you in regard to it. He tells me you are treating him splendidly.

I wrote to the people in Astoria, Oregon, at the time of his trial. Mrs. Higgins was anxious that he not be given so long a sentence. She is a kind woman at heart and did her best to help him. I always try to do as my correspondents ask me in reason for I find that they they try to please me in behaving better. Will you advise me, Warden, about your opinion? Just what is best to do about Mr. Baldwin? He wants to go to South America and try to do better. I will get him literature on the subject so he may study up the country. Hoping I may hear from you in regard to the matter.

I remain very sincerely,
Elizabeth Novell

Warden Murphy shared with all wardens the occupational chore of answering the letters of good and well-meaning women who would, if they could, bring a ray of sunshine into the gray ugly prison routine. He must have smiled at Elizabeth Novell's calm assertion of "Jeff's" innocence in setting fire to the flax mill. But Murphy was a good man, and he provided her with a crisp and friendly, if somewhat tangential, answer:

I beg to acknowledge receipt of yours of the 21st inst. relative to Jefferson Baldwin, an inmate of this institution.

As noticed by you, there has certainly been a change in Baldwin within the past few months and he has evidently made up his mind to do the right thing and get out in an honorable way. He has often mentioned the fact that it was his desire to go to South America and I am sure he would appreciate any literature on this country. He has been suffering so with rheumatism here of late, but other than this he is getting along fine.

Very respectfully,
Warden C. A. Murphy

Murphy was a correctional pioneer who scarcely realized his accomplishment. His minor disappointment in the school was, in any case, only a forerunner of things to come. But, meanwhile, the prisoners watched and the custodial staff waited as the new warden plunged ahead with his experiments.

Complaints began to mount from the townspeople of Salem as the hostility of law-enforcement ranks began to express itself. A well-known show business personality, T. G. Bligh of the Old Grand Theater in Oregon, helped organize "shows for the cons." Fun was poked at a policeman in a minstrel show put on by the inmates. There were more escapes, and many who read of them did not hear the warden's statement that more than eighty-five percent returned next day. His regime was held together partly by the respect of lawmen and old-line guards for his military record. They sensed a hardness underneath Murphy's push for prison change.

In September, Panzram began a series of events that altered the picture.

There was a big hospital close by where there were a lot of women nurses working. They used to write mash notes and try to date me up for a good time. I used to go out once in a while and one night while I was with one of these girls, having a good time with a bottle of booze she had, I, not being used to drinking much, got loaded to the eyes. I was pretty drunk and the girl was very pretty and affectionate. I stayed too late and then being drunk I thought I was a pretty dumb slob to stick around there when I could be having that kind of a good time all the time. The night was warm and the moon was shining bright. A freight train was whistling down in the yards—calling to me, I figured. Anyway, I answered.

Panzram's disappearance was more that just an embarrassment to Murphy. It gave credence to the critics who had maintained all along that his experiments would, sooner or later, explode in the administration's face. The public, well aware of Panzram's reputation, was alarmed.

Murphy's chagrin turned into shock a week later. Panzram, after hiding in the woods and working his way down the valley, stole a bicycle near Shedd and rode it into the farming community of Tangent. With a sheriff's posse in close pursuit, Panzram broke into a house and stole food, clothes and a loaded pistol. In Albany a few hours later, Chief Deputy Sheriff Joseph Frum recognized Panzram and tried to arrest him. A gunfight ensued. After Panzram emptied his pistol at the deputy, he was captured and placed in the back seat of the sheriff's car. During the ride to the station, Panzram grabbed the deputy's gun and tried to shoot him. The gun failed to fire. Panzram was knocked out and later returned to Salem in chains.

After I robbed that house I felt that I would rather die than be brought back to the prison to face Spud Murphy. I guess that's the reason I had courage enough to put up a gun battle in the middle of town, me alone against the sheriff and the rest of the town. Anyway, that's what happened. I fired and fought until my gun was empty of bullets and I was empty of courage.

Panzram's escape attempt after six months of changed behavior, the consequent violence in the gun battle and the attempted murder of Deputy Frum upset the precarious equation that had allowed Murphy's program to continue. It also upset Murphy himself. He had Panzram placed in the bullpen and made an example of him by hanging him cuffed to the cell door for eight hours every day during the last three days of September 1917. There is no record of any complaint from Panzram.

The change of policy introduced uncertainty into the prison. Inmates took advantage of the nettling distractions to work out escape plots. Although none succeeded at this time, their efforts evoked the usual political concern in high places. The governor began to require daily reports from the deputy warden he had placed under Murphy,

Charles Burns. Burns reported that inmates had tried to ram a railroad car through the prison gate. One convict, working out his own private escape scheme, stuck a piece of garden hose in his mouth and jumped into the mill race with the idea of sawing through the bars under water. He was thwarted unwittingly by three other inmates who believed he was drowning and insisted on rescuing him.

Two prisoners were cut with knives in the dining hall. Several guards quit, accusing Murphy of failing to back them up in conflicts with convicts. The flax mill foreman resigned.

Murphy, who had been riding high and secure a few weeks before, suddenly found himself faced with a two-front rebellion in his prison and hostility in the statehouse. The Marion County grand jury, manipulated by an ambitious district attorney, launched an investigation.

Panzram, silent in his cell, waited for his trial on December 3 for burglary and assault.

Murphy had taken a new look at Panzram and at his prison. He received a letter from Sheriff Bodine of Albany recommending the limit of sentence for Carl Panzram. Murphy addressed a letter to Judge P. R. Kelly of the Circuit Court in Albany:

> I am commanded to have Jeff Baldwin [Panzram] in your court Monday morning for trial and wish to say this man is desperate and will undoubtedly try to pull some desperate stunt during the trial, as he has been heard to say that he does not intend to serve any of the time proposed, and while I know it is not considered to be just the thing to iron a man in the court room, I would respectfully request that he be brought in irons and have them taken

off during the actual trial, but I would like very much to have your permission to put them back on before leaving the courtroom with him because if he tries to get away we would have no opportunity to kill him, which we would certainly have to do.

Yours very respectfully,
C. A. Murphy, Warden
OSP

Kelly gave Murphy permission to put irons on Panzram in the jury room. The day before the trial was to take place, Murphy furnished Kelly with a brief summary of Panzram's record, including the two terms in the Montana State Penitentiary and the wrecking of the jail in Astoria. "This is all we have record of, but I am of the opinion that he has served most of his life in reformatories and prisons," Murphy wrote. "He has been in more or less trouble since his confinement at this institution, has spent considerable time in solitary confinement and has made numerous attempts to escape."

Panzram had two trials, one in the morning for assault with intent to kill and one in the afternoon for burglary. He pleaded not guilty to both indictments and refused to allow the court to appoint an attorney to defend him. Both juries convicted him. Three days later he was sentenced to eight years for assault and two for burglary. Judge Kelly said the sentences would run consecutively. Panzram had escaped from the penitentiary facing four years. Now he faced fourteen.

Back at the prison, Murphy must have felt like a man sitting on a rock slide. The bleak history of Oregon State Penitentiary—the old stone, the smell of caged people, the decades of recurrent punishment and the return of hate despite his efforts—became a hostile presence. His own accomplishments, which had seemed solid, now appeared as tentative as the grass struggling through the abandoned clay of the bullpen.

Murphy discussed his reactions in an unusual letter to Judge Kelly:

> Baldwin's [Panzram's] fall has done more to hurt the cause of the honor system than any other one thing that I know of. If he had made good it seems to me that the rest would have been easy, because he was such a notorious criminal. I think this reformation after all he had gone through and all the grief he had caused other wardens would have shown there was some good in every man if you could find it.
>
> I hardly know what my future course will be regarding Baldwin. I know for certain I will never trust him again, but what steps to take towards reformation, I do not know. I am inclined to think it is hopeless.
>
> Yours very respectfully,
> Charles A. Murphy, Warden
> OSP

Panzram was brought back to the prison and locked in a cell. A few months later he was put to work in the kitchen. Late in April, a snitch passed word to Deputy Warden Burns that Panzram and four other men were planning an escape.

Guards located a cut bar in a window leading to the prison basement. On the other side of the basement was another barred window leading to the front lawn of the prison. Burns figured that Panzram and the others would use that route. He stationed armed guards in a grove of trees a few yards away to shoot the convicts as they came out.

Panzram got wind of the plan. The guards waited in vain. But the day the guards were removed, Panzram learned of the change and proceeded to carry out the original escape plan. He didn't tell the others.

Sawing his way into the basement, he put on the white uniform of a trusty cook. A bar spreader—a screw-jack made from a heavy nut and bolt and a short, notched piece of pipe—took care of the bars in front. Panzram strolled out of gun range before the wall guards opened fire.

I made a clean break. I have never been back since. I still owe 14 years there. That happened in May 1918.

XIV

CARL PANZRAM stepped across the Oregon state line late in September. He was now a man of twenty-seven, with fourteen years on his head. Several hundred handbills were posted and mailed throughout the country; they offered a fifty-dollar reward, not a small sum in those days, for his apprehension. Panzram's height, weight, scars and tattoos were listed. His true name was not given; his aliases, used in Oregon and Montana prisons, were listed as Jefferson Baldwin—7390, Jeff Davis and Jefferson Rhoades.

There was feverish wartime activity on the railroads as Panzram rode cars that were crowded with itinerants heading east. He was now a thoroughly prisonized, totally alienated fugitive, an engine without brakes, fueled by hatred and revenge. His chance for an altered pattern of life had gone glimmering with his break from Oregon prison and Warden Murphy.[41] Panzram had attempted murder, committed arson, robbery, burglary, sodomy-rape and mayhem.

His hatred, however, had not yet come to envelop him, and he had not yet directly taken human life. He was now to spend the longest time of his curious career outside of prison. If he was seeking punishment, it eluded him. He was a lone fugitive, moving in the war-absorbed world of 1918 and in the Armistice-wild and disillusioned era that ushered in the twenties.

The war was on at that time and the country was pretty hot. Every once in a while I was picked up and either turned loose or broke loose. I took the name of John O'Leary [42] and I registered for the army draft at Meyersdale, Pennsylvania. They put me in Class 1-A. That didn't sound good to me, so I kept moving. I moved into Baltimore where I worked for a few days at Sparrows Point and then went into Baltimore, bought a gun and met a nice boy. The boy told me a good joint to stick up at Frederick, Maryland. There we went to the hotel where I registered as John O'Leary. What the kid's name was, I don't know or care. At two o'clock that morning we went down into the lobby of the hotel and stuck up the joint. My end was better than $1,200 and the kid got about a couple hundred in small bills and about 10 pounds of silver. Where he went I don't know.

I went to New York to see what made the lights so bright there. I found out. Later I joined the Y.M.C.A. in New York, and Marine Fireman's Oilers and Water Tenders Union. Those papers with my membership card in the Fireman Oilers' Engineers were sufficient to get me a Seaman's Identification Card. Armed with those credentials, I joined a ship, the *James S. Whitney* of the Grace Line. Went to Panama and from there to Peru where I jumped her and went up to the copper mines at Cerro De Pasco. Worked until the strike and then went to Chuquicomatti, Chile, where I worked for the Braden Copper Corporation a short time, then back to Panama where I signed up as a labor foreman for the Fortification Division, U. S. Government.

A short time there and I went up the coast of Panama to the island of Bocas Del Toro, where I worked driving niggers for the Sinclair Oil Company. They sent me to take charge of a gang way up in the Talamanca Indian country. Not long there until I was fired for fighting anybody and everybody all the time. This was in 1919, and I was still using the name of John O'Leary. I burned the oil well rig at Bocas Del Toro for which the Sinclair Oil Company offered $500 reward but no one ever got it yet.[43]

I learned a little about uncivilized people while I was up in the Talamanca country in Costa Rica and Panama. What I learned I liked and wanted to learn more about them, so when I got back to Colon, Panama, I inquired around a bit and found out all I could about a race of Indians who had not been contaminated or civilized yet by the other civilized people. Those Indians were a tribe called the San Blas Indians who lived in the Darian country in the mountains and on the islands down the coast of Panama. At Panama City I got a legation passport issued to me by the U. S. Ambassador there. But I had to get down the coast and not having the money to buy one I set out to steal a small schooner. I hunted around until I found one I liked. Then I hunted around until I found a hard-boiled sailor who would listen to me. Between us we concocted a scheme to steal that schooner and kill the owner, captain and crew. There were six of them on board of her.

The two of us got all ready to do the business but the other fellow got to drinking and while drunk, he went alone to the schooner and killed all of the six men, but he was too drunk to handle the schooner and the consequences were that he got caught. He was tried in the court at Colon, Panama, and the court sentenced him to 18 months for his crime. I was in the clear. I stayed that way by getting on a Panama ship, the *General Gothals* or the S.S. *Colon,* I don't know which. I came to the States on her and joined the S.S. *Houma,* an oil tanker and went from New York to Port Arthur, Texas, and from there to Glasgow, Scotland. There I robbed the ship and everybody on her for which I got a short bit in Barlinnie Prison at Glasgow, Scotland. When I got out of there I had money and my old Panama passenger's passport.

I went to London, to Southampton, crossed the channel to Le Havre in France and up to Paris. Had a good time but was soon broke, so back to Le Havre where I joined a ship to Hamburg, Germany, and a few other ports in Europe and then back to the States. Landed broke and went to Bridgeport, Connecticut, where I robbed a jewelry store. I got about $7,000 worth of stuff but my end after peddling the lot was $1,500. Then I signed on the S.S. *Manchuria* and went to Hamburg, Germany, and had a hell of a time with my 1,500 American dollars and German marks at 60 to the dollar. In nine days I was broke and came back on the same ship.

Back in New York in the summer of 1920 I think—June or July but maybe August. Five days after I got back broke on the *Manchuria* I went up to New Haven, Connecticut. There I robbed the home of someone in that place. I got about $40,000 worth of jewelry and Liberty Bonds. They were signed and registered with the name of W. H. Taft and among the jewelry was a watch with his name on it, presented to him by some congress or senate while he was the Governor General of the Philippine Islands. So I know it was the same man who had given me my three years in the U. S. Military Prison when he was Secretary of War about 1906. Out of this robbery I got about $3,000 in cash and kept some of the stuff, including a .45 Colt Automatic. With that money I bought a yacht—the *Akista*. Her initials and registry numbers were K.N.B.C., 107,296.[44]

On my yacht I had quarters for five people but I was alone for a while. Then I figured it would be a good plan to hire a few sailors to work for me, get them out to my yacht, get them drunk, commit sodomy on them, rob them and then kill them. This I done. Every day or two I would get plenty of booze by robbing other yachts there. The *Barbara II* was one of them. I robbed her and a dozen or so others around there. I was hitting the booze pretty hard myself at that time. Every day or two I would go to New York and hang around 25 South Street and size up the sailors. Whenever I saw a couple who were about my size and seemed to have money, I would hire them to work on my yacht. I would always promise a big pay and easy work.

What they got was something else. I would take them and all their clothes and gear out to my yacht at City Island. There we would wine and dine and when they were drunk enough they would go to bed. When they were asleep I would get my .45 Colt Army Automatic, this I stole from Mr. Taft's home, and blow their brains out. Then I would take a rope and tie a rock on them and put them into my rowboat, row out in the main channel about one mile and drop 'em overboard. They are there yet, ten of 'em. I worked that racket about three weeks. My boat was full of stolen stuff, and the people at City Island were beginning to look queer at me so the next two sailors I hired I kept alive and at work. One was named Delaney and the other was Goodman or Goodwin.

The three of us on my boat pulled out one day and went as far as Graves End Bay, New York, where I robbed another yacht. They knew it but I figured on killing them both in a day or two. But we only got as far down the coast as Atlantic City, New Jersey, where my yacht was wrecked, with everything on her lost. The three of us got ashore alive. The other two I paid off and where they went I don't know or care. I was sick at that time and a Dr. Charles McGivern took care of me there at his home for a week or so. Him I gave a few pieces of jewelry of Old Man Taft's. I also gave him the .45 Colt Automatic that I done the killing with. I left his home and went back to Connecticut looking for another $40,000, but I got six months in the can at Bridgeport, Connecticut, instead for burglary. I done that six months and while there I borrowed $100 from my doctor, Charles McGivern. When I got out of the can I went to Philadelphia. There I got my Colt .45 back from the doctor.

Then I joined the Flying Squadron of the Seamen's Union who were on strike at that time. A few days later I got into a gun battle with some scab sailors and the cops. The cops won. I got pinched and held for the grand jury under the charges of aggravated assault and inciting to riot. I got out on bail and immediately jumped it. I went to Norfolk, Virginia, got a ship to Europe and robbed and jumped her when I got there.

From Europe I went down to Matidi [Matadi] in the Belgian Congo, Africa. From there I went to Luanda Angola, Portuguese West Africa. There I went to work for the Sinclair

Oil Company, driving niggers, and I sure drove the hell out of them too. I wasn't there long before I decided to get me a nigger girl. I got one. I paid a big price for her. I bought her from her mother and father for 80 eschudas [escudos] or about $8 in American money. The reason I paid such a big price for her was because she was a virgin. Yah, so she said. She was about 11 or 12 years old. I took her to my shack the first night and took her back to her father's shack the next. I demanded my money back because they had deceived me by saying the girl was a virgin. I didn't get my money back but they gave me another and younger girl. This girl was about 8 years old. I took her to my shack, and maybe she was a virgin but it didn't look like it to me. I took her back and quit looking for any more virgins. I looked for a boy.

I found one. He was our table waiter. I educated him into the art of sodomy as practiced by civilized people. But he was only a savage and didn't appreciate the benefits of civilization. He told my boss and the boss-man fired me quick, but before he did I licked the hell out of him. They chased me out of the jungles of Quimbazie where that happened and I went back to Luanda. There I went to the U. S. Consul, a Mr. Clark, but he had heard all about me and my ways and he would have none of me. I left his office and sat down in a park to think things over a bit. While I was sitting there, a little nigger boy about 11 or 12 years old came bumming around. He was looking for something. He found it, too. I took him out to a gravel pit about ¼ mile from the main camp of the Sinclair Oil Company at Luanda. I left him there, but first I committed sodomy on him and then killed him. His brains were coming out of his ears when I left him and he will never be any deader. He is still there.

Then I went to town, bought a ticket on the Belgian steamer to Lobito Bay down the coast. There I hired a canoe and six niggers and went out hunting in the bay and backwaters. I was looking for crocodiles. I found them, plenty. They were all hungry. I fed them. I shot all six of these niggers and dumped 'em in. The crocks done the rest. I stole their canoe and went back to town, tied the canoe to the dock and that night someone stole the canoe from me.

To some people of average intelligence, killing six at once seems an almost impossible feat. That is because of their ignorance of the full details. It was very much easier for me to kill those six niggers than it was for me to kill only one of the young boys I killed later and some of them were only 11 or 12 years old.

In Africa there are bull buffaloes that weigh 2,000 pounds and have enormous strength, yet a crocodile 12 or 15 foot long can kill and eat a buffalo. Any of these 6 niggers that I killed could kill and eat one of those crocodiles. Armed with no more than some small sticks and a bit of grass and a piece of rotten meat they do that trick every day all over Africa. I was forearmed with the knowledge that I had gained and also a 9 millimeter German Luger automatic pistol and plenty of bullets. The seven of us were in the canoe, the other six in front of me where I sat in the stern. The canoe was about 22 feet long, 4½ foot wide and 2½ foot deep.

The niggers expected nothing. They all had their backs turned to me. I am a crack shot. I fired a single shot into each nigger's back, and then reloaded with a new clip and fired another shot into the brain of each one as they lay dying or dead in the bottom of the canoe. Then I threw them all over board and the crocodiles soon finished what I had left of them. This canoe was registered and licensed. It must still be in existence. If it is, there are two bullets imbedded in the wood, one in the bottom near the stern and one on the port side near the middle. These niggers were all full grown men with families who must be still alive and who still remember me as dozens of people saw me at Lobito Bay when I hired them and their canoe.

The pistol with which I did that killing, I brought back to the States. There is a record of it at the Maxim Silent Firearms Co. at Hartford, Conn. where I sent it in the winter of 1922 and 1923, from Yonkers, N.Y. under my name of Captain John O'Leary. Under that name and address, 220 Yonkers Ave., I sent the pistol to them and they sold me a silencer for it. All of this must be on the books of that Company's records. The Port Police and the Belgian Consul at Lobito Bay can verify the rest of the Lobito Bay end of it. I thought that the pistol wasn't deadly enough as it was so I got a silencer for it to be able to do a bigger and more efficient business in the murder line. And, believe me, if that heavy calibered pistol and the silencer had only worked as I thought it would, I would have gone into the murder business on a wholesale scale instead of being a piker and only killing 21 human beings. My intentions were good because I am the man that goes around the world doing people good.

Next I bought a ticket on that same Belgian steamer and went back to Luanda where I again went to Mr. Clark, the U. S. Consul, and bummed him for a ticket to Europe, but he gave me the air and set the cops after me. That night I went to the house of a Spanish prostitute and robbed her of 10,000 eschudas. She also set the cops after me so I beat it. I couldn't get out of there by rail or by ship as the cops were looking for me so I hiked out. I hiked north for the Belgian Congo, 300 miles away, through Ambrizett and Ambreeze, up to the mouth of the Congo River at San Antonio. There I hired a canoe and paddlers who took me across to Point Banana. There I bought a ticket on a French ship to Boma and from there up to Matidi. There I stayed about a month. Then broke, I couldn't get a ship. I stowed away on a U. S. ship, the *West Nono*. They carried me as far as Axime on the Gold Coast and dumped me there. I walked to Secondee [Sekondi] and there robbed some lime juicers and bought a ticket on the S.S. *Patonie*. On her I got as far as Las Palmas [Canary Islands], and there the U. S. Consul didn't know me and I gave him a lot of bull and he bought me a ticket on a Portugese ship to Lisbon, Portugal.

When I got there I at once went to the U. S. Consul to try to get a ship out but I got hell instead. He knew all about me. A Mr. Crandall, a director of the Sinclair Oil Company, had been there a few weeks before on his way from Luanda, and he told the Consul all about me. That afternoon I stowed away on an English coal carrier that took me to Avenmouth, England. A day or so later I signed on a U. S. ship as a consul's passenger to New York. This was in the summer of 1922.

Just as soon as I got to New York I took my old license as captain and owner and my bill of sale which had been given to me in the Customs House in New York City for my old lost yacht, the *Akista,* that I went and saved all of this time from 1920 until 1922. I got a new license and set of papers by turning my old ones in to the Customs House in New York City. I kept these new papers and began looking around for another yacht of the same size and kind so I could steal her, take her name and number off and put mine on.

In July at Salem, Massachusetts, I murdered an 11 or 12 year old boy by beating his brains out with a rock. I tried a little sodomy on him first. I left him laying there with his brains coming out of his ears.[45] Went down towards New York—robbing and hell-raising as I came. That same summer and fall I went through Philadelphia to Baltimore where I bought a ticket to Jacksonville, Florida, on a boat. At Jacksonville, I signed on a ship and went to Baton Rouge, Louisiana, paid off there and went to the Marine Hospital at New Orleans. I stayed there a month or two and when I left this hospital, I robbed their drugroom of two suitcases full of drugs, cocaine, morphine and opium. Sold some in New Orleans, some in St. Louis and the rest in New York. In January or February 1923, I got a job as a watchman at 220 Yonkers Avenue, Yonkers, New York, for the Abeeco Mill Company. While there I met a young boy of 14 or 15 years whose name was George and whose home was and is in Yonkers. I started to teach him the fine art of sodomy but I found he had been taught all about it and he liked it fine. I kept him with me until I left that job in April 1923.

A month or two later I got a job as watchman and caretaker of boats at the New Haven Yacht Club at New Haven, Connecticut. I took very good care of their boats, so much so that I robbed one the next night. The name of the yacht I don't know but the owner of it was the Police Commissioner of New Rochelle, New York, or some place near there. Part of my loot was his pistol, a .38 Colt double-action side-break gun.

A few weeks later about May or June I stole a yacht at Providence, Rhode Island, and sailed it as far as New York. I was alone until then. At New York I picked up a kid about 18 or 20 years old, took him on the yacht with me as far as Yonkers. There I let him go back to New York. At Yonkers I picked up my other kid, George. I took him along on the yacht to Kingston, New York. There I painted the yacht over, changed the name and numbers to correspond to my papers. I tried to sell the boat there. While doing so, I met a fellow who said he wanted to buy my boat but instead of that he got out on the yacht with me where we were laying at anchor. There he tried to stick me up but I was suspicious of his actions and was ready for him, and I shot him twice with the same pistol I had stolen from the Police Commissioner's yacht at New Haven a short time before.

After I killed him I tied a big hunk of lead around him with a rope and threw him and his gun overboard. He is there yet so far as I know. Then I sailed down the river, stealing everything I could as I went. I got as far as Newburgh, New York. There the kid, George, got scared and I let him go home to Yonkers. When he got home he told the police all he knew about me which wasn't much but it was enough for the cops to come looking for me. They caught me and my yacht at Nyack. They took me, boat and all my plunder to Yonkers in jail there. Charged with sodomy, burglary, robbery and trying to break jail there. I got a lawyer there, a Mr. Cashin.[46] I told him the boat was worth five or ten thousand dollars and that I would give it to him if he got me out of jail. He got me out and I gave him the boat and my papers. When he went to register the boat he lost her because the owner from Providence came and got her.

A few days later I went to New Haven where I killed another boy. I committed a little more sodomy on him also and then tied his belt around his neck and strangled him, picked him up when he was dead and threw his body over behind some bushes.[47] Went to New York then and got a job as a bathroom steward on the Army Transport, *U. S. Grant,* going to China, but instead of me going to China I got fired for being drunk and fighting. The next night I robbed the express office at Larchmont, New York, and got caught in the act, put in jail and indicted at White Plains, New York, for burglary. I at once saw that I could be convicted so I immediately saw the prosecuting attorney and with him made a bargain. He promised me that if I would plead guilty and in that way save the county the expense of a trial, he would agree that I would get a very light sentence in return. I kept to my side of the bargain but he didn't. I pleaded guilty and was immediately given the limit of the law, five years. At once I was sent to Sing Sing.

XV

AUTUMN REDS and browns flamed along the banks of the Hudson River as Carl Panzram was unloaded from a train and marched through the armored south gate of Sing Sing prison. Judge Bleakley in Ossining, New York, had sentenced him to five years for third-degree burglary. Panzram had used an axe to pry open a window in the baggage room of the New York, New Haven and Hartford Railroad. He was, it developed, "wanted badly" in Oregon, where he owed fourteen years. A hold was later placed on the prisoner which would keep him available to serve the time in that state after he had done five years in New York. Were he to serve the entire sentence in both places, he would be fifty years old upon release.[48]

This violent fugitive had now ended the longest time he had ever spent outside of reform school or prison since he was twelve years old. He was no longer a young tough in his twenties, prone to violence but shaken by the kindness of Warden Murphy. Carrying the flag in front of the Oregon prison band was now only an ancient memory.

Panzram was thirty-one. Except for a few irrelevant days in jail, he had been free for five years. During that time he had grossly murdered, burned, raped, robbed and stolen with a kind of fateful impunity. He had seen thirty countries, pursuing an obscure pattern of destruction that had begun in his childhood. His anger had been fused into him by violence. He had been whipped, beaten, seduced, raped, dosed with salts, hosed with water, sapped, frozen, overheated, cuffed, ironed and isolated.

His hatred of the human race had deepened after his first murders, and he himself, as a member of the race, was not exempt from that hatred. His life seemed impulsive, happenstance; yet, paradoxically, his crimes were carefully planned. Was he seeking punishment? If so, his capture had been strangely delayed.

But now he *was* captured. He faced the years of imprisonment society had accumulated for him. They began when he was checked into Sing Sing, quarantined for the required period and put to work on the prison coal pile.

Panzram kept an eye on the guards, but none of them offered him trouble. They wore crisp blue uniforms and went around the prison unarmed. A tough but enlightened young warden, Lewis Lawes, had banned holstered revolvers and abolished the carrying of clubs.[49] A career guard, Warden Lawes was beginning to surprise penologists with the effectiveness of his more liberal administration. His talks and writings on the subject of capital punishment laid the groundwork for New York's abolition of the death penalty forty years later. Lawes expanded the honor system and permitted inmates a degree of self-government. Prisoners were allowed more yard exercise.

Built around a rock quarry hewn from the Hudson's east bank, Sing Sing's century-old cells were tight, sunless relics whose dampness in humid seasons required newspapers spread upon the floor to soak up moisture. Lawes allowed prisoners in the older cellblocks to attend a nightly silent cinema in the mess hall. This was largely a health measure, at first, to combat the high incidence of pulmonary diseases in the damp quarters.

Panzram's stay in Sing Sing was shortlived, however. His background and record had come under review by prison authorities. Before the end of October, he and a dozen other prisoners were hurried through breakfast and readied for transfer to a dead-end bastille in northern New York, the Clinton prison for incorrigibles at Dannemora.

Panzram and the others were handcuffed two by two and fitted with leg irons. A heavy chain was passed through the irons, forcing prisoners to keep step as they clanked to Sing Sing's east portico and boarded a special coach on the New York Central Railroad. Ten hours later, after exchanging three locomotives, the train pulled high into the Adirondack Mountains to a stop in a small village less than twenty miles from the Canadian border. The future residents peered through dirty train windows to see soiled gray walls rising sheer from the other side of the town's single street. The sign on the train station said: DANNEMORA.

As soon as the train stopped, the uniformed Sing Sing

guards disappeared. Tough-looking men in civilian clothes jumped aboard carrying shotguns and steel-tipped canes.[50] Some wore hunting jackets or mackinaws. They didn't smile.

Panzram and the others were ousted from the coach under a torrent of growls and curses. They kept in step on the uphill climb to Dannemora's walls. As they passed through the single, rust-colored gate, they could see guards with rifles looking down at them.

The procession halted inside a large building where another dozen guards strode purposefully with canes while the manacles and leg irons were removed. The newcomers were ordered to strip and were quickly searched. Other guards kicked through their extra clothing, removing items which were overlooked at Sing Sing. Pencils, magazines, safety razors, wedding rings, pictures, rosaries, religious medals, letters and keepsakes were confiscated. There were no explanations and no exceptions.

An officer told the naked arrivals the fundamental rules. Silence. No talking in line, at work or at meals. No getting out of step. No moving around the prison except in marching units under the supervision of a guard. No malingering, no complaining. Any prisoner wishing to address an officer must approach within six paces, take off his hat and keep his arms folded tightly across his chest while stating his business. Rule violations would be punished by lockup and loss of good time.

The prisoners were given gray uniforms and new numbers. Panzram, Sing Sing #75182, was assigned Dannemora #17531. He was ordered to a cell in North Hall.

Panzram's course of violence and revenge was being

tested by America's worst prison in the corruption-ridden twenties. A pain-and-punishment mill of almost legendary repute, Clinton Prison had virtually lost its name years before in favor of Dannemora—a mournful sound to prisoners. Even as early as 1905, it had been known as the Siberia of America, a prison set in beautiful mountain countryside, with trees and clear air which the inmates could see and smell as they lifted their faces from the dusty yard. Troublemakers, escapees from Sing Sing, drug addicts—anyone hard to handle—would be shipped to this prison. Dannemora carried a symbolism that was replaced nationally by Alcatraz in 1934 and, for a brief interval in infamy, by Tucker Prison Farm in Arkansas after Alcatraz was abandoned in 1961.

What made Dannemora different from its numerous fierce competitors in sadism and cruelty among prisons of the North (always to be distinguished from the curiously earthy horror of the chain-gang man-destroyers of the South) was the presence of a multigeneration dynasty of guards and their families. In the isolation of their wilderness, they set up traditions and patterns of repression and a value system which they transmitted through sons and relatives to their successors.[51]

The oldest cellblock in Dannemora had been constructed in 1845 and had been little changed since that time. There was no plumbing and little light. The new men, bundles tucked under their arms, were marched in silence through the central rotunda and on through an archway into a vast hall with a high ceiling. On one side were tall, dusty barred windows; on the other side were four enormously long rows of cells, stacked one on top of the other. The closely barred gates of the cells were recessed in the wall, giving each cell the appearance of having been cut from solid rock.

On a barked order from the guard, the prisoners hurried up the narrow maze of stairs to look for their new homes. Panzram's cell, identical to the others, was too small for anything except sitting or lying down. The width was forty inches—just space enough for a man's legs between the iron cot and the wall. On the bed was a stained, bedbug-ridden straw mattress and pillow.[52] A blanket was folded over the end rail.

Each cell in Dannemora was lit with a twenty-five-watt bulb dangling from a cord in the low ceiling. The light was too dim for much reading, even if the prisoner happened to obtain a book. There was no running water and no toilet. A tin cup hung on a nail. Some of the newcomers gagged as they lifted the lids of the strong-smelling iron buckets to relieve themselves.

Food was plain and poorly cooked. The allowance on the budget was six cents per meal, the same as in 1868. No fresh fruit or vegetables were included in this diet.

Of all the New York prisons, Dannemora was the only one designed specifically to punish. The guards did their part. They worked twelve-hour shifts and had to pay twenty-five dollars to the ruling political party to get the job.

Men who tried to escape or who faked insanity were put in a small stone building at one end of the prison yard. There they were cuffed up, beaten or tortured by solitary confinement until they begged to return to their regular cells.[53]

Prisoners whose minds actually broke were taken down

the street to the State Hospital for the Criminally Insane.[54] Transgressors either remained there for life or were brought back to the prison, when their sanity was restored, to resume serving their sentences. At Dannemora, the hospital for the insane was more dreaded by many prisoners than the "Box."[55]

Panzram soon decided that he would not serve five years in Dannemora.

I was there only a few months when I made a time bomb and tried to burn down the shops. The screws found it but didn't blame me for it. They put the blame on a couple of other guys and put those two in isolation. Then I tried to murder a con. I sneaked up behind him as he was sitting in a chair and I hit him on the back of the head with a 10-pound club. It didn't kill him but he was good and sick and he left me alone after that. Then I was locked up for a few months more.

Because of my many convictions and my bad record as an escaped man, I was very closely watched, and at the least infraction of the rules, I was severely punished. I was put to work in the worst workshop in the prison. I had a task to do eight hours work every day, six days a week, for which I was allowed 1½ cents per day. In this prison the work wasn't very hard but very monotonous and wearing on the nerves. The discipline was very strict. The food was very bad. After six months of this I was feeling pretty hot and very disgusted. I attempted to escape. I failed in my attempt but in doing so I fell about 30 feet to a concrete walk, breaking both of my ankles, both of my legs, fracturing my spine and rupturing myself. In this condition I was carried to the prison hospital where I lay five days and was carried out and dumped into a cell without any medical or surgical attention whatever. My broken bones were not set. My ankles and legs were not put into a cast. In fact, nothing was done except give me a bottle of liniment which would have done no good if I had been able to rub it onto myself. The doctor never came near me and no one else was allowed to do anything for me. In that condition I was left for eight months. At the end of that time the bones had knitted together so that I could stagger around on a pair of crutches. After a few more months on crutches, then a cane for a few months. At the end of 14 months of constant agony, I was taken to the hospital where I was operated on for my rupture and one of my testicles was cut out.[56] Five days after my operation I tried to see if my sexual organs were still in good order. I got caught trying to commit sodomy on another prisoner. For that I was thrown out of the hospital and dumped into a cell where I suffered more agony for many months. Always in pain, never a civil answer from anyone, always a snarl or a curse or a lying, hypocritical promise which was never kept. Crawling around like a snake with a broken back, seething with hatred and a lust for revenge, five years of this kind of life. The last two years and four months confined in isolation with nothing to do except brood upon what I thought was the wrongs that had been done to me. Not allowed to receive letters or visits from friends. One lady friend traveled 1,000 miles and spent hundreds of dollars to come and visit me.[57] They allowed her to see me for ½ of an hour only, although she stayed in the town for one solid week trying to see me again. My incoming and outgoing mail was held up or destroyed. I was not allowed to complain to any of the higher officials. Whenever I tried to do that, the letters I wrote were torn up and returned to me.

When the prison inspectors came to investigate conditions and complaints, they were told I was a degenerate, that I suffered from delusions and that I was insane, so they would pay no attention to anything that I or anyone else ever complained of. This went on for all of my five years, and the more they misused me, the more I was filled with the spirit of hatred and revenge. I was so full of hate that there was no room in me for such feelings as love, pity, kindness or honor or decency. I hated everybody I saw.

Hardship in Dannemora grew worse with overcrowding. Passage of the Baumes Laws in the mid-twenties sent four-time losers behind bars for life in New York. A rising public rage against convicts led to a tightening of New York's parole and probation policies.[58]

By 1927, 1,534 desperate prisoners were crowded in Dannemora into quarters intended for only 1,160. Nearly a hundred inmates were forced into the prison's tubercular wing to make room for the extra bodies. Segregation cells were kept full.[59]

As longer sentences were handed down from the bench, more problems grew inside the prison. Dannemora guards seized a box of guns and ammunition that had been shipped to one of the prison industries. It was the forerunner of a bloody explosion to come.[60]

My whole mind was bent on figuring out different ways to annoy and punish my enemies, and everybody was my enemy. I had no friends. That was the frame of mind I was in when my five years was up and I was turned loose to go anywhere I wanted to go. My intention was to rob, rape, and kill everybody I could, anybody and everybody. It was my intention to commit enough burglaries to get a few hundred dollars together and with that to go to a place I had picked out at a railroad tunnel between Meyersdale, Pennsylvania, and Cumberland, Maryland. There I intended to wait until a fast all-steel Pullman train, the Capitol Limited or the National Limited, came along. I intended to have a large contact bomb in the middle of the tunnel fixed so that when the engine struck the obstruction, the bomb would explode and wreck the engine and block up that end of the tunnel. The explosion would set off and burst some large glass containers of formaldehyde and other gas and also set fire to a few hundred pounds of sulphur. The gas fumes thus generated and let loose in the closed tunnel would, in a very few minutes, kill every living thing on the whole train in the tunnel. I would be stationed at the rear entrance to the tunnel behind a barricade and armed, ready to shoot down anyone who had life enough to try to get out of the tunnel.[61] As soon as I was assured that all were dead, I would put on a gas mask and an oxygen tank, such an outfit as is used in mine rescue work, then enter the cars to rob the train. Another precaution that I intended to use was to place a time bomb on a bridge or tressel, 12 or 15 miles back up the line from the way the train had come. This bomb would be set to go off just about the same time that the train would be wrecked in the tunnel. I intended that if this racket had worked out according to the way I figured that it would, I would have at least 1½ hours in which I could work unmolested, and in that time I could gather up 50 or 100,000 dollars from three or four hundred dead passengers in money and jewelry. Then I would go a few miles away and plant everything in a prearranged hiding place. Then go away and remain quietly in hiding for a month or two and at the end of that time I would return, lift my plant, go on to New York and turn everything into cash. With unlimited funds in my hands I then intended to steal millions of dollars and kill millions of people. This I intended to do by starting a war between England and the U.S.A. Sounds fantastic, all right, but I am positive I could have done it. The way that I figured on doing this was to work through numerous brokers on Wall Street, playing the stock market ahead of time with the knowledge that I alone would know that England and the U.S.A. would soon be at war. Forearmed with this knowledge, I would know exactly which stocks would rise and which would fall in value. Then with all my money placed with the proper instructions with the different brokers for investment at the proper time and place, all that would be necessary for me to do would be to start a war between England and the U.S.A. This I intended to do by waiting until diplomatic relations were somewhat strained between the two countries. Then I would quietly sneak up and sink some great British battleship while in American waters on a peaceful mission. This could be done very easily. All I need to do would be to wait until some British ship was laying at anchor in the Hudson River at New York. Some fine night I would come up the river with two gasoline launches made fast to each other, side by side, with one launch filled with TNT with a 15-minute fuse attached to it. In the bomb boat I would have an anchor and a long line. When I reached the proper position about five yards ahead of the battleship, I would light the fuse, drop the anchor of the bomb boat and cast off the lashings of the two launches. In my launch I would go on my way up the river while the bomb boat would slowly float down alongside the battleship where it would explode and sink the ship with all hands, except maybe a few survivors who would be able to tell that they saw two launches which looked like U. S. Navy boats with Navy flags flying, run by a man dressed in a U. S. Navy uniform, who disappeared in the night. If this succeeded it would start a hell of a row between England and the U. S., just as the sinking of the U.S.S. *Maine* did in '98 between Spain and the U.S.A. But if this didn't start a war, then I would go down to the British West Indies, buy a small British schooner, keep her under British registry with all British captain and crew. I would load her with a few tons of explosives, covered with an inoffensive-looking cargo, send her to the Panama Canal where I would place a time bomb in the hold set to go off in some one of the locks of the Canal. I would leave the boat to proceed to her doom and the doom of the Panama Canal. That would be very sure to start a hell of a big war, and in the meantime I would be salting away millions of dollars through speculating on stocks on Wall Street. I have worked on boats and ships and also for the Fortification Division and the Cattle Industry on the Panama Canal as a labor foreman where I handled a great deal of explosives in blasting operations, also I can make any kind of a bomb. These schemes may sound fantastic and grandiloquent and impossible of accomplishment by one man, but I feel sure that it could be done and I also feel sure that I could have and would have done just exactly as I planned if circumstances and luck had not been against me.[62] (I was only out of prison one month and six days, but during that time I committed 12 burglaries and one murder. I had a goal in view and was working toward it as quickly as I could.) If anyone is in doubt as to these facts, then just get the Pennsylvania Railroad timetable, look up the schedule of either the National Limited or the Capitol Limited. Look up the map and you will find that there is a tunnel just as I have described between Meyersdale and Cumberland. I have been there and I know all about where to get the dynamite and fuses.

I used to spend all my time figuring how I could murder the most people with the least harm and expense to myself, and I finally thought of a way to kill off the whole town: men, women, children, and even the cats and dogs. I intended to buy up about a barrel of arsenic poison. Then I was going to get me six or eight hogs, starve them until they were all ravenously hungry and then I would give them all a big feed of flour, water, mash and arsenic poison, all mixed in one mess. They would all dive into it and fill themselves full, and in an hour or two the poison would begin to work through their systems. Then I was going to hang them all up by their hind legs with a wash tub under them to let the slimey poison and froth drain out of them into the wash tubs. That I would strain and dry out, and then I intended to get some clay and make three big clay pots, each one to fit inside the other and each one a little bit harder than the next one. Then I was going to fill all three pots with poison. I was going to put the lot all in one and put that in the bottom of a small creek that flows into the reservoir that supplies the town and prison all their water.[63] That would have fixed a hell of a big bunch of them at one time, for by the time they found out what was wrong with them it would be too late for all the damn doctors in the world to cure 'em. Lucretia Borgia used this racket on a small scale but I figured on a few extra improvements so that I could do a better job than the Borgias done. They were pikers. They didn't kill half enough. They should have killed everybody and left this world for the only good thing in it, Nature. This would be a damn fine world if man was out of it.

When I was discharged I was told that I was as pure as a lily, free from all sin, to go and sin no more. Eighteen days later I committed six or eight burglaries, two days later I committed a murder in Baltimore, and 12 days later, a burglary in Washington, D. C. The next day or two I committed two more burglaries in Baltimore. Then I was arrested there and brought back to Washington, D. C.

XVI

THE ENTRY of arrest on the Washington, D. C., police blotter on August 16, 1928, was almost routine—"investigation housebreaking." Detectives located the suspect's address in an information tradeoff with a young informer and occasional fence, Joe Czerivinski. Czerivinski had been caught pawning a radio stolen from the residence of a prosperous dentist. The informer was released and the officers staked out a decrepit rooming house in a hot, afternoon rain. Later they pushed into one of the rented rooms and turned up a revolver, heavy burglary tools and a strange-looking, bear-like man with a limp, a heavy black moustache and agate-hard eyes that watched them sleepily but made them move with care. As the handcuffs clicked shut on his heavy wrists, the man answered Officer Bradley's first question with his true name and age: Carl Panzram, thirty-seven. He described his occupation as "thief," admitted stealing the radio, and characterized the charge as a "joke." Bradley studied the burly suspect and asked him why he felt the charge was a joke. Panzram replied that he had killed too many people to worry about the charge.

The officers dismissed this as the flippant boast of a caught thief. Later the district attorney supported their feelings that Panzram was what was known in the police parlance of that day as a chiseler, a man who tried to get extradition to another state by claiming commission of a crime there.

They noted attentively, however, Panzram's statement that he had spent time in prisons. He told them that people were better off dead, and he mentioned two dates and places with a clarity that caused them to write down details. But their skepticism was plain. Panzram suddenly took on a "con face" and began a taciturn silence which continued through booking, quarantine and quartering in a four-man cell in the Washington, D. C., jail.

The Washington District Jail was and is an ugly, huge red stone pile, built in 1880. It has served, over decades of time and construction revision, as an all-purpose, maximum-security, racially segregated, federally run prison. During the tenancy of Carl Panzram, the accommodations ranged from drunk tanks and overnight vagrancy quarters to Isolation cells, a death row and an electric chair.

Panzram's cell was located in the south wing on the second tier. This, during the early evening shift, was the province of Henry Lesser, a young, inexperienced guard of twenty-five. On August 20, 1928, Lesser was riding to work on one of Washington's battered green and yellow streetcars. He was about to begin, in the sense of a mission, the longest journey of his life.

Lesser had become a jail guard almost as inadvertently as he would now happen upon one of the strangest killers to wander across the face of this century. He was born in 1902 in a small Jewish and Portuguese settlement in Fall River, Massachusetts, where his Russian-immigrant father, Lazar, earned a precarious living as a door-to-door salesman of frames for religious pictures. Unlike Panzram's parents, Lazar Lesser never punished his children, and his wife, retreating into herself, would occasionally take to her bed, convinced that she was dying. But she was deeply religious and the children watched her light the candles on the eve of every Sabbath.

Henry was similar to Panzram in being the youngest in the family, and one who trailed his two larger brothers and his sister. He was graven in his father's image, a quiet, handsome boy with curly hair and large gray eyes.

Miserable for years in classes, Henry discovered that he could avoid being called upon by sitting in the back of the room and keeping quiet. Recitation caused him agonies of embarrassment; his self-consciousness extended to the synagogue where his bar mitzvah was a near disaster, saved only by heroic prompting from the rabbi.

Henry, the *schrechidicher,* the fearful one, struggled for status within the family. He was aware of his parents' financial straits, and he watched with envy as his brothers organized newspaper routes to bring in extra nickels. Hoping for similar approval, Henry joined a Victory Garden project at school, where boys were paired off to raise potatoes. Henry's partner was a large ninth-grader named Uzzie, who slipped away to smoke cigarettes while Henry toiled. Henry was fascinated as the new potato sprouts emerged under his patient work, but his progress reports on this miracle won him slight attention at the family table. On the appointed day of harvest, Henry ran to the potato patch with his largest sack, only to discover that the *gonif* Uzzie had arrived earlier and taken the crop. Nothing else was ever said about the potatoes.

In the middle of the tenth grade, Lesser quit school. He was shunted to work in a clothing store, moving to similar employment in Washington, D. C., the city where his able brothers had climbed into accounting and law.

Sales work for Lesser was misery. He "related" to his customers, but his shy friendliness was not translated into high sales. Managers totaled his receipt books with faint disdain. Their disapproval turned to raking sarcasm as sales pressures rose. In that day customers were quoted a fifteen-dollar price for suits known as "Lesters" and then were allowed to bargain down as far as ten dollars, with suspenders thrown in. Lesser developed a nervous cough and was depressed.

The misgivings of store managers about their young clerk took on a different meaning as Lesser's resentment propelled him into the retail clerks' union. He became active in the union's affairs. In the antilabor twenties, this effort was the most unrewarding imaginable. Management was hostile, and clerks were—and are—proverbially hard to organize. Clerks' salaries were microscopic. But the difficulties of union efforts were irrelevant to Lesser, who had meantime discovered through the organization a measure of identity and some idealistic new friends. His attitude toward learning changed; he became a hungry reader.

Plunging fervently into union work, Lesser tried to better conditions in the store where he worked by organizing fellow clerks. The enraged manager engaged Lesser in a fistfight, then fired and blackballed him. Lesser was not greatly concerned; his interests had widened and he found a job as an attendant at St. Elizabeth's Hospital. He was inquiring about juvenile probation work when he discovered, and was accepted into, a vacancy as a guard in the District Jail.

Lesser enjoyed the job. He had automatic status in the iron order of the prison; and since he was interested in the downtrodden, here was a chance to help. At the same time, and for the first time, he was in power—the master.

The Washington, D. C., jail was situated in a poor part of the nation's capital, in the south section. In the hot, late afternoon, Lesser watched from the streetcar window as the neighborhood grew shabbier, thinning out into tenements interspersed by vacant lots. The 1928 presidential election was on, and he saw posters of Al Smith in his brown derby. Smith was to be defeated by Herbert Hoover as the Roaring Twenties neared their end in the market crash of 1929.

When the car ground to a stop on Nineteenth Street Southeast, Lesser stepped off with a stream of the ragged infirm who were headed for the government-run hospital next to the District Jail. This was a part of town few people visited without good reason.

Lesser was eager about the prison, but he was new to it. His nose wrinkled at the steamy smell of human sweat and disinfectant as the prison's barred gates opened after the turnkey's look and identifying buzz, and then shut behind him. He pushed back his stiff, railroad-conductor cap with its brass shield that identified him as a guard and adjusted his hot, sweaty, blue serge, double-breasted uniform with high collar and brass buttons.

Lesser looked neat and almost dapper, and his gray eyes were friendly behind thick glasses. He had been trained in the prison policies which emanated from the office of Superintendent W. L. Peak. Peak was a thin, lanky, cold-looking former military officer who hired large, warm, muscular guards. Meticulous order was kept in the Washington, D. C., jail. Oddly enough, Lesser, who avoided flaunting force, had earned staff respect. There had been something tough and persistent about him in several brief "status" encounters which had gained him the respect of fellow guards, and he was known to mind his own business. There was seldom any trouble in South Wing during Lesser's shift.

Once up the iron stairs, Lesser strode quickly along his tier of four-man cells, each an oblong, barred box which was part of a larger square composed of tiers of these cages. The whole structure was a larger box inside the high roof and stone walls of a still larger box. The murmur of voices, the functioning of washbasins and lidless porcelain toilets provided a constant backdrop of noise.

Lesser was to remember later his first awareness of something unusual in one of his prisoners. On the western side, against the setting sun that burned into the tall, dirty barred outer windows, Lesser saw the silhouette of a large man framed by a second set of bars. Lesser was struck by the way he carried his large, round, lowering head. The young guard was affected in a way he could not explain, except to state decades later that "there was a kind of stillness around him, how he looked." He remembered the prisoner's name, C. Panzram. The name was as odd as the man.

As Lesser turned to walk away, he had a peculiar feeling. He turned to see Panzram watching him, his huge hands on the bars. He could hear conversation in the shadows of the cell and knew that two other men were there—a wizened safecracker, Hal Levin, and a pudgy lawyer in for estate fraud, Stanley Furley.

"When is your court date?" Lesser asked casually.

"November eleventh," Panzram said coldly, studying him. The hardness of the convict's face was so striking that Lesser assumed a gang connection.

"What's your racket?" Lesser asked, smiling.

"How did you know?" Panzram said. "What I do is I reform people."

Lesser responded vaguely and moved away uneasily. He thought he heard faint sounds of laughter from the cell.[64]

When the tier fell out for weekly showers two days later, Lesser watched Panzram, noting the scarred and welted body, the insignia tattoos[65] on both sides of his muscled breastbone and the strange prancing limp with which he walked.

Panzram ignored the young guard as he fell into the jail routine. Prisoners were allowed out of their cells only for meals and for a half hour of exercise during the afternoon. Trusties in white trousers were allowed to live in unlocked cells in return for carrying out many prison tasks. They would also run errands—for a price. It soon became clear that Panzram had nothing—and no use for "snitches in white pants." His cellmates alternated in providing Panzram with tobacco and makings, but otherwise they let him alone. Panzram paced and said little.

The day before Furley and Levin were to make a court appearance, Lesser unlocked their cell to allow them haircuts. Although it was against jail rules for a prisoner to receive a haircut except on an appointed day each month, Lesser somehow made sure that his men were neatly barbered and shaved before going to court. Prisoners believed it sometimes made two or three years difference in the judge's sentence.

During the next three weeks, Lesser sensed a buildup of tension in the south tier. Levin and Furley, usually pleasant with the young guard, became shifty-eyed and evasive.

Lesser was puzzled by their reticence. He did not know that they had watched Panzram working tirelessly on one of the bars of his cell, pulling, wrenching and twisting with his powerful hands to loosen the concrete in which the bar was embedded.

Conversation between Lesser and the burly prisoner continued on a wary, impersonal level. Guards and convicts kept apart, and violators earned a deadly ostracism from their respective groups. Lesser, however, was unable to restrain his curiosity about Panzram. He was intrigued by Panzram's description of himself as a man who "reforms people." Late one afternoon Lesser asked Panzram just how he went about doing this. An odd grin widened on Panzram's face until a gold-capped upper tooth showed. Panzram told Lesser that the only way to reform people was to kill them.

Lesser broke off the talk to cover his feelings. He was shocked, but he also felt a strange inner response to the convict. The talk had been quiet across the bars, but Lesser wondered whether Panzram's cellmates had heard. He wondered about Panzram's record.

Early in October, Superintendent Peak called the jail captain and lieutenants to his office and informed them that information had been received advising that Carl Panzram was a dangerous criminal who had done time in different prisons, including Dannemora.

Peak warned his staff to exercise strict disciplinary measures upon observing violations of any kind, especially from those prisoners with records because they were the ones who should know better. Peak was a believer in the efficacy of punishment to cure criminals. His convictions differed little from those of many custody-oriented officials then or now. Punishment is a perennial favorite with the public, helping officials to survive and conferring upon them a moral rectitude. It also, in the case of Peak, sanctioned brutalities inconceivable to the outside world. Peak refused to hospitalize drug addicts, preferring them to suffer withdrawal pains in their cells as a salutary reformative device.[66] Other events, it was whispered among prisoners, took place in a basement room, although this area was routinely shown to grand jury members and visiting church groups as a laundry room.

Later on the same day, guards shook down the entire tier. Two guards entered the cell which housed Panzram,

Furley and Levin. Furley and Levin lay on their bunks pretending sleep. Panzram crouched in a far corner, watching. One guard stood while the other tapped the bars on the rear of the cell with a short iron rod. One bar gave out a dull sound.

The guard smothered an exclamation, and they both looked at Panzram. They ignored Levin and Furley, locked the cell and reported to the captain of the guard. They returned with handcuffs and removed Panzram, who offered no resistance, to a one-man cell in the segregation unit which was composed of six cells functioning variously as solitary confinement, death row or cells for psychotics, depending upon circumstances. The cells were in a short corridor, separated from the south wing by a screened door. Each cubicle was bare except for a sewer hole and a straw tick.

Panzram was locked into the first cell and handcuffed to the door. Four guards came for him at seven o'clock that evening and brought him, tightly handcuffed, downstairs to the basement. They carried saps, and one guard trailed with a stout rope. Panzram offered no resistance. He did not know where he was going.

In the basement of the jail, Panzram was pushed backward against one of the posts, about eighteen inches around and nine feet high, which supported the iron beams running under the ceiling. His wrists were uncuffed, then joined together behind the post and recuffed. A rope was slipped through the cuffs and tied around the post a few feet above his head so his arms were extended upward. The rope was tightened to lift Panzram's heavy body so that only his toes touched the floor. The stretching joints with arms wrenched backward over the head caused instant and indescribable pain.

A short time later, the prison physician, Dr. Harris Berman, appeared with his assistant, a prisoner. Berman was a young, near-sighted career doctor with a pitted face and wiry hair. He had learned to follow orders.[67]

He wore a crisp white coat, and a stethoscope hung from his neck. He looked impassively at Panzram, fitted his stethoscope to his ears and placed it on the suspended man's chest. Panzram swore softly. The physician nodded, shrugged and left. He returned at intervals throughout the night to repeat his heart check.

"Panzram was kept in this position for about twelve hours," Henry Lesser wrote in his notebook. "The next time the doctor came to put his stethoscope on his heart, Panzram taunted him with a charge of committing sodomy on his assistant. The doctor was shocked and voiced intense disapproval. Panzram, in his suffering, shrieked and blasphemed, hurling vilest epithets at the doctor and everyone present, and expressed his desire to kill them. He cursed his own mother for bringing him into the world and yelled that he would kill her and everything human."

A gray dawn light was creeping through the round Roman arches of the jail as the trusties dragged Panzram up the iron steps and locked him in his Isolation cell. He was lying on the floor when Lesser saw him hours later. Lesser saw that both wrists were abraded and bleeding from the handcuffs. Scabs of dried blood covered Panzram's mouth. His huge arms were covered with bruises.

Lesser felt angry and ashamed. He asked Panzram if there was anything he could do but received only muttered curses and imprecations. Lesser backed out of the short corridor, shaking his head.

"During the course of that day," Lesser wrote, "Panzram saw Officer Pratt, one of those who had taken him to the post, peeking in at him. He called Officer Pratt a son of a bitch. Knowing the guard as I do, [I think] Pratt must have been overjoyed at this opportunity for further torture. He wrote an insubordination slip to Peak and that evening four burly guards opened Panzram's cell door. The prisoner resisted and was knocked unconscious with a blackjack. Eyewitness prisoners say that he was kicked and punched by other guards. Panzram was put to the post again and stood there all night."

According to Lesser, Dr. Berman disapproved of two consecutive nights of this torture, but he said nothing. In prison, reticence is a bread-and-butter proposition.

Sometime after midnight, prisoners in other parts of the jail were disturbed by faint, persistent yowling and tortured shouts of defiance. There was speculation when, a few minutes later, Peak was seen hurrying toward the basement.

By dawn, word was out through the grapevine that Panzram had spent the night confessing to the murders of three boys. One of the trusties, who had been assigned to pull on the rope, whispered to a jailmate that Panzram had gloated over the murders, which he said took place around Boston, New Haven and Philadelphia. Panzram had described how he had raped a boy and strangled him with his own belt. He had bellowed that he would kill everybody down there and that he enjoyed killing people.

Although Panzram had told detectives and others about

the murders, his claims had been dismissed as idle talk. But when he narrated the same story under torture, he was taken more seriously, since the statements seemed to be forced out of him. Peak called in the press, and Panzram's admissions were outlined in a story in the Washington *Post*.

Henry Lesser, feeling in his bones the brutality of the punishment, headed for Panzram's cell as soon as he reported for work. Then, remembering his earlier reception, he called a trusty named Simpson and handed him a dollar to pass on to Panzram.

In his seven months as a guard, Lesser had learned that one of the worst things that can befall a man is to spend any length of time in jail without money. In jail, the dollar would buy cigarettes, candy, a newspaper, an extra sandwich—any number of things which relieved the iron boredom of prison routine and prison food.

When the convict tiersman told Panzram that Lesser had sent in a dollar for him, the bruised prisoner thought a joke was being played on him. When he realized the gift was sincere, tears came to his eyes. Later on, when Lesser came by to check cells, Panzram limped to the bars, smiled and spoke civilly to him. With obvious effort, he thanked the younger man, saying that no screw had ever done him a favor before. Panzram told him that reporters had been around for his story, according to the grapevine, but he had refused to see them. He asked when Lesser was going to question him about his life. Lesser replied that when Panzram wanted to talk about it, he probably would.

Panzram studied the young guard. His slanting eyes were cold but speculative. "I'm going to see that you get the story of my life. All of it. Just keep me fixed with pencil and paper."

"We became friendly," Lesser wrote in his notebook, and added a curious expression: "A spirit of *entente cordiale* prevailed between us." He thought about it for a long time. He sensed that he was not only violating a prison rule but was also taking on an obligation.

The next day, Lesser hid the writing materials underneath his blue jacket and smuggled them to Panzram, who quickly hid them underneath a mattress, the cell's only furnishing. "I'm not much for writing, but you come here every night after midnight and I'll have something for you. I may leave here anytime for some big house, mad house, or death house. I want to write it out before I kick off so I can explain my side of it. Even though nobody ever hears or reads it except one man."

It was 2:00 A.M. before Lesser got a chance to slip into Isolation to pick up the first batch of writing. He stayed to converse for a few minutes, catching his first glimpse of a strong if uneducated mind. The young guard was surprised to learn that Panzram had read Schopenhauer and shared that philosopher's pessimism about human affairs.

Intrigued by the pages that rustled underneath his jacket, Lesser walked straight up to the jail barber shop, turned on the overhead light and sat down in the big wooden chair.

The narrow, lined tablet pages were still fresh with carefully penned words which stretched tightly in a slow, even hand, from one edge to another. The top of each page was neatly numbered.

After reading Panzram's account of some of his early experiences in reform school and on the road, Henry Lesser began to feel the nudge of something unusual. Lesser could not find words for what moved him. He felt the grip of a life and the horror of a personality flexing the heavy muscles of retaliation and revenge. He determined to save the prisoner's writings.

XVII

WITH PANZRAM's trial for housebreaking less than three weeks away, federal authorities mulled over requests for extradition from other states, based upon Panzram's confession.

In Massachusetts, the Salem police said that the Boston murder described by Panzram fit closely the details of a 1922 slaying in which twelve-year-old Henry McMahon was beaten to death with a rock.

In Philadelphia, Panzram was indicted for the unsolved murder of Alexander Luszzock, a young newsboy, on the basis of details which could have been known only to the murderer.

Chief Phillip T. Smith of the New Haven police department notified Superintendent Peak that the youth whose body was found on a road leading from New Haven to Bridgeport in August 1923 may have been the victim described by Panzram as the murder he had "enjoyed most."

This victim, said Smith, was gagged with a handkerchief and choked with a belt as Panzram claimed.

Pennsylvania asked for Panzram's extradition.

Meanwhile, the Salem, Massachusetts, police department sent witnesses to Washington in an attempt to link the prisoner positively with the murder of the McMahon boy. On November 1, Mrs. Theresa C. Parsons and Mrs. Bertha Luxton unhesitatingly picked Panzram from a seven-man lineup as the individual they had seen walking along a road with the boy shortly before his body was discovered. The women had told detectives that the man they saw with the boy was carrying something white in his hand as they disappeared into the woods.

Asked casually whether he was carrying anything in his hand at the time he killed Henry McMahon, Panzram replied, "Yeah, I think it was a copy of the *Christian Science Monitor.*"

Still Panzram refused to give further details of the crime, repeating, "I'll speak my piece in open court."

Wary federal authorities, however, decided at the last minute to ignore extradition and to prosecute Panzram on the housebreaking charge.

To Lieutenant Ed Kelly of the District Police, Panzram's recalcitrance was further proof that his murder admissions were a ruse. "Panzram's a chiseler," he told avid reporters who asked about the murder indictments. "You can't believe anything he says."

Panzram shrugged at the news that extradition was out. He penned his manuscript secretly each day, refusing to talk further to detectives, except to deny any connection with an unsolved Rhode Island murder.

November 11, 1928, rolled around as a dark, blustery day in Washington. Panzram limped angrily in his cell. He refused Lesser's offer of a pretrial haircut.

In the early morning hours of November 12, he hastily penciled several more pages of manuscript, handing the narrow sheets through the bars to Lesser. "When you read this," he said, "you'll wish you had blown my brains out instead of blowing me to smokes and eats.'

Lesser gasped at the number of sheets which Panzram handed him. The guard had talked with Panzram casually about crime, the code of the underworld, underworld slang and the like; but Lesser was unprepared, in that more censored day, for the brutal impact of one of the remarkable crime documents of this century. Panzram's rhythmic litany of crime terms and his rude analysis of the crime problem, although written in the twenties, reads as though it were expressed just yesterday by a shrewd, reflective criminal without a structured education.

The underworld code is very simple. It is: Never squeal. Don't be a stool pigeon, a rat or an informer. All crooks want everybody else to believe that they are square. Cops are the same. They all wish everybody else to think they act from principle. They are always telling everyone they meet all about how much principle they have. It's against their principle to do this or not to do that. The queer part of this is that they not only want others to believe this but they even believe themselves. But the real truth of the matter is that they deceive themselves and mistake policy for principle.

When crooks are square with anyone, it is because it is

for their own interest to be so. It is good policy. When it ceases to be to their own interest to be square with one another, then it becomes time to change their tactics, and they are not slow in doing it either. It makes no difference to them who they snitch on, no matter if they have been loyal to each other thru a whole lifetime as partners and friends. No matter if they send their friends to prison or to hell by way of the rope or chair. That cuts no ice. They are looking out for their own precious skins. If they can benefit themselves at the expense of someone else regardless of what the others have to suffer for their treachery, they will sure break the law of the underworld and open up and sing grand opera. I have known cases where men have been loyal pals and friends, have gone thru every crime on the calendar, murders, rapes, robberies, in jails and in freedom, in health and in sickness, riches and starvation and privations. Years and years together and always loyal and square with each other, but when the time came for the test of the first law of nature, self-preservation, everything went overboard. They all squeal sometime. Big crooks and little crooks. They all squeal when it is to their interest to do it. The greatest crooks I ever knew or ever heard of, they all do it.

I have met every kind of a crook there is. I have worked and lived both with and against them. Coppers the same. I know their tricks inside and out. I have associated with every sort, both in prison and on the street. They and their works and their thoughts are like an open book to me. I know them well to my sorrow. I have been mixed up in every kind of a crooked deal there is with every kind of a crook there is. Con-men and gang men. Prowlers and boosters, stickup artists, can-opener artists and sometimes face artists, peter-men and box-men, paper-hangers and crape-hangers, hustlers and rustlers, pimps and McGimps, hookers from the big town and hookers from the sticks, big shots and pikers, dynamiters and sodomiters, fruiters and poofters, dingbats and gay-cats, shiv-men and gunmen, needle pumpers and snow snifters, hop heads and jug heads, wise guys and dumbbells, bootleggers and rumrunners, wolves and gunsels, dips and short-card gamblers, home guards and boomers, booze fighters and cop fighters, and last but not least muzzlers and guzzlers. I have put in twenty-nine years in the game of hooks and crooks. There is no angle of this game that I haven't tried at some time or other.

My kind have their names for each other: Booster—shoplifter; prowler—burglar; stickup or heister—holdup man; jug head—dumbhead; hophead—dope fiend, a smoker of opium; snowbird—cocaine sniffer; needle pumper—hypodermic user; con-man—confidence man; shiv-man—knife man; can opener—outfit of tools to rip a safe; peter-man—box-man or safeblower. Sometimes used to describe a man who slips a peter or knock out drops in another's drink (a Keeley). A pimp is a pimp and a McGimp is both or worse than either. Paper-hanger—forger; crape-hanger—either a gloom or killer. Catting up a scatter or ginmill—to hold up a saloon. Mob is the same as a gang. A gunsel is a punk and a punk is a poofter and a poofter is a pratter and a pratter is similar to a fruiter. The only difference between the two is that one likes to "sit" on it, and the other likes to "eat" it. A face artist is an exceptionally well-experienced fruiter. One who knows his bananas better than an amateur. A face artist is one who goes downtown for lunch and nose-dives into the bushes when he's hungry. Croaker—a prison doctor and a very appropriate title it is too. Big finger—warden;

second finger—P. K. or deputy; screws—the big finger's dogs; dance hall—death house; big house—hoosegow, stir or college. To pull off a hot prowl is to turn off a trick in a private or a joint that is to be kipped or bugged; that is to rob a place where people are sleeping or that is wired. To get a stretch in stir—to do a bit in the hoosegow; to make a lam—to crush out of the hoosegow. A big shot is a leading light of crookdom. A wolf is one who has a preference for a gunsel. Sometimes they fall madly in love with each other and then the green-eyed monster stalks abroad.

I have met thousands and thousands of my kind in every different degree, from the king pins and the biggest of big shots down to the greasiest of grease-balls and without exception, one and all insist on deluding everybody else and themselves also, that they are square, that they have in their make-up the sparks of principle and honor. That they keep the code of the underworld. That they never squeal. Anything and everything against anybody and everybody is quite all right and permissible at any time or place but the one rule that must be kept by all, regardless of anything else is that they must never sqeal. No matter what happens, no matter what pressure is brought to bear on them to get them to open up and squeal. If the coppers work the old mother and Jesus racket on them or give them the third degree, a wrong rap with a big stretch in stir or even the rope or the chair, still they are supposed to keep their traps shut and never squeal.

I have never met or heard of anyone yet who ever admitted that they were wrong and that they were stool-pigeons, squealers or rats. They all insist that they are right guys and square crooks. Even when they are caught right in the act of going on the stand as a witness for the State against their pals, they won't admit it. One and all insist that they are men of honor and that they act from principle only. They all swear that they are loyal to the first law of the code of the underworld.

In theory this seems to be the case. That the average person really believes this to be true and that most crooks believe it also. The average superficial observer only sees a very small part. He sees nothing of what goes on behind the scenes and under the surface. The actual facts of the matter are that none of the crooks are square with one another or with anybody. They are not square with the coppers and the coppers are not square with them.

The coppers are a pretty dumb lot. Most of them are well supplied with big flat feet and a big fat head, which is usually sadly lacking in gray matter. The coppers I have known and I have known plenty of them, too damn many, in fact, were and are a bunch of dumb-bells who couldn't track an elephant in a snow bank unless they first had some rat or stool pigeon to lead them to it, and point it out. Most of them have plenty of brawn but few have any brains. With all of the forces of the law behind the coppers, all the steel bars and stone walls, their guns and clubs, all would avail them nothing if it wasn't for their rats and stool-pigeons. The third degree and the rats are the best and worst weapons that the cops have. Yet they will never admit that they have or use either. Perhaps it isn't generally known but it is a fact nevertheless that during the World War every man in this country was classified all according to their mental and physical and moral conditions. The crooks and coppers were both put in the same class, which was pretty low down in the scale.

Few people know that gangsters and gunmen in New York

City have on several occasions made special reservations and very expensive trips to and from the Clinton Prison or that they have invited the warden and the second finger [second warden] and 8 or 9 screws at a time to come down to the Big Town where they were wined and dined at the Silver Slipper and other night clubs, all at the expense of those gangsters and gunmen. All of these things are matters of common knowledge among the underworld. Many coppers know these things. The Silver Slipper and the Cotton Club are the special hang-outs of both cops and crooks. Anyone at any time can verify these things. Therefore, it stands to reason that the coppers and the crooks are all working together and all double-crossing each other at the same time. And yet each and all of them are always yelping about their honor and their great principles.

Honor among thieves is the bunk.

Crime. This country is having a war right now [1928] and very few people even realize the fact. War, in the final analysis, is merely murder and robbery and the expenditure of life and property. This country today is having a crime war. Many thousands of lives and billions of dollars worth of property are lost every year. Crime is increasing 10 per cent each year. All society is up in arms to combat crime and criminals. They are using every possible method that the law can devise. The best thing they have been able to do so far is to build bigger and stronger jails and prisons and fill them full of criminals. Just as soon as a prison is filled to capacity, they start right in building more and more. And they are all full. But still there are more criminals every day. There is no end to them under the present system. Even the most superficial investigator of this question of crime knows this to be a fact. All of your police, judges, lawyers, wardens, doctors, National Crime Commissions and writers have combined to find out and remedy the cause and effect of crime. With all of the knowledge and power at their command, they have accomplished nothing except to make conditions worse instead of better. This is not a theory. This is a fact. Statistics prove it beyond any possibility of doubt. This being the case then they and their system must be wrong. Those who make and enforce the laws are more guilty than those who commit the crimes against the law. The criminal does not profit by his crimes. It is the law makers and the law enforcers who do profit the most. They, in reality, are the real cause of the most crime. They know it, too. That's why there is so much crime in this country today. Those who roar loudest about putting down crime are the very ones who cause the most crime.

I am 36 years old and have been a criminal all my life. I have 11 felony convictions against me. I have served 20 years of my life in jails, reform schools and prisons. I know why I am a criminal. Others may have different theories as to my life but I have no theory about it. I know the facts. If any man ever was a habitual criminal, I am one. In my life time I have broken every law that was ever made by both man and God. If either had made any more, I should very cheerfully have broken them also. The mere fact that I have done these things is quite sufficient for the average person. Very few people even consider it worthwhile to wonder why I am what I am and do what I do. All that they think is necessary to do is to catch me, try me, convict me and send me to prison for a few years, make life miserable for me while in prison and then turn me loose again. That is the system that is in practice today in this country. The consequences are that anyone and everyone can see crime and lots of it. Those who are sincere in their desire to put down crime are to be pitied for all of their efforts which accomplish so little in the desired direction. They are the ones who are deceived by their own ignorance and by the trickery and greed of others who profit the most by crime. Much depends upon the point of view of the persons who express themselves on the crime question. Those who roar the loudest and are therefore the most heard are the writers, judges, lawyers, and would-be expert criminologists. All of these people make a nice, soft living out of crime.[68] Therefore, they are directly interested in that subject. They don't produce a damn thing. All they do is to shoot off their mouths and push a fountain pen. And for doing this they live nice and soft. They wear good clothes, eat the best foods, live in nice homes, have the best of everything the world produces. They have a nice, soft graft, and they know it, too. They are not a lot of chumps like the criminals. Don't think for a minute that they are going around really meaning to do as they say they wish to. Put down crime. Not a chance. There will be no pick and shovel for that sort of people. That's what would happen to them if they really did put down crime. There is two sides to every question. My point of view is just as plausible and a damn sight more probable than all of the hot air that has been published about this question. Others who have expressed their ideas in print on this subject have all been either directly or indirectly interested in receiving some sort of profit or benefit of some kind from what they say or write or do about this crime question. Some have good jobs which they want to keep or perhaps they are trying to get a better one or perhaps they are merely incensed and prejudiced against criminals because they or their friends have been robbed or murdered. I, on the other hand, have not a single thing to gain by writing this. My life and my liberty are forfeited. I cannot gain a single thing in any way for writing this.

I am not writing this because I expect some benefit by doing it. I am not trying to do myself or anyone else either harm or good. My only motive in writing this is to express myself and my beliefs. My point of view. Perhaps I am altogether wrong but, on the other hand, I may be right and you may be wrong. Let the facts speak for themselves and then judge the results. Under the present system, the best and the worst you can do is just as you are doing now and that is making bad matters worse. Before you can ever put down crime you must change the system a whole hell of a lot. Also you must change your educational system. You must absolutely divorce the schools and prisons from all politics. As things are now, you are making criminals much faster than you are reforming those who are already in existence. Every child has some criminal tendencies. It is your place to correct those traits and teach them the right way to live while they are young and their minds are forming. Then when they do reach the age of reason and action, it will be quite natural for them to live clean, upright, honorable lives. In that way you will stop crime at its source before it begins.

As for the criminals that are now in existence and working at their trade or those that you now have in prison, you can reform those who are capable of being reformed and those few who are incapable of any kind of reformation, you can keep them where you have them now, in prison where they can do no harm. These two things you can do or you can keep on doing as you are now. Either make things better or worse. If you think that you can stop crime by catching us, locking us up, punishing us by brutal treatment, hanging or electrocuting us, sterilizing or castrating us, then you are a fool for thinking that way. That only makes bad matters worse.

A child is very easily led. Any child, if properly taught, will live the way he is taught to live. All criminals are merely overgrown children. It is in your hands to make us or break us. We, by our own efforts, are failures in life, simply because we don't know any better. We don't know how to live decent upright lives. Heredity has very little to do with the shaping of our lives. The main causes of why we are what we are is because of our improper teaching, lack of knowledge and our environments. Every man's philosophy is colored by his environments. If you don't want us to rob, rape and murder you, then it is your place to see that the mental and moral misfits are properly taught a sufficient amount of useful and sensible knowledge and put into the proper environment where they can be best fitted to exist in life. Otherwise, they will be misfits and failures and you are the actual cause because they don't know any better, and you do. My own case is very similar to many thousands of others. I was born a normal human being. My parents were ignorant, and thru their improper teachings and improper environment, I was gradually led into the wrong way of living. Little by little from bad to worse. I was sent to a reform school at the age of 11 years. From that day to this, all of my life has been lived among moral and mental misfits. All of my associates, all of my surroundings, the atmosphere of deceit, treachery, brutality, degeneracy, hypocrisy, and everything that is bad and nothing that is good. Is it unnatural that I should have absorbed these things and have become what I am today, a treacherous, degenerate, brutal, human savage, devoid of all decent feeling, absolutely without conscience, morals, pity, sympathy, principle, or any single good trait? Why am I what I am? I'll tell you why. I did not make myself what I am. Others had the making of me.

If someone had a young tiger cub in a cage and then mistreated it until it got savage and bloodthirsty and then turned it loose to prey on the rest of the world, to go anywhere and kill anyone it wanted to, then there would be a hell of a roar from those in danger of the mad tiger. Everyone would believe that to be the wrong thing to do. But if some people do the same thing to other people, then the world is surprised, shocked and offended because they get robbed, raped and killed. Yet this is exactly what is being done every day in this country. They done it to me and then don't like it when I give them the same dose they gave me. They do it to thousands of others and the others in turn retaliate by robbery and murder. If you don't like to be robbed, raped, burned or killed then stop your own injustices, your own dirty work. Stop your lying and hypocrisy. Live decent yourselves and teach others who are not able to do right unless they are taught right. If you get abused, robbed or killed, you have it coming to you, so don't blame it all on the one who harms you. Some of the blame is yours for not making it your business to see to it that such conditions should not exist among your fellow men. If you put a lot of powers in the hands of your public servants and they misuse their power, then you are at fault also. I have only a little knowledge but I have as much intelligence as the average person and I know that I was taught wrong. I could have been taught properly, and if I had been, I feel sure that I would have led a far different life than I have done. You are to blame more so than I. That's my belief. If you are going to go on teaching others as you have taught me, then you must suffer the same as I.

XVIII

LESSER'S SHIFT had already ended by the time Panzram was locked into a chain of prisoners headed for the Washington District Court. The ancient oaken chambers were packed with spectators eager for a glimpse of the strange man who boasted of multiple murder.

Shortly before ten o'clock the courtroom was silenced by the entry of the heavy-set prisoner whose prancing gait drew attention. Flanked by two of the huskiest deputy marshals in Washington, he was securely handcuffed and was not freed until the party was inside the gate separating the court area from the crowded pews. A third marshal stationed himself at the gate.

As the links were slipped from his wrists, Panzram turned slowly and surveyed the inquisitive throng. His eyes had a smoky stare. His expression was contemptuous behind the huge black handlebar moustache. The deputies breathed easier as Panzram drew up a swivel chair and threw his legs under the counsel table.

"All rise!" ordered the bailiff, rapping the gavel smartly for the entrance of Justice Walter I. McCoy.

Panzram busied himself with a toothpick and studied the details of the courtroom as the judge arranged his black robes and stared with annoyance at the scowling defendant.

"Do you have a lawyer?" inquired McCoy, glancing at his copy of the felony indictment for housebreaking.

"I'll be my own lawyer," said Panzram.

A jury was impaneled as Panzram sat impassively, cocked back in his chair. His head did not move, but his eyes followed each venireman as he took his seat.

Prosecutor William H. Collins called witness after witness without cross-examination from the agate-eyed defendant. Collins concluded the government's case with testimony from the small-time informer who had been caught trying to pawn some of Panzram's loot. Joe Czerivinski's Adam's apple bobbed as Panzram looked him in the eye.

"Take a good look at me," growled Panzram. He lifted a huge finger and drew it across his throat. "I've promised it to you and you'll get it. Now get away from here."

The judge rapped for silence.

Later, Panzram asked McCoy, "I take the stand now, do I? I have a few words to say."

On the stand, Panzram's eyes slid toward the table where his pistol and burglar tools lay. Prosecutor Collins whispered to an assistant, who hurried over and removed the exhibits to a safer place.

The arms of the witness chair disappeared under Panzram's huge hands as he faced the jury, ignoring everyone else in the courtroom.

"You people got me here charged with housebreaking and larceny. I'm guilty. I broke in and I stole. What I didn't steal, I smashed. If the owner had come in I would have knocked his brains out."

Panzram's eyes took on a strange depth as he watched the jury.

"There's something else you ought to know. While you were trying me here, I was trying all of you, too. I've found you guilty. Some of you, I've executed. If I live, I'll execute some more of you. I hate the whole human race," he said evenly.

A juror gasped. Panzram's round head suddenly swung toward the prosecutor, who looked alert and suspicious.

"You think I'm playing crazy, don't you? I'm not. I know right from wrong. No delusions. I don't hear anything you don't hear. My conscience doesn't bother me. I have no conscience. I believe the whole human race should be exterminated. I'll do my best to do it every chance I get."

The courtroom was numb as Panzram turned to the jurors once more. "Now I've done my duty. You do yours!"

As Panzram stood up, Collins broke the silence.

"Wait a minute," he barked. "Did you serve five years in Dannemora for burglary?"

"I did."

Collins read off a partial list of prisons, jails and reform schools. Panzram acknowledged each one. None of the offenses involved murder.

Collins smiled and sat down. "That's half of 'em," Panzram snorted. Collins refused to argue the case to the jury. Judge McCoy asked Panzram whether he wished to make a final argument.

"No," said Panzram, "they understand it. Let them go and vote."

The jury filed out and returned with a guilty verdict in

one minute, apparently the shortest deliberation time in the courts's history.

"Are you ready for sentence?" McCoy asked Panzram.

"Suits me," the prisoner said.

"I hereby commit you to the custody of the warden of the federal penitentiary at Leavenworth, Kansas, for a term of twenty-five years."

There was a hush in the courtroom at the sentence.

Panzram's face broke into a frightening grin. Fixing the judge in the eye, he lifted his right hand and repeated the gesture he had made for Czerivinski. "Visit me," he said. The judge paled, banged his gavel and adjourned the court.

The jail grapevine brought news of the twenty-five-year sentence to Henry Lesser even before Panzram was returned to his cell.

Lesser didn't know what to say to his friend. He gave him an extra package of cigarettes and mentioned rumors of the impending formation of a new Federal Bureau of Prisons which would, to Lesser's young mind, undoubtedly mean drastic prison reform in line with the most progressive thinking of the day. He discussed with Panzram the ideas of Harry Elmer Barnes, Sheldon Glueck and Hyman Lippman. To Lesser's surprise, Panzram was well read in these theorists. He worked with concentration on the manuscript, thanking Lesser politely for extra cigarettes and other small favors. When trusties and other guards came around, he growled at them.

Toward the end of November, word circulated among the guards that Panzram was in an agitated mood again. They were more than willing to let Henry Lesser tend to the strange prisoner.

The young guard had witnessed Panzram's new blowup

shortly after a letter from a New Jersey farmer arrived at the jail. Lesser had delivered the letter with pleasure because it contained two dollars. But instead of being delighted with the money, Panzram's face darkened as he tore the letter to bits and threw it through the bars.

He explained to Lesser that he had once worked for the farmer for a short time and had recently written a letter demanding ten dollars in back wages.

That evening, Panzram handed Lesser a letter that enclosed the two dollars the farmer had sent. "See that this gets out!" urged Panzram, his huge fists squeezing at the bars. The letter suggested that the farmer use the money to buy some potassium cyanide, and that he swallow half of it and send the rest to Panzram.

Panzram's rages waxed and waned as he awaited transportation to Leavenworth. Lesser noticed the huge prisoner pacing his cell, jingling coins in his pocket and exclaiming: "I would give anything for just one hole!" At this, Lesser said, Panzram would gesture with his fingers to show what he meant.

Panzram's hatred of Peak was well known among the guards. The superintendent discreetly stayed out of the south tier. Panzram boasted that he would murder Peak with his bare hands if given an opportunity.

Word came down after Christmas that a chain of prisoners would be transported to Leavenworth on January 30. Henry Lesser found his name posted as one of the guards to accompany the prisoners. The sergeant told Lesser that his job was to "babysit that dingbat."

Peak grew edgy as the transfer date neared. He gave an order to check the bars in Panzram's cell daily.

The task was assigned to Henry Lesser, who unhesitatingly appeared in the Isolation wing with a short iron bar. Panzram became alert as he caught sight of the object. His face froze as he studied Lesser. The young guard was smiling.

"Gee, Carl, did you ever see such a beautiful sunset?" asked Lesser, pointing to the bars in the back of Panzram's cell.

To Lesser's surprise, Panzram reacted by jumping backward, eyeing the iron rod warily. "Why did you want me to turn my head?" demanded Panzram suspiciously.

Lesser looked down in amazement at the bar in his hand. "I've got to test that window. That's all."

Panzram considered this. His eyes brimmed with suspicion and pain. Gradually he seemed to relax. "I thought you were trying to get me to look the other way so you could hit me with that. Others have done it before."

Lesser shook his head and looked at the bar again. "I would never do that, Carl."

Lesser took a brass key and opened the cell. He walked inside, aware that the prisoner had edged behind him. Slowly, Lesser raised the iron rod and tapped each bar in the window. "I'm sorry I called your attention to the sunset," Lesser apologized. "I guess you're in no mood to appreciate it right now."

Lesser walked slowly out of the cell, locking the door. He heard Panzram draw near the bars behind him. "You're brave," said Panzram in a low voice. "But don't ever do that again. Turning your back on me like that."

"I'm not brave, Carl," protested Lesser. "I knew you wouldn't harm me because we're friends."

"Yes," replied Panzram. "You're the one man in the

world I don't want to kill. But I'm so erratic I'm liable to do anything."

On January 30, 1929, Panzram was one of thirty-two federal prisoners loaded on a train for Leavenworth. The men were handcuffed in pairs, then shackled in two long lines with leg irons and chains. It was to be a long trip by day-coach, with each movement surveyed by shotgun-wielding guards. A spindly suitcase thief was unhappy to find himself handcuffed to Panzram. "Just don't bother me," rumbled Panzram.

On the way out of the jail, Panzram jerked the line of prisoners to a halt as he grabbed for Peak's personal trusty. This was the same prisoner who had taken down Panzram's confession at the post. He spat on the trusty, who fled as Panzram was shoved back into line. Panzram was heard muttering that he wanted Peak and would wreck the train. A guard whispered to Lesser, glancing up at the emergency brake cord as the prisoners settled into the train, guards following. Lesser nodded. Panzram intended to grab the emergency brake cord as the train rolled at high speed, in hopes of producing a derailment. On Peak's nervous advice, the conductor had disconnected the emergency line in the prison car.

Dr. Berman, who had examined Panzram's heart at the post, also heard a tip that Panzram planned to break loose somehow and get to the warden or some other official. Berman, according to Lesser, stood up all night keeping a constant watch on Panzram lest this occur. Panzram gazed at the doctor in contempt. He made disparaging sexual references about Berman and shrieked similar accusations at Peak each time the warden put his head into the car.

"Whenever Panzram saw Peak," Lesser recalled, "his eyes blazed. He had a lust to kill Peak."

At a way station in Missouri, Henry Lesser looked up from the back of the coach and saw Panzram staring through an ice-rimed window at two small boys who peered up curiously at the prison coach. Panzram thumbed his nose at them, pulled his cap down over his eyes and slept. Lesser also looked at the boys and shuddered as he remembered Panzram's confession.

Later that day—February 1, 1929—Lesser heard the iron wheels of the prison train click more slowly as they ground against the rust of switch and spur. He opened the coach door and stood between the cars, breathing the frigid air of the winter plains and gazing at what lay ahead.

Rising from a low hill just inside the Kansas state line, the great squat silhouette of one of the world's most formidable prisons was visible. From the train's unsteady platform, Leavenworth Penitentiary appeared dismally impressive—a twenty-two-acre expanse of red-hued masonry surrounded by a thick wall ranging from thirty-one to forty-two feet high. On this gray winter day it was decorated with a crust of sooty snow.

Guards and convicts alike, bearded and bleary-eyed from the trip, watched in silence as the train made its final switch, rolled through the gaping portals of the east wall and rumbled down "Railroad Avenue" to the red brick heart of the prison. Leavenworth was called the Big Top by the underworld, in contrast to the Little Top—the smaller United States Military Prison nearby.

Carl Panzram may have recalled how he handled this same red stone and brick more than twenty-one years before:

as a sixteen-year-old army prisoner, shackled to an iron ball and chain, he had broken rock to help build the Little Top. He had been in many prisons and at one time summed up his impressions:

> I have been in two reform schools, nine big prisons and hundreds of jails. None of them were any different from the others. All were run under the same system by the same sort of people and the results were exactly the same in all of them. My last term in prison was exactly the same as my first, and the results were the same in each case. And my own case is exactly the same as many thousands of others.

XIX

AUTHORIZED BY Congress in 1895, Leavenworth was constructed by two generations of convicts laboring under armed guard. In a cruelty of history little known and often denied by officialdom, the first contingent of 400 prisoners was marched in shackles from the prison at Moundsville, West Virginia, to the Leavenworth plain, a distance of 1,250 miles.[69] Those who balked were taken out of line and whipped. The silence system was enforced during the long march and the work which followed.

The great wall of Leavenworth was begun in a hand-excavated trench, thirty feet deep. Stone was quarried from the adjacent hills and wrested into place by groaning labor gangs watched by guards carrying Spencer repeating shotguns. Native clay was fired into brick at the rate of a quarter-million units a month at peak production. During the biting cold of Kansas winters, wood fires were built to keep mortar from freezing in the wall.

Survivors told of standing in ranks in winter as guards

counted and recounted prisoners. Men on the wall lost fingers and toes from frostbite, and there were deaths from an epidemic of meningitis during the second winter.

The harshness bred by these early conditions was to become a tenacious part of Leavenworth's legacy. It was later modified only by the corruption of the twenties.[70] R. W. McLaughry, a bristle-bearded Scotsman and former Chicago police chief, took over Leavenworth at the turn of the century, and it was he who forced the construction of most of the wall and the prison cellblocks as well. He was tough, fair and totally punitive, but paradoxically not unkind. One of his statements was, "Leavenworth is hell, and I guess I'm the chief devil."

Guards had orders to shoot any convict who came closer than six paces or moved farther away than twenty.[71] Silence was enforced during meals and at work, and it was a serious offense to be discovered with an unpermitted pencil. McLaughry's tenants received a ninety-rule booklet, with penalties for the violation of any regulation. More serious offenses against the booklet called for cuffiing to the door, beatings and the always sinister rigor of the universal total punishment—the Hole.

When Leavenworth's first permanent building was completed—a one-and-a-half-story structure near the west wall—the first fifty prisoners were housed there. Soon after, a second building was mortared up and more prisoners housed. That summer, the rattle of new chain was heard as 250 dusty convicts marched in from Fort Smith, Arkansas. Others were shipped the following year from San Quentin, California.

With the completion of the new two-story Isolation

building with its triangular dungeon cells, federal officials held a dedication ceremony and turned the old military prison back to the army. Worn down in the prairie, as a permanent reminder of Leavenworth's history, were four smooth, parallel paths traversing the two-and-a-half-mile line of march between the two penitentiaries. Among the thousands of shoes which trod this earth smooth were those of Private Carl Panzram in the years 1907 to 1912.

The prison train came to rest between two long rows of brick buildings. An icy blast of fresh air jolted against the rank smell of the car as the new bodies groaned and stirred. Panzram limped down the aisle, broke a glowering mask and shook hands quickly with Henry Lesser. They promised to write.

The parting had been brief. Impressed in Lesser's memory was the odd gentleness in the two powerful hands that shot out in the manacles, and the incongruous warmth of a smile that lifted the enormous black moustache now showing the first faint gray streaks of approaching middle age.

A Leavenworth officer took the visitors in tow as the new inmates were marched away. During a tour of the prison, Lesser gaped at the huge, five-tiered cellhouses which, despite their size, bulged with inmates. On the eve of the Depression, he was seeing in Leavenworth one of the most seriously overcrowded large prisons in the country. Drugs, gang crime and multiplying statutes passed by a frightened Congress had swelled the inmate population to 3,700 in space designed for 1,640. With the new dead-end bastille of Alcatraz still five years away, Leavenworth served as the abode of a large number of hardcase long-termers mixed with wispy addicts, income tax evaders from the business world, a few military prisoners, minor gangsters and confidence men.

On tour, Lesser was able to peer through the mesh-covered bars of a comparatively large cell. He saw a tall, stoop-shouldered inmate wearing a green eyeshade and moving about among a hanging multitude of cages, each of which contained at least one live canary. The prisoner, who was used to prison tours and being pointed out as a "convict reforming," was Robert Franklin Stroud, a lifer in his thirteenth year of solitary confinement for killing a guard. Later he would become known to Lesser and the world as the "Birdman of Alcatraz."[72] But long before this, the canary-breeding prisoner would cross paths with Carl Panzram.

Superintendent Peak took care of the paperwork of handing over the Washington prisoners and paid a courtesy call on Leavenworth's warden, T. B. White. A tall, strong-willed and personable Texas Ranger, White had taken over the prison in 1927, after a scandal in which the chief clerk had committed suicide and the staff doctor had resigned. Over lunch, White relaxed and listened courteously as the tight-faced Peak described Panzram's dangerous character and urged that the new inmate be placed in Isolation at once.

The suggestion was unusual, and the tense gravity of Peak's manner in making it surprised White. He consulted with his deputy warden, who ran most of the inside of the vast prison. Fred Zerbst, former head of the Atlanta Federal Penitentiary before Republicans replaced him with an Ohio politician, was a career official of thirty years' standing. He had an odd, monkey-like face and an eccentric manner, but he knew his business.

Although Zerbst's precise reaction to Peak's advice can only be surmised, the deputy warden must have felt that many dangerous prisoners were confined in Leavenworth and not all of them could be segregated. In any case, neither White nor Zerbst acted on Peak's strong recommendation. The superintendent rounded up his guards and returned to Washington. Less than six months later, he would enjoy the satisfaction of telling the press that he had tried to warn the Leavenworth officials about Carl Panzram.

Panzram was processed routinely and outfitted in a gray Leavenworth uniform stamped with his new number, 31614. He watched with indifference as the admissions clerk misspelled his name: "Panzran."[73]

Later, the burly convict was led to Zerbst's office in the Isolation building, where the deputy warden addressed him by his new number, lectured him on what was expected and assigned him to a job in the laundry.

Panzram stared at him impassively. Then he shrugged his heavy shoulders. "I'll kill the first man that bothers me," he said matter-of-factly.

The statement, which Panzram had repeated already several times, must have been lost on the busy Zerbst. He was used to dealing with prisoners who looked and acted tough. Backed up by guards and orderlies, Zerbst reprimanded Panzram coldly and told him to get out and get to work. But he had assigned Panzram to a man who welcomed refractory prisoners.

In most prisons, a laundry assignment would have been

routine. In Leavenworth, it was something the well-informed inmate tried to avoid.

The foreman of the prison laundry, located in an ill-ventilated basement across "Railroad Avenue" from Isolation, was a stout, moon-faced civilian named Robert Warnke, often known as R. G. by his fellow staff. Warnke was a veteran of many years standing and was active in the Leavenworth Ku Klux Klan, a strong force in Kansas in those days. He was known to the inmates as very good when he was good, but otherwise as a "pencil artist," someone who wrote up inmates on report, accumulating damaging data in the prisoner's jacket.

Warnke apparently felt no inner warning as the sullen prisoner was signed over to his charge in mid-February of 1929. A trusty led the way to the laundry. Panzram stopped, folding his arms in careless imitation of prison rules, as he drew near a short, plump man wearing a civilian suit and vest. The trusty handed Foreman Warnke an initialed slip with Panzram's name and number on it.

Frowning through gold-rimmed spectacles, Warnke took out a worn pad and pencil and copied the information. He motioned Panzram to work on a machine near a small, withered burglar, Marty Rako. Warnke strolled away and Panzram's look followed him. Rako glanced once at the cold, slanting stare of the new prisoner and allowed himself a slight nod. He sensed trouble. Years later, he would make a taped interview of what he saw and felt in the ensuing weeks.

At large in the prisoner population, on the yard and at meals, Panzram was marked immediately as a loner. He did his work, spoke seldom and spent most of his spare time reading. He shared a cell in D Block with another long-term prisoner who was illiterate and unkempt, and little conversation passed between them. Much of the time the thin, untidy cellmate found himself looking at Panzram's gray-shirted back as the massive newcomer rooted endlessly through books from the Leavenworth library. Panzram preferred philosophy books, which were few in the slender store of the library. His letters show that his grade-school education hampered, but did not stop, his interest in complex concepts. He read Nietzsche and Schopenhauer.

In the laundry, a co-worker made a joking remark about his choice of reading matter, then felt his smile slip as Panzram studied him carefully before limping away.

Panzram's cellmate was due for a similar signal. One evening, the man was staring absent-mindedly at Panzram when the huge prisoner glanced up and caught his eye. It was, as the man later recalled to Marty Rako, a strange sensation. Panzram said quietly, "I think you'd better move, plan to get out of here. Now, do you want me to write out the transfer or do it yourself?"[74]

The cellmate swallowed and found his voice. He would, he said, go.

In Washington, Henry Lesser had been absorbed with the Panzram manuscript. Eleanor Trott, the roommate of a girlfriend, took an interest in the writing and volunteered to type some copies verbatim for submission to a publisher. Lesser had decided to send the material to H. L. Mencken, the celebrated editor of the *The American Mercury* and probably the most heeded American critic in the late twenties.

Lesser wrote enthusiastic letters to Panzram describing his faith in the confession despite the horror it contained. Mail censors at Leavenworth destroyed some missives, but the young guard had friends, and soon there was correspondence between the two men. To protect his job in the District Jail, Lesser used the pseudonym "Henry James"—perhaps to reflect his new literary hopes—and used Miss Trott's Northwest Washington apartment as a return address. But in his excitement, Lesser may have failed to perceive the dangerous soundings in his former prisoner's letters. Panzram's first two letters from Leavenworth, deceptively even-sounding, revealed important details.

Post Office Box 7 — Leavenworth, Kansas
31614 — April 1, 1929

Mr. Lesser:

Your letter of March 30th was handed to me this evening and I am answering at once to thank you for it and its enclosure of one dollar. Your letter was quite short but straight to the point as usual. I enjoyed reading it and I expect to enjoy the spending of your dollar. I never got the post card which you sent me.

This is my first letter since I have been here. I shall be glad to hear from you at any time you care to drop me a line. You can write to me without sending me any money. I'll be glad to hear from you just the same and I'll always answer you.

There is very little news that I can give you because there is none to give so far as I know. I have been here 2 months today. Nothing very unusual has happened to me so far. I have no complaints of any kind. What the future may have in store for me I don't know or very much care. Your postscript in regards to Allen [the only policeman Panzram admired][75] was the natural result to be expected considering the conditions and circumstances in which he was situated. He will be the gainer in the long run. That sort of a man will always be up in front sooner or later.

I believe you know the regulations about my privilege in letter writing. So please don't ever send me anything unless you're sure I'll get it. I don't need anything and I think I can manage all right. My wants are little and I think I can satisfy them. I have met a number of my old pals in here who knew me years ago. I still have my perpetual grouch and I don't believe it will ever wear off until I pass out completely. That time can't come too quick for me. Just at present I pass my time in sleeping, eating, working, reading and thinking. And the last is not the least.

I have wondered about you a number of times, and since reading your letter, the thought has occurred to me that you may be keeping house or getting ready to. The name sounds English. Kind of musical, too. I had hopes tho that you by this time would have found yourself in a better job with more congenial surroundings and a cleaner atmosphere. Take my tip and drop that job like you would poison. That's no kind of a job for you. You are built for better things than that. How is your lady friend and yourself getting along in your writing the Biography of the meanest man you ever knew. I have been passing my time away by scribbling a bit now and then. So far I have written about 30 or 40 thousand words. Should you ever come to this institution and if you cared for it I would gladly make you a present of my little contribution to the world's worst literature. You owe me nothing but I consider myself under some obligation to you.

Well, I'll wind up this tale of woe, by saying so long and best wishes.

I am very truly,

Carl Panzram, 31614

Leavenworth, Kansas
April 15, 1929

Sir:

I received your letter of March 30th and the one dollar enclosed. I answered your letter the day after and am now sending another one.

I did not receive your post card, so don't send any more of them. But letters are permitted and yours will be appreciated by me.

I'll be glad to hear from you at any time and will always answer you if I am able to.

There is something I would like to ask you and as soon as I hear from you I'll drop you another letter.

No more at this time, so, so long and good luck.

I am,

Carl Panzram, 31614

I forgot to tell you that when you write me a letter, you should use plain smooth paper and sign your full name and address and then I'll be assured of getting your letters. Another thing is that when you see Sinclair you can talk to him and verify what I told you about his wells at Panama, Costa Rica and Angola, Africa. He probably won't know me but he will have heard of me from Superintendent Mowriss in Panama, his director Crandall and Mr. Williams, his Superintendent at Loanda, Angola, Portuguese West Africa. He will have heard of me and my wicked ways. Just as a matter of curiosity I should like to know what he has to say about it.

If you should get my letters all right I wish you would let me know, because if you don't get them there isn't much use in my writing. I am not writing letters just to pass away the time for the benefit of anyone else except you and me.

I shall be careful and not write anything that is not permitted, so there will be no good reason why you shouldn't get my letters.

You also in your letters to me must observe the rules as they are here and not write anything that isn't allowed.

Just use plain smooth paper and sign your full name and address on the bottom of your letters as I do here and now.

Carl Panzram, 31614

Henry Lesser received another letter about this time that was to lift his spirits over many years:

THE AMERICAN MERCURY
730 Fifth Avenue
New York

May 25, 1929.

Dear Mr. Lesser:

This is one of the most amazing documents I have ever read. Obviously, printing it in a general magazine would be impossible. Moreover, I doubt that it could be done as a book for general selection The man to handle it effectively is Dr. Murchison. I hope that you let him see it. Meanwhile, my best thanks for sending me the manuscript. I can't recall reading anything more shocking.

Sincerely yours,
H. L. Mencken

XX

Carl Panzram was settling into Leavenworth when he learned, possibly from newspapers but more probably from convict circles, that the Washington, D.C., jail might shortly entertain perhaps the richest man in America ever to serve a prison sentence. By one of the curious ironies of life, Panzram had worked for his oil company, and Henry Lesser was still employed in the prison that would hold him. The judge who had sentenced Panzram had sentenced him, and the prosecutor of Panzram had prosecuted him.

The man was Harry F. Sinclair,[76] an oil millionaire fifty times over. He had been tried and convicted for felonious contempt of the Senate and for shadowing (following) a jury.[77]

Sinclair was chairman of the Sinclair Consolidated Oil Corporation. His conviction came as an aftermath of the fabled Teapot Dome oil-lease giveaway scandal. It was a rape of public holdings of such magnitude that the scandal created anger in a populace jaded by gang murders and multiple political chicanery, cronyism and corruption of the Harding era.

Now one of the rare occurrences of world prison history was about to take place. People were wondering what would happen when fifty million dollars went to jail.

On the evening of May 6, 1929, the Washington, D. C., jail staff, prisoners and a small mob of newspaper reporters had been waiting for more than an hour, peering through the spring drizzle, when three black limousines with headlights ablaze drove around the ugly red stone jail three times and stopped. A liveried chauffeur descended and held an umbrella for Sinclair as the portly, well-hatted oil tycoon emerged, blinking pleasantly in the white glare of camera flashguns. He slipped, caught himself and advanced up the jail steps with a slight limp as his brother and an attorney followed. The chauffeur trailed with two black-grained leather suitcases. He was met by a United States marshal and by G. Ratherdale, captain of the watch, and walked quickly into the prison as the double steel outer door then slammed on the noses of the clamoring reporters. Sinclair was ushered into the office of Superintendent Peak, who then returned to the waiting press.

"Mr. Sinclair has informed me," said Peak, "that he doesn't wish to see the press." Sinclair, the superintendent affirmed, would be treated the same as any other prisoner. He would not be assigned a job until his "qualifications" had been checked. Peak did not know exactly where the oil magnate would be housed. That would depend upon circumstances.

Sinclair's luggage had been picked up by guards and,

in the jail proper, was turned over to a trusty. Henry Lesser followed the entourage of guards and trusties who found it natural to fall behind the large, balding, handsomely imperious man of middle age.

Lesser noted that Sinclair was neither "printed," "mugged" (photographed), strip-searched nor required to take a bath, nor were his clothes examined for vermin in the usual procedure. He was not limited to the five dollars allowed other prisoners.

"Not a dime was taken from Sinclair," wrote a convict observer. "He went to his bunk that night with his hip pocket containing a roll of money so thick that it couldn't go into a side pocket. He had his traveling bags and his toilet articles." Although clad in pink silk pajanas, Sinclair did, however, spend his first night in the prison dormitory. But someone had already found a sick screen to give him privacy. Henry Lesser later heard the gentle snore of fifty million dollars in new surroundings. He was vaguely troubled.

Curiously, the treatment accorded the handsome and loaded guest did not anger the prisoners. Grinning, they accepted this foray into penal surrealism as a lark. Convicts used it to verify their contentions about the essential idiocy of prisons everywhere and waited with suspense to see how far the jail officials would go.

On the following day it was discovered that Sinclair had once enjoyed pharmacy training. This made it inevitable that he would be employed as a trusty in the pharmacy of the prison hospital with Dr. Berman. It was only natural, then, that Sinclair would have a hospital room rather than a prison bunk, and, since there was really little space for anyone else in the room, he couldn't be expected to share it.

Only bars and lack of curtains spoiled the effect as Sinclair turned his quarters into a temporary board room of Sinclair Consolidated Oil Corporation. Peak, aware of the exigencies of worldwide operations, allowed Sinclair to expand into two rooms as important bankers and corporate executives flowed through the jail at odd hours. White visitors were barred from the prison, however, on visiting days for Negroes. The racial protocols of that day proved stronger than the needs of Mr. Sinclair.

On May 16, jail staff and convicts alike shared Sinclair's satisfaction when their 531st convict, #42060, was re-elected *in absentia* chairman of the board of Sinclair Consolidated.

Henry Lesser occasionally strolled by Sinclair's suite, watching for a chance to talk privately with the illustrious inmate. He would watch Sinclair pad by, pink-faced in a monogramed dressing robe, always moving, always knowing where he was going and rarely alone. Lesser was amazed at the swiftness with which Sinclair had been able to reverse the process of punishment for wrongdoing and to substitute for it the pleasant sojourn of a visitor to a strange setting where he was treated as a guest. The guest was invariably courteous. Whenever he made a request, it was accompanied, where feasible, by a five-dollar bill.

Lesser saw large tips handed out as Sinclair's routine needs were serviced. His dirty clothes, for example, were picked up weekly by his chauffeur and sent to the A. Sulka Company, then a special laundry in New York.

Prisoners had arguments, which sometimes grew

dangerous, over who would perform tasks for the millionaire. A convict meeting was finally held, and the prisoners settled on a strict seniority system, listed according to each convict's booking date.

A former Pullman cook landed the job of preparing Sinclair's favorite green salads. Another inmate, whose lucky name was Herbert Hoover, nailed down the shoeshine franchise. When important visitors arrived on corporation business, five-dollar bills disappeared into pockets as trays of catered food were delivered to the hospital suite. Baskets of fruit, which arrived periodically from well-wishers, went home with deserving staff members.

Sinclair ate steak, squab and hot-house strawberries; fellow inmates ate sowbelly and prunes.

Lesser, who had been absorbing socialism with some newfound friends in Washington, slowly became indignant at the bizarre privileges extended to Sinclair. At the same time, he was puzzled at the lack of indignation among guards as well as convicts. Did walls a prison make, when they housed this many million dollars? Henry then smiled wryly, feeling a lump inside his uniform coat pocket. It was the thick, rich Havana cigar he would enjoy at home. Any officer who wished had received one from a box left by Sinclair's chauffeur with the turnkey. It seemed to Lesser that whenever anyone, guard or inmate, opened his mouth or hand, Harry Sinclair put a cigar or money into one or the other.

Trouble, however, developed for Sinclair when Superintendent Peak, with a sudden flourish accompanied by a statement to the press, removed Sinclair's cash money. Peak's regime had been embarrassed by newspaper interviews of released inmates, who had traded stories about Sinclair for a dinner, a dollar and a drink.

"Major Peak, whose kindness of heart is known to many unfortunates, received Mr. Sinclair in his office" for a discussion of problems, the New York *Times* reporter wrote evenly. The ring of services around Sinclair, however, increased and tightened. Lack of ready cash was no problem for Sinclair, because convict lending circles rated his credit as adequate.

It was impossible, really, to dislike Sinclair. He drew a grudging respect from the prisoners, since in their view he had gone to jail essentially for refusing to talk, even though his powerful interrogator was the Congress itself.[78] He also gained favor with inmates because of his genuine indignation at his lot.

"I was railroaded!" Sinclair would assert, his blue eyes blazing with conviction as the prisoners nodded approvingly. He pledged with profane eloquence a campaign to defeat the senator he held responsible for his indictment.

Later during his term (which lasted six months and fifteen days of a one-year sentence), the United States Parole Board turned down his application. Sinclair made strong statements to the press. These were long, and the reporters shortened them. In a haze of rich cigar smoke, his favored friends among the inmates slyly winked as Sinclair, with a majestic flourish, condemned the press *in toto* for omission and distortion of his true words.

Henry Lesser waited for a chance to talk privately with Sinclair about Carl Panzram. It was difficult because Harry Sinclair arose when he wished, and sometimes he wished to rise at noon. Lesser had talked to a red-faced guard who had made the mistake of shouting at Sinclair to get up when the bell rang. There was no answer and Sinclair did not get up. Nothing was done about it.

One day late in May, Henry Lesser found Harry Sinclair alone in the pharmacy. Clad in a white hospital jacket, he was sitting on a high stool, counting quinine pills.

Lesser told Sinclair about Panzram, "a former employee of the corporation," in Leavenworth. He described Panzram's trial and twenty-five year sentence before informing Sinclair about Panzram's work in Angola and Bocas del Toro.

Sinclair bent forward, listening intently. Lesser hesitated, and finally produced a letter from Panzram.

"Panzram got into a fight with one of your foremen and—well, he fired up one of your oil rigs, I guess."

"He *what*?" Sinclair exclaimed. "Let me see that letter!" Lesser was discomfited by the oil man's sudden anger when his property interests were at issue. Reluctantly Lesser produced the letter.

Post Office Box 7 — Leavenworth, Kansas
31614 — May 24, 1929

Your comment about Sinclair's aroused interest in the oil well in Bocas Del Toro, Panama. Tell him not to blame me even tho I am the one who touched it off. A big man by the name Mowriss was the real cause. He canned me when I was doing all right and everybody else was satisfied. His mistake cost Harry a hundred grand. Years later I heard from other fellows like myself that Harry was and is a pretty good old scout to my kind of people. But being sorry didn't rebuild his oil rig. Maybe I earned a part of it back for him by the work I done for him on his oil field down in Angola, Portuguese West Africa. If you will take the trouble to look up the back files of the Saturday Evening Post for 1923 and 1924 you will find a series of articles written by a Mr. Marcosson about the oil business, among them you will find my picture, taken at Quimbazie, way up the Quanza River.[79] I was driving a team of 80 big buck canibals and they were hauling a boiler on a long rope, hooked up two abreast just like oxen. Only they didn't have as much brains as an ox. If you look these things up you must remember that at the time I was sailing under the name of Capt. John O'Leary. Harry may not know me but surely will have heard of me from a Mr. Crandall, one of his directors in his Co. Or Mr. Williams his Supt. in Loanda, Angola. Old man Mowriss sure knows me to his sorrow. He must have wanted me pretty badly when he offered $500 for me. I would like to hear him roar when and if ever he does hear that I am the one who put such a crimp in his plans. I done it because he was bull-headed and wouldn't let well enough alone. Well I have gossiped enough for now so I'll quit writing and start walking up and down the floor talking to myself, cursing a blue streak and every once in a while having a good hearty giggle. But what I got to giggle about I can't figure out yet. But that cuts no ice. . . . So long

Carl Panzram, 31614

Sinclair handed Panzram's letter back to Lesser.

"I do remember that there was a fire in one of our

installations in Central America. I remember Crandall . . ." The oil man's grim look slowly relaxed. He looked slowly around and seemed to recall where he was. The expensive memory of his arson-fired oil well was forgotten.

"You say this man is in prison for twenty-five years? What crime?"

"He broke into a house," Lesser said, "and stole a radio." Lesser saw the look of total incredulity on Sinclair's face. "But there were complications," Lesser added quickly.

"Well," Sinclair said, "that's a long time. Are you asking me to give him some money?"

"No," Lesser said. "I just want to confirm that you know about it. I'd like to write Panzram that you have no hard feelings."

Sinclair was smiling now. "Of course not. I will have that reward offer taken down at Bocas del Toro, if it is still posted. And I wish him well. Twenty-five years! By the way, do you know what Bocas del Toro means?"

Lesser shook his head.

"It means Mouths of the Bull," Sinclair said.

Later, Sinclair overheard an office man comment that a prisoner was only in jail for thirty days and that that was not very long.

"Not very long?" Sinclair exclaimed. "Hell, the only time thirty days doesn't seem long is when it's on a note." Sinclair on several occasions hired legal counsel for prisoners he deemed worthy.

The "Great Presence," as the prisoners called Sinclair, was prone to large gestures and a charmingly informal manner. But whenever he passed a guard who was strong

Carl Panzram, twenty-one, booked into Montana State Penitentiary as Jefferson Rhoades. (Montana State Penitentiary)

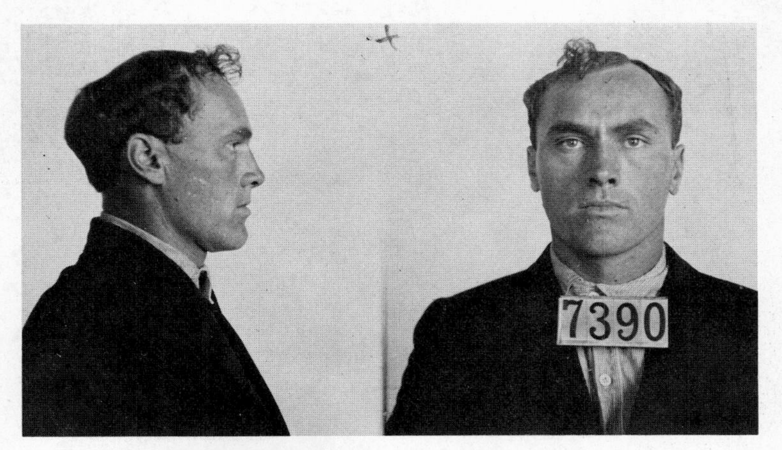

Carl Panzram, twenty-three, in Oregon State Penitentiary. (Archives, State of Oregon)

Carl Panzram, thirty-seven, following arrest for burglary by Baltimore police department. (Police Department, Baltimore, Maryland)

Henry Lesser in 1938, three years after he left federal prison service.

Charles A. Murphy of Oregon State Penitentiary, a correctional pioneer. (Portland *Oregonian*)

William L. Peak, superintendent of Washington District Jail. (Harris & Ewing)

Harry F. Sinclair (left) arriving at Washington District Jail to begin serving his term for contempt of the United States Senate. (International Newsreel Corp.)

Minnesota State Training School, Red Wing, Minnesota, 1906.
(Minnesota State Training School)

Quasi-military uniforms and formations were part of the routine at Minnesota State Training School, 1906. (Minnesota State Training School)

Young inmates of Minnesota State Training School stand barefoot at widely separated workbenches, 1906. (Minnesota State Training School)

Oregon State Penitentiary, Salem, Oregon.

Cellblock, Oregon State Penitentiary, during the administration of Warden Murphy. (Portland *Oregon Journal*)

Cell, Oregon State Penitentiary, 1957. Floor, walls and ceiling are steel; bars admit little light and no fresh air. (Portland *Oregon Journal*)

Bullring, Oregon State Penitentiary. Recalcitrant prisoners were forced to walk ceaselessly around the circle. "Open-air" punishment cells are under the porch overhang. (Portland *Oregon Journal*)

Clinton State Prison, Dannemora, New York, in the mid-twenties. Slitlike apertures at left are entrances to narrow cells. (New York Department of Correction)

Washington District Jail, Washington, D. C., 1929. (International Newsreel Corp.)

Death Row, Washington District Jail. Panzram occupied the last cell, near the window, and wrote his confession there. (International News Pictures)

Stripe-suited prisoners constructing huge cellhouse for the new penitentiary, Fort Leavenworth, Kansas, early in century. (United States Bureau of Prisons)

on military ways, he invariably gave a snappy, deadpan military salute. The inmates knew that Sinclair was amusing himself, and they watched the satisfied guards with covert smiles.

Sinclair soon found a knowledgeable bookie and spent many hours with him in a learned discussion of one of his principal hobbies. The Sinclair racing stable in Rancocas, New Jersey, had five excellent colts, any one of which might be a winner in the next Preakness. The racing world was familiar with the green-and-white track colors of Harry Sinclair.

The country was still wild and bright in the summer of 1929. Sinclair's financial problems, and those of the entire country, seemed trivial in the mounting prosperity. Few were prepared for the financial catastrophe which was then gathering momentum, like a gigantic wave, to break and fall upon the country, ending an era during that autumn. Before the end of his brief sentence, Sinclair would know the frustration of seeing all this from a jail. When he finally emerged, Harry Sinclair would walk grimly into a different age.

XXI

Outside, the world of the twenties moved gaily ahead with little awareness of the country's decaying prisons. As spring thawed in 1929, Americans bent to their radios and heard the distant crackle of President Herbert Hoover expressing confidence in his predictions of a new era of profit. Borrowed cash and extended buying on margin sent the stock market roaring on its last dizzy ascent as the unaffluent joined the national rush to wealth. Busboys, retired teachers and widows emptied their savings into shares of anything within reach.

But in the country's deep underbelly, the vise of poverty was being paradoxically tightened. Unemployment was rising as small farmers throughout the country, already the hidden victims of the postwar years, abandoned their homesteads and set out for the nearest cities. Vagrancy laws were tightened and petty crimes increased.

Meanwhile, the disaster of Prohibition had nurtured a

vast army of violators, creating a climate in which local law enforcement broke down in spasms of graft and accommodation. Hoodlums fought each other openly for control as Congress, now thoroughly alarmed, passed new statutes reinforcing the police powers of the federal government. In Washington, young J. Edgar Hoover was polishing the fledgling F.B.I. into shape, and on March 2, 1929, the Jones Law went into effect, making bootlegging a federal felony.

The load of new laws staggered the already overcrowded and neglected federal prison system. Drug addiction had already changed the complexion of the prison population, and now these unwelcome additions were joined by petty gangsters and small entrepreneurs.

As new prisoners stacked up in Leavenworth and as the season grew warmer, Panzram had fewer chances to isolate himself. In the laundry, he warned other convicts to "quit talking about him," and delivered a veiled threat to a prisoner he saw looking at him. Panzram felt pushed by the crowding and the growth of the vermin problem. Prisoners were thrown into makeshift quarters with little sanitation, and this was combined with worsening food.

With the crush of new inmates, the Leavenworth dining room was filled and emptied nine times daily. Overworked cooks rushed out daily kettles of steamed rice mixed with tomato sauce. Inmates who could afford it relied on the prison commissary to provide variety. Wealthier convicts—fallen bankers, businessmen and judges—paid for the luxury of a steak, a bleached bedsheet or a shoeshine. The prison "merchants," in turn, converted this cash into payment for a side of stolen beef or commissary fare. To earn a few nickels for smokes and food, Panzram began laundering extra handkerchiefs. Rako noticed this and warned him in quiet whispers not to let Warnke find out. Panzram shrugged.

He wanted pocket money and he had already warned both the deputy warden and the foreman about what he intended to do to the first person who crossed him.

Before long, Warnke got wind of the handkerchiefs and inspected Panzram's machine. The next morning Panzram was reduced to third grade and sent to the Hole.[80]

Reduction in grade was serious punishment in Leavenworth. Third-grade prisoners coming out of the Hole were celled in a separate section on the top tier of D Block and were subject to the silence system and a variety of oppressive rules. They were not allowed to use the commissary, attend a prison movie or receive ordinary mail. Any infraction of rules by a third-grade prisoner meant automatic time in the Hole. Panzram had been told it was hard to get out of third grade in Leavenworth.[81]

But the punishment meted out by Zerbst had an attractive possibility for Panzram: it was the usual practice of the deputy warden not to send a third-grade man back to the work supervisor who had written the report. Few prison employees, under ordinary circumstances, wished to come in contact with a man being punished in this manner on their account.

Panzram served his brief time in the Hole and came out expecting a work transfer from the laundry. He was not to get this wish.

For some reason, the normal Leavenworth procedure was not followed in Panzram's case—possibly because he had threatened openly to kill Warnke, and the laundry foreman had not wished to lose face by appearing fearful. Face in any prison is of vital importance, and Leavenworth was no exception.[82]

When Panzram was transferred back to Warnke's control, Rako noticed that the huge prisoner was acting peculiarly. Rako on one occasion saw Panzram stop work and glower at a group of prisoners who were talking and glancing in his direction. Panzram walked over and said something Rako couldn't hear. The men stared, and as Panzram walked away, one smiled. Rako was later to comment: "He [Panzram] told them many times, 'Leave, don't ride me, leave me alone, you're going to get hurt.' And they didn't listen. They thought he was kidding. But he wasn't. He was a very serious man."

Zerbst turned down Panzram's new request for a transfer. Warnke had refused to aprove it.

In the middle of June 1929, Panzram seemed calmer, according to inmate observers. He faded into the prison background. But Panzram's face had changed. He had made a decision.

June 15, 1929

Your letter of June the 8th reached me the other day. That was a pretty nice letter all right. Full of news and all of it good. I was a bit surprised to read what Mencken wrote to you. I don't have much faith in the thing being worth while, but if anyone like Mencken says it's good I must believe it. You use your own judgment and do just as you like about it. It's yours and what you do with it is O. K. by me. I should like to read the article in *The Nation* about [Fremont] Older, but that's out of order here. Send no clippings. I am still on my same job and like it less each day. *I am getting all set for a change. It won't be long now.*

I think you're out of luck for the other 75,000 words I wrote here. That's out of order also. Glad your friend was pleased with the watch chain and charm. I made it out of an old fiddle bow and a peach stone. Next month I'll send you a bead necklace.

Surely you're not going to wait until you get the same as Allen got. You're the same type as him and you must expect the same kind of a deal if you stay in your same line of business.

When you do write me again I wish you would tell me as much as possible about Mr. Mencken's reply to you. In your last letter to me you asked me if I wanted any books or reading matter and if I would be permitted to receive any. The type of reading matter which I prefer is taboo here and I intend to get myself a dictionary and encyclopedia in 6 volumes as listed in Montgomery Ward Co. catalog. It costs 8 dollars and if I ever get that amount of money together I intend to get one of those sets.

While browsing thru an old batch of miscellaneous magazines the other day, I struck an exceptionally interesting article in the *American Magazine* of the March 1929 issue. Look it up and let me know what you think of it. Its title is, "My Seven Minutes in Eternity" and it was written by Bill Pelley. I think it will be of interest to you.

That's all for this time. So long and good luck. I am,

Carl Panzram, 31614

As June 20, 1929, dawned hot and bright in Leavenworth, Panzram marched down to breakfast with the third-grade gang. This group was the first out of the dining hall.

Dew was still on the brick as the early men swung down the street, paced by a guard, and filed off to their jobs. Panzram descended the stairs to the stilled laundry, limped past the empty barber shop and shower room and headed for a partly assembled washing machine near one of the large steel posts bracing the first floor.

Several opened packing cases were near. Panzram's eyes searched for something he needed.

In the next five minutes other men began to arrive. A prisoner named Amos Malone walked in and began checking the soap supply. Two others, Neil Maxwell and Jim Kasoff, also walked in. Nobody had noticed that Panzram was not in his usual place.

Guard Louis Guenther had checked off a half-dozen names and was leaning idly against a wall as the work crew appeared. He walked into another room, brushing past the foreman who had just arrived and was making his own check with notebook and pencil. Foreman Warnke began strolling slowly down the aisle past the steel supports.

Meanwhile, across the prison, Deputy Warden Zerbst was making his way to his own office. He was nearly at the Isolation building when he remembered something he wanted to tell Guard Captain Fred "Bull Durham Shorty" Morrison. He turned and walked into Morrison's office.

In the laundry room, Foreman Warnke drew abreast of the steel support near the packing cases. He looked for a moment at the debris, then turned slowly around. He found himself gazing into the face of Carl Panzram. A small frown had hardly gathered on Warnke's face when the ten-pound iron bar in Panzram's fist came smashing down.

Panzram's bellow of hate froze the laundry. Men looked around, still uncomprehending, as Panzram dashed the bar again and again on the bloody head of the foreman, who had fallen to the floor. His body quivered spastically; the shattered gold-rimmed glasses were knocked against a wall. With a roar, Panzram turned and began chasing fellow inmates in the laundry. There were yells of fear as they managed to elude the mad, limping prisoner waving the iron bar.

The prison street was clear as Panzram emerged from the basement. Crimson flecked his face and made dark spots on the gray Leavenworth uniform. His hand was smeared bright red.

Then Panzram, limping along more slowly, the bloody bar still in hand, walked twenty yards across the prison street to the blocklike Isolation building. Dale "Red" Ballard, a new guard, glimpsed Panzram as he passed but nothing registered.

Panzram walked into Zerbst's office, hoisting the bar. He stared at the empty chair.

There were muffled voices behind a door leading to the package mailroom in back. Panzram opened the door and came inside. His first swing with the bar missed, and there was pandemonium as the clerks fled.

Panzram went back into Zerbst's office. As he did, a convict runner entered at the same time. Panzram chased him as far as the corner of the dining room. Once more, Panzram turned and went back to Isolation. This time

Ballard was on his feet, gaping. A thick steel door was between him and the enraged, bloody prisoner.

"I just killed Warnke," Panzram said. "Let me in."

Ballard stared in disbelief. He looked at the iron bar. Finally he said, "I will never let you in with that in your hand."

"Oh," said Panzram, looking at the bar. "This is my lucky day." He hurled the bar away.

Ballard yelled for help and opened the door. Panzram stepped inside and, with a relaxed expression, walked into the nearest cell.

XXII

FRIGHTENED TRUSTIES, under the direction of guards, wheeled the smashed, sheet-covered body of R. G. Warnke to the hospital. Dr. C. A. Bennett immediately examined the remains. He was able to distinguish five deep wounds in the face and head. Any three of them, he later testified, were capable of causing death.

While Panzram paced nervously in an Isolation strip cell, prison authorities held an emergency meeting. Warden White's face was a cold map of inquiry. Deputy Warden Zerbst sat pale and silent. He had been threatened by Panzram and might have been killed if he had come into the hall at the expected time.

Warden White ordered the laundry shut down and the men sent to their cells. His immediate concern was for the safety of the prison and the possibility of riot. There was a curious quiet, familiar to longtime staff and prisoners, before the fact of death. But it was not the charged and ominous quiet that presages violence, the quiet that guards with "trouble sense" learn to feel. And so the huge prison simmered on in the deep heat of the Kansas afternoon, and the routine went on with little change.

Some long-timers felt a deep satisfaction in the death of Warnke, whom they had hated. Hundreds of others did not know him, and almost no one among staff or inmates had heard of Panzram. Those who had, considered him a ding, unpredictable and homicidal, someone to be avoided in the tight relationships of prison survival.

It quickly became clear that the killing of Warnke was an isolated incident. Nevertheless, some of the guards and prison staff, terribly aware of their small numbers in the overcrowded prison, walked along the narrow edge of hysteria. No one could feel sure of the situation.

Warden White immediately notified Washington and prepared to face the press. A Department of Justice investigator, J. R. Burger, set out for Leavenworth from Topeka to interview witnesses and wrap up evidence. Warden White's demeanor reflected the heavy responsibility which follows a staff death by violence. It was his job to let nothing happen that would interfere with the operation of justice through the trial, sentence and, it was to be hoped, execution of Carl Panzram.

It was White's first experience with serious trouble in his prison. Reviewing his vast empire of red stone, holding hot and desperate men, where vermin multiplied in the cell walls and in the mattresses, where the food was bad and help was short, he may have felt a warning of worse trouble to come, a riot which was now only a few weeks away.

In his dark cell, behind meshed bars and a heavy outside wooden door shutting out sound, Panzram waited and fully expected guards to unlock his cell door and kick him to death.

Later, guards did come to his cell. He watched them narrowly and was ready to exact a heavy toll for his demise. But he saw nothing in their faces to give him pause. He saw no blackjacks, no clubs. They escorted him to a wider cell, No. 13 cell in the Isolation tier, with a bed and mattress and standard equipment. Panzram was given clean, beltless clothes and flannel prison slippers. His new cell was thoroughly shaken down and he was placed in it. No words were spoken.

Panzram was left alone. He sat quiet, dazed by the unexpected treatment. The Isolation section was a prison within a prison. Yet in the midst of the worst overcrowding in the prison's history it held only three prisoners, two of whom had killed guards. Compared to the cellblocks, it was calm and almost comfortable.

Panzram limped back and forth, then stopped, listened and shook his head like a puzzled animal. He was hearing a strange and beautiful sound, clear trilling music on a rising cadence which rose to break in a shower of notes.

He could smell faintly an earthy odor mixed with disinfectant. Then he remembered the "canary con" he had heard about when he was living in the larger prison. At this time, Robert Stroud was at his pinnacle of success, both with birds and with prison officials. Reprieved from the hangman for the murder of a federal guard in 1916, Stroud was in his thirteenth year of solitary confinement, a man "legally dead" and encased in a stone tomb where he was allowed to raise canaries. He was becoming an international authority on canary diseases, and enjoyed high-status privileges at this time. He had unrestricted special-purpose mail privileges. He received as many as a hundred letters a week. Prominent visitors saw him when on tour in the prison. Stroud was considered dangerously homicidal by officials, and the bitter paradox of his life in prison was well underway. There were decades of time yet to test his endurance.[83]

Panzram sat impassively in his cell, buried in constant reading of books and magazines available through the prison library. He was allowed no exercise. Although Panzram and Stroud were not allowed to meet, Stroud's tall, thin figure could be seen passing daily down the corridor, under escort, for his exercise period in the yard, a small, walled area. As a high-status convict, Stroud expected new prisoners to make the first move toward acquaintance. Communication could take place through loud conversations with the tier guard—talk which could be overheard by another prisoner—or by passing whispers. Less frequently, contact was made by risking a "kite" (note). But Panzram took no initiative whatever. He kept to himself.

Stroud was puzzled by Panzram and grew interested in him. Years later, Stroud was to write about Panzram and the Warnke murder in an enormous manuscript on the history of federal prisons. Stroud's accurate observations, combined with his almost grotesquely mistaken inferences about the mysterious and morose Panzram, form one of the striking studies of character in confinement.

Word about the murder reached Washington, D. C., in the afternoon *Daily News*. The account was brief and inaccurate, but there was no doubt about the death of Warnke.

Its inevitability was not lost on Henry Lesser, who read the account during his shift at the District Jail. Rigid faces in the guardroom reminded him that his friendship with Panzram was remembered.

Lesser experienced, as he later related, conflicting emotions over the news. He felt sadness and frustration about Panzram, the monstrous product of violent punishment. But as a guard, he also felt a deepening anger over the needless and useless death of a fellow staff man, caused by the failure of Leavenworth officials to heed multiple warnings by Major Peak and by convicts, as well as the direct threats of Panzram himself to Deputy Warden Fred Zerbst and to the victim, R. G. Warnke.

Lesser, with growing frustration, perused lengthening newspaper accounts of the murder, including Peak's self-congratulatory statements about how he had warned federal authorities. An editorial in the *Herald* drew a wry smile from Lesser when it complimented Peak and questioned the judgment of federal officials in Kansas.

Lesser received a short letter from Panzram written three days after the tragedy.

June 28, 1929

This is merely to let you know that I am all right, or at any rate as well as could be expected, considering all of the circumstances.

Should you read anything very unusual in the papers about me, you mustn't take it for granted that it is all true.

I have no pen or ink at this time so you must excuse the pencil and my bum writing. I am a little nervous just now but I guess you can read what I write.

Later on I shall write to you and try to explain some things which are probably puzzling you just now. In the meanwhile, I'll be waiting patiently to hear from you and wishing you good luck. I am,

Carl Panzram, 31614

It was several days before Lesser wrote to Panzram. He wrote several letters without waiting to receive answers. There was something about the warmth of his correspondence which would surprise and perturb the prisoner. (Lesser's letters, unfortunately, were not preserved.) Panzram's reply reflected his feelings, and a good deal else.

I received your letter of July 9th this evening, and am answering it at once. Your letter contained quite a bit of news. I was glad to get it. I have been puzzled a good bit about the general tone of your letters to me. Your superscription especially has me wondering. The generally friendly tone all thru your letters. All of 'em. I can't help but believe you're sincere in your protestations of friendship for me. But what gets me is how in the heck any man of your intelligence and ability, knowing as much about me as you do, can still be friendly towards a thing like me, when I even despise and detest my own self. That's what puzzles me. Wonders will never cease. So Allen got himself reinstated in the good graces of the law. How come that Right came out on top of Might. Doesn't seem reasonable to me. Even tho he is the Law and no friend of mine, I can and do respect him if I can't like him. Yes, I read about the demise of one of my old companeeroes, Frank Marlow of Silver Slipper fame. He isn't the first of that mob to be taken for a ride, and if I know anything of his crowd, he won't be the last. He is one of the push that hoisted the S.S. *Mullhouse* for a million in booze, 8 or 9 years ago. If you keep on reading the newspapers you'll see some day where some more of his click will be taken. Eighteen men pulled that *Mullhouse* trick and not a one of 'em ever done a day, even tho everybody in New York, including the coppers, knows it. They are too strong for the law but they are not strong enough to keep on fighting among themselves and prosper at it. I don't wish any of 'em any bad luck but I hope they all go out like the Kilkenny Cats did. Say, I want to tell you something—you know in my letters to you I have been grousing about my job here. I didn't like it and wanted a change. Well, I got a change, all right, but I had to kill my boss to get it. That makes either 21 or 22 that I have to my credit. You can put that down in your little story book, and if I keep on living much longer I may have some more to put in my graveyard. For the past two or three weeks I have been pretty well upset. Things all went wrong for me. My plans have been all shot to pieces. I thought for a while I would soon be either free or dead but I haven't had any luck either way. I am still alive and locked up tighter than I was before. But patience works wonders and time makes all things equal. I know a lot of laws but I only know one thing is a sure worker. That's the Law of Compensation. That one will sure work. Say, about those things I was going to send you, the bead necklace and the bead handbag. You're out of luck for those, I guess. I had 'em, all right, but when I went on the war-path a couple of weeks ago, I lost them and everything else I had and damn near lost my life with them. Too bad I didn't. But maybe I can lose it or throw it away yet. I have hopes. Now, I have another murder charge against me besides those in Massachusetts, Pennsylvania and Connecticut. I am bound to be tried somewhere for murder and then maybe the Law of Compensation will catch up with me and cook my goose. Maybe the Law will do me one favor in return for all the misery it has caused me. I look forward to a seat in the electric chair or dance on the end of a rope just like some folks do for their wedding night. Well, it's time to cut this thing short and for me to start walking up and down my cell floor, talking to myself and trying to figure out the quickest and easiest way out of this damned world. How are you making out with your dime novel. Don't Hearst want it? He did once, at least his editor [Arthur] Brisbane, did. So long.

Carl Panzram, 31614

Lesser responded on July 29 with a cheerful letter containing news of his becoming acquainted with the eminent Harvard professor, Sheldon Glueck,[84] and how, on editor H. L. Mencken's recommendation, Dr. Glueck was now reading Panzram's autobiography. Panzram fired a letter back immediately.

August 4, 1929

I received your letter of July 29th all O. K. I wrote you three others since the 12th of July. I write one every week now. I hope you get all of 'em. I believe that I get all of yours all right. Your last letter had quite a lot of news and, as usual, all of it good. Too bad that all of mine can't be that way also, but you know enough about me by this time that wherever

I go there is sure to be bad luck and hard times for somebody and sometimes for everybody. I am old bad-luck himself. The last time I stopped anywhere long enough for the people to know me very well was in Dannemora. There I had a lot of different people ask me at different times who I was and what good I was. My answers were all the same. "I am the fellow who goes around doing people good." Asked what good I had every done anyone: Again my answers were the same to all. "I put people out of their misery." They didn't know that I was telling them the truth. I have put a lot of people out of their misery and now I am looking for someone to put me out of mine. I am too damned mean to live. If your friends, the Glueck Bros. from Harvard, should ever express their real opinions to you about the causes of my mean disposition, then I wish you would let me know their versions of it. So Mencken is still interested in Lucky Baldwin's autobiography. More power to him at it. You remember, I once told you that I wrote about 75,000 words along that line. Well, in your last letter to me you expressed the desire that you would like to have that also. The truth of the matter is that I am afraid you're out of luck for these reasons. In the first place, it is against the rules to write anything like that and also against sending it out. When I wrote it, I was in a different position then than I am now. Then I could see and talk to many people, now I see very few and talk to less than that. Then I had plenty of time, pens, ink and paper. Now I have only time. I haven't even a pencil. The one I am writing with now, I borrowed and must return it. I have no money to buy anything with. On the other hand, if I did have everything I needed including permission from the officials here, then I would gladly spend a month or two in putting down on paper the things I know and also the things I think I know. But I can't do anything myself. Perhaps you can tho. That's up to you if you care to write to the Supt. or Deputy Warden here. Those are the only ones who can give me this privilege. You must use your own judgment. Anyway, I couldn't do anything about it just now because I expect to go up for trial next month and I would have to wait until I see if I get my wish then. Well, so long and good luck. From

Carl Panzram, 31614

Panzram's letter expressed his hope of going to trial in a month. "I would have to wait," he wrote, "until I see if I get my wish then. . . ."

What wish was Panzram referring to? As his own words make clear, he was from youth a "dedicated man"—dedicated to destruction by *lex talionis,* an eye for an eye, since he was twelve. And the law had been working itself out, in bloody precision, and the latest result was a new mound of earth in a nearby cemetery.

Now, however, Panzram's hatred of humankind seemed to go into neutral gear, leaving in the drive-train of action only a resolve to achieve his own death. He had learned long since, in his expectation to fulfill this wish, that for him death was an elusive quarry to be wooed with persistence and cunning.

The convict's inquiry about whether the Glueck brothers would shed light on his condition naturally went unanswered. It would have been unprofessional for either of the eminent brothers to hazard a psychological opinion of Panzram, even if they had one. But Henry Lesser was set aglow with the letter he received from Dr. Sheldon Glueck concerning Panzram's autobiography, even though the chances of its reaching print seemed as remote as ever:

112 2d Ave., Belmar, N. J.,
7/24/29

Dear Mr. Lesser:

I have read the remarkable document written by Carl Panzram. Of all criminal autobiographies it is unquestionably the most striking, and in many ways the criticisms he makes of the existing penal system are justified.

I don't know what you plan to do with this manuscript. If you plan to publish it, there are passages which are too revolting to include, however much one wants to retain the statement in the exact state in which it was written.

I should like to know something of the way in which you induced Panzram to write this, and of your own work and interests. If Panzram is still alive, he would make a fascinating psychoanalytic study. Merely to classify him as one type or another of offender or psychopath is not an illuminative process; he should be studied by a skilled psychiatrist over a long period of daily contacts.

I should like to keep the Ms. a little longer, as I may get a chance to show it to my brother, Dr. Bernard Glueck.

Thanking you for letting me read this document, I am

Sincerely yours,
Sheldon Glueck

The heavy-set prisoner, fattening from lack of exercise, had also responded to Lesser's query about the manuscript, now virtually book-length, which Panzram claimed to have written in Leavenworth. There was no way that Panzram could have passed even a friendly prison censor if he had stated that his writings were confiscated at the time of his transfer to the Isolation cell. He did, however, make such an inference inevitable. He also made it clear that he could no longer easily kite anything out. He sensed the highly critical nature of prison censorship, especially in the more political climate of federal penitentiaries.[85]

XXIII

IN THE long hot prison summer of 1929, federal authorities proceeded carefully with the murder case against Panzram. Even in the rush of prosperity, the public was aroused by riots that swept Dannemora and then erupted in a chain of explosions in Auburn Prison and in the overcrowded bastions of Michigan and Ohio. Desperate men, acting in mass, were carrying out a violent retaliation. The growing casualty list included prison personnel.

Security precautions for Panzram were tight. Deputy Warden Zerbst, with Warden White's concurrence, ordered an Isolation guard stationed at a desk immediately across the corridor from Panzram's cell. A night-and-day watch was maintained for the prisoner's safekeeping, including prevention of suicide.

Federal authorities were determined to keep their prisoner in good shape for the hanging they anticipated. But getting him to the gallows would require a conviction for homicide, and this made a showing of premeditation mandatory. Such a showing might go far toward neutralizing a plea of insanity.

Federal investigator J. R. Burger had already come and gone, collecting basic information for the federal prosecution. Now he returned to Leavenworth. Along with Deputy Warden Zerbst, he went to Panzram's cell to ask some carefully framed questions designed to tighten the government's case.

Panzram ignored the indirect questions. Burger finally put his sheet aside.

"Did you intend to kill Warnke when you hit him with that iron bar?"

A look of disbelief crossed Panzram's face. "Sure I intended to kill him. What the hell do you think I hit him for?"

Developments in August, however, stepped between Panzram and an early date with the federal judiciary. Sensitive political centers in Washington and Kansas already felt the beginning of pressure from capital punishment groups, which had detected rumors of a hanging. Volunteers rushed forward with opinions that Panzram must have been insane. The harassed federal authorities, sitting on potential insurrections in their boiling prisons, hastened to nail down this aspect of their case.

Unknown to them, Panzram was as determined as they to remove any doubts of his sanity. But he had a sweeping, Swiftian irony, and it occasionally got out of hand.

Dr. C. B. Van Horn, psychiatrist at the Kansas State Training School for Boys, was sent out to obtain a mental history of Panzram. Van Horn was routed from Isolation by Panzram's bellows and profanities; he settled for photostats of an official prison record and a copy of Panzram's last will and testament, deposited with Warden White, leaving his body to the dogcatcher of East Grand Forks, Minnesota, and bequeathing a curse to mankind.[86]

During the next few weeks, Leavenworth authorities were perturbed when Guard Ballard passed word that Panzram was talking eagerly about his expected hanging. The young guard wore out pencils as he summarized for the warden some of Panzram's sodomy and murder claims, which Panzram described in revolting detail.

But now the old suspicion of federal authorities returned. With his claims of other murders, Panzram could be playing for insanity by appearing to wish for his own execution. The evidence might, in the hands of a shrewd attorney and a psychiatrist, be used to prove the prisoner's total incompetence.

Halfheartedly, with their bird already heavy in hand, authorities began to investigate the truth of several of Panzram's asserted murders. They discovered that witnesses had recognized Panzram as a man walking away from the murder of Henry McMahon in Salem, Massachusetts. Extradition proceedings had been requested. But when authorities were unable to pinpoint the veracity of many of Panzram's claims, due to lack of time and resources, the entire matter became less conclusive. They worried about mental competence all over again.

Panzram's letters were carefully screened for proof of sanity—a procedure misinterpreted by Panzram, who was afraid that his sanity, the one human quality he felt he had left, would be questioned. In his next letter to Henry Lesser, on August 20, he revealed his deep sense of the main obstacle to his plan for self-destruction at the hands of the state.

I received your last letter July 29th. This is my third letter since then. What's the matter? Don't you get all of my letters or don't you care to answer them. If you don't want to write to me, just say so and I'll not bother you any more. I believe that you would write to me, all right, if you got my letters, but it looks to me as tho you don't get 'em all. But why you should get some of 'em and not all is what I can't understand. All of my letters are alike. I write just exactly what I think and believe that I obey all of the rules in regards to letter writing. Of course, there are a lot of things I would like to write about that is verbotten here so I write only what I think will pass the censor here. Maybe the fault is that I don't know what's all right and what's all wrong. I always believed, I do yet too, that I knew right from wrong. It looks to me as the others do not agree with me. There are some folks who actually believe I am just a little bit nutty. But I don't worry about that because they don't know me like I know myself.

I know myself far better than anyone else knows me and I am firmly convinced that I am not crazy. What got me started along this line of thinking today is an article I read in the *New Era,* the prison paper published here. The issue of August, '29. I am sending it to you in a separate cover along with this envelope. The article to which I refer is on page 14. Paragraph No. 1 in Column 2 is what steamed me up. This does not mention me by name but I am the one that is meant, all right. I don't know who wrote it and don't care, but I do care when he or anyone else thinks or says I am insane. I wish you could get a publisher for that story of mine. I would like to have a copy of it when I go to trial. I expect to go up for trial next month or maybe October. I don't care what they do to me just so they don't try to prove I am crazy. I don't want no part of that.

Let 'em hang me, burn me or anything they want, but I am going to see that they don't bug me. I am not very good on trying to explain things by talking, especially in a court room. I get mad and fly off the handle too easy, but if I can get a copy of what I wrote in Washington, D. C., and then produce it in Court, I am sure I can convince anyone who is even half way open to reason that if the Law is right then so is

Carl Panzram, 31614

But now there was another delay in Panzram's trial; inmate patience came to an end on the burning plains of Kansas.

XXIV

As PANZRAM elaborated his bill of hate in the best accommodations he had ever experienced, the big prison broiled in the Kansas heat. Temperatures in the summer of 1929 reached 115 degrees in the shade. Guards working in the open wore pith helmets, making the Leavenworth compound look like an African desert outpost. Prisoners grew weary and desperate as overcrowding continued and food grew worse. Rat feces and mealworms were found in the oatmeal. Even the thin milk soured in the heat. Rumors moved through the prison that Warden White had turned back $200,000 in surplus food money to the federal treasury. It was not as widely observed that one reason for this was the refusal of many hundreds of prisoners to eat the prison food. They came to the dining room to pick up bread and purchase bootlegged steaks from kitchen convicts who stole whole sides of beef from the prison freezers. The operation was well organized and only the poorer inmates were forced to endure the food lines.

At noon on August 29, 1929, trouble began in the Leavenworth messhall. Gagging on a watery meal of leftover spaghetti and "Spanish rice," men banged their spoons and were soon throwing plates and breaking windows. Captain Carney, a well-liked officer, managed to quiet the mob by promising no write-ups and better food by suppertime. They responded by leaving the messhall. But instead of going to their jobs they raced into A Block along the front of the prison, fanning out into the huge radiating wing of C Block. Tension carried through angry whispers and reached into Isolation, where prisoners and guards alike felt something unusual going on. The normal cadence of the prison was replaced by tingling quiet. The huge prison ground slowly to a stop.

Panzram could hear angry voices in the laundry and shoe factory, sixty feet from Isolation. Guards made themselves scarce. By 2:00 P.M., in the deepening heat, these nearby voices were drowned by the distant hair-raising moan of convicts going into mad violence in A and C Blocks. The walls echoed a frenzied smashing of glass and the dull thuds of cell doors which were somehow pried off and used as battering rams.

Guards tried grimly to save the prison. With the situation touch and go, several of the custody staff talked the men in the shoe factory into going to B Block where, they promised, an emergency meal would be served. As the marchers passed the wing of D Block, they could see the rioters. In B Block, a dozen guards tried to urge the gray convict column into cells; the cons eyed the guards angrily and began to roar. Soon they were smashing B Block.

Warden White heard the new din. The metal shrieked as pipe railings were ripped from the galleries in B Block and used as levers to pry off entire tier gates, which were hurled to the concrete floor below. Pipes burst in geysers of water and steam.

White shook his head and realized that he was in danger of losing the prison. Leavenworth's huge steam siren began to blow, gathering a wail that could be heard fourteen miles away. Off-duty guards and extra policemen rushed to the prison. Newspapers and wire services sent out reporters.

The men in B Block raced through a connecting hallway and flooded into the kitchen and dining room. Someone began smashing coils in a huge refrigerator and soon the prisoners were driven back by ammonia fumes. The smell spread over the compound as the riot continued.

By sundown, a rumor had spread through the prison that sixty-five inmates were planning to strip naked, blacken their faces and bodies for disguise, and capture White and the prison steward. The plan, heard in hoarse psychopathic frenzy, was to force the prison cooks to cut up the hated officials into steaks and then fry them on the huge range. Naked, blackened cons could be seen rushing back and forth in the torn cellblocks, but White and the steward by now were safely out of reach.

Inside Isolation, Panzram noticed the lights slowly fading as steam pressure dropped. Through a barred window, he could see guards standing on the lawn outside A Block to keep the rioters from coming out.

At 11:00 P.M. the prison was almost pitch-dark execpt for searchlights. The officials had been organizing, and now a squad of marksmen entered the gun gallery in B Block. Through a megaphone, officers ordered the men into their cells.

Elsewhere in the prison, there was a sudden roar, a sound of gunfire, and then silence.

Immediately Warden White, Deputy Zerbst and a dozen armed escorts entered B Block at one end. A con in one of the cells halfway down the main floor gallery stuck his foot out. It was blasted off with a shotgun.

Mike Martinez, a young bank robber from Texas, looked over a railing on the top gallery and was shot dead with a pistol by someone in the White party. The riot was over.

XXV

EARLIER IN his career, Henry Lesser had had occasion to attend a meeting in St. Elizabeth's Hospital in Washington, D. C. There he met the late Benjamin Karpman, M.D., a psychiatrist-criminologist of note, whose strongly held views, research and writing ability made him a valuable resource in the primitively manned field of penology. Karpman liked Lesser and used his expertise to help the young guard with some personal problems. Avid for new views in criminology, Lesser attended Karpman's lectures and tried to overcome the handicap of his less-than-high-school education.

Dr. Karpman was an early advocate of the view that virtually all criminals are sick and should be hospitalized. The idea that "offenders" should be "treated" was comparatively new, even in the staff cadres of prisons where services were beginning to be known under the new-old term of "corrections."

Ben Karpman was a nervous, excitable man who seemed to have unending trouble with his automobile. Nurses whispered that he had "no mechanical sense." He wore a beard and was known as a rude, peremptory person, not likely to waste time. But he was a prophet ahead of his day, and Henry Lesser felt his time well spent with Karpman, whose discourses upon the all-motivational character of the libido were a byword.

At this time a picture of Sigmund Freud, the great Viennese founder of psychoanalysis, was standard equipment in the offices of psychiatric hospitals and New York psychiatrists. Freud's all-embracing theory of the libido and its sexual core was deeply established in professional thinking. It was central in the outlook of discussions which Henry Lesser had with Dr. Karpman concerning the bizarre convict named Carl Panzram, following the murder of R. G. Warnke on June 20, 1929.

Dr. Karpman had a proposal to make. He suggested that since Lesser had a good rapport with Panzram, the guard might be in a position to put to the prisoner certain questions, formulated by Dr. Karpman, which would perhaps shed some light on the sexual basis of violent murder.

Lesser had described Panzram to Karpman as the only man he had ever heard of who had raped boys and then killed them with a rock. Yet Panzram had killed in other ways as well. He was historically unusual—a mass murderer who clearly expressed a philosophy of hate. And yet he had shown great intelligence and seemed capable of friendship, even, in Lesser's own case, with a guard.

Henry Lesser put Dr. Karpman's questions, without

mentioning the source, in his next letter to Panzram. The response, on September 28, was immediate.

Yesterday evening I received your letter of September 25th. In it you asked me 8 questions. It would take 10 or 15 pages of paper like this for me to fully answer all of your questions. That can't be done. You should already know the answer to most of 'em. Read your manuscript over again and you will understand. You surely know the facts if anyone does besides myself. If you don't know, you probably never will understand. I wrote it plainly and distinctly enough for anyone to understand. All except 2 of your questions. The last one about the murder which I committed in here, you might not understand.

You asked me why I done it and if I got a kick out of it. I had not one good reason for doing it, but about 47 reasons and each one of them was a good reason. Good enough for me anyway. You know the deal I got in the D. C. can from Superintendent Peak. Did you think I would forget and forgive that? I told you all then while in my cell, again in the open court, again when I came here, I told everyone I came into contact with that I would sure knock off the first guy who ever bothered me. I even told that to the deputy warden here and the man I killed. I warned 'em all to lay off me and leave me alone. They didn't leave me alone and I killed one and tried to kill a dozen others. The way I figure things out is this way. If it was all right for the law to do the things to me that it has then it's all right for me to do the same thing to the law.

Peak was the one I waited 5 months to get but he didn't come here, so I stepped out and got another one just like him.

You asked if I get a kick out of killing people. Sure I do. If you don't think so, you do as I had done to me, 5 or 6 big huskies walk in on you and let 'em hammer you unconscious, then drag you down in a cellar and chain you up to a post and work you over some more, and then if you feel like forgiving and forgetting all about it, write and tell me about it, will you. I have had 22 years of this kind of stuff, and you know it, and yet you're chump enough to wonder why I am what I am. Don't be so dumb. Judging by the tone of your letter, you now figure I am a bug of some kind. A fire bug or a homicidal maniac. That's where you're wrong. I am no bug, even if I do get a kick out of things which would have the direct opposite effect on you.

Another thing, you asked about sending me some cigars. Now you know better than that. That's high treason. If you're going to send me money, that's all OK. At the same time, you can have the Haldeman Julius Co. send me their catalog so I can buy some of their books.[87]

Carl Panzram, 31614

The implications of this letter, and one to follow, would afford more insight into the mind of a murderer than any prior account. Clearly, it would be wrenching reality to impute a sexual motive, or even an aura of eroticism, to the murder of Warnke. Panzram did not, however, discuss his feelings concerning the murder of the boys he had raped. Was this a "repression?" Some awareness of this was shown in his next letter, which the restless convict sent off on October 6.

Post Office Box 7 Leavenworth, Kansas
31614 October 6, 1929

I received your letter of September 25. I answered it at once but was unable to fully answer some of the questions which you asked me. I'll try to answer some of 'em in this letter.

You asked me as to my motives in doing some of the things I have done. Surely you know that I am very impulsive, very vindictive and absolutely unscrupulous. Those are reasons enough to explain my actions. You also know why I feel and am that way. As for the kick I get out of it, I meant figuratively and not literally. What ever possessed you to think that me or anyone else ever had a sexual-like feeling when we commit a crime like a murder or arson. That's the bunk. I myself have intelligence enough to know the feeling but I haven't knowledge enough to explain it so that you could understand it. The only way I know of for you to find out just what sort of a kick I get out of it is for you to do as I done.

Experiment: go buy yourself a box of matches, or go get an ax and bop some guy on the back of the neck. Its easy when you know how. Besides you put em out of all their misery when you knock em off.

Now then for your question about my ideas of any dreams I have had and their effects on me. Sure I have dreams but they have no effects whatever on my actions during my waking moments. What started you thinking about that was probably my questions about Bill Pelley's article in the

American Magazine for March '29. Just forget it; you probably have already, because you never answered my question. Since I read that I have read some more of his writings and I have come to the conclusion that he is some kind of a bug or more probably a hop-head. I am neither. I can reason things out just as logically and clearly as anybody. I can see the truth and I can admit it where a great many other people are unable to see the truth and are unwilling to admit it even if they do see it. Well that's about enough of my philosophy for this time.

Now about you. I would like to know when if ever you're going to quit that Lousy Job and get a real one. That job is doing you no good. Its doing you harm. If you stay with it long enough you'll be as bad as That Great Criminologist [Superintendent Peak] who studied his subject for 28 years and then thought that he knows it all. If you don't believe it ask him. You know who I mean. That great Christian and Military hero. The Major. Now then as for the money and cigars which you promised me: just forget it or wait until you peddle your manuscript and then if you get a real bankroll, "donate" to

Carl Panzram, 31614

Panzram, however, still was not satisfied. On October 11, he wrote a third letter. In this the convict devoted more of his limited space to describing how his predictions of prison riots were being fulfilled.

I wrote two letters in answer to yours of September 20th. This is my third and yet I haven't had room to answer half of the questions which you asked me in your letter of that date. But before I do that I want to ask you something. Do you remember what I told you and the predictions I made to you in regards to the conditions and the probable results and the consequences of it in New York State? Especially in Dannemora and Auburn. Now you know that what I said would happen, has happened. You know why too. But that's merely the beginning and not the End. The worst is yet to come. Colorado was no surprise to me. Neither would it have been to anyone else who has kept back of that place since and during the regime of Warden Tynar. Here is another little tip for you. History repeats itself. Just keep your eye on Texas, Rusk and Huntsville. They are both due for the blow-off. The same of Eastern and Western in Pa., Baltimore is due for a jamb and so are a good many others.

When Jeff City and Lansing tear loose there will be noise and smell enough so that the people must see and hear the truth whether they like it or not. The powers that be are beginning to get it in the neck the same as any other crooks. The prisons all over the country are beginning to close their gates on Officers, Chiefs of Police, Sheriffs, Lawyers, Judges, Governors and a good many others who make the laws and those who are supposed to enforce them.

People who have been asleep for a generation or more are now beginning to wake up to the fact that laws are made to be obeyed by all and not by all except those who make them or enforce them on others.

I sure used to get a good kick out of it, before I got into my last jamb, when I could sit down in the messhall here, right beside some other kind of a copper. Believe me, I never missed an opportunity to tell 'em what I thought. That's one privilege I sure enjoyed and took full advantage of. But I can't do it anymore. Now I have no one to talk to except myself. But I like that fine. I can say just what I want to myself without any fear of being contradicted or having my block knocked off. So you see everything has its advantages. Even solitary confinement.

I am as contented now as I have ever been or ever expect to be. I have a large, clean, airy cell, plenty to eat and pretty good eats too, far better than I have ever had in any hoosegow before. I have a bed to sleep on, magazines and newspapers to read, twice a week a good barber gives a good shave, a good hot and cold shower bath every week with a clean change of linens, plenty of tobacco to chew and smoke. No work to do, and no one for me to bother about and no one bothers me in any way, not yet anyway. But still I am not satisfied. There is one thing I still lack and that's a nice comfortable grave to be dumped into. When I get that I'll be fully contented.

Carl Panzram, 31614

Later in October, Panzram answered one of the questions which concerned his early life. His responses were consistent with the writings of his confession and the verified data of his background. But he added some detail about his mother which was omitted in earlier writings.

Leavenworth, Kansas
October 20, 1929

I received your letter of Oct. 9th. Glad to hear that you got both of mine, of the 25th of Sept. and the 6th of Oct.

I wrote you another on Oct. 11th. I am glad that you didn't take any offense at my crankey letters.

You're a pretty level-headed sort of a fellow and you know I am always in a bad humor just like a mad dog. Still for a little while after I got your last letter I felt pretty good. Almost human.

Yes, I have read in the papers about Allen and his stirring up a row there. He is a pretty clever guy for a youngster but he is battling a bunch that is not only clever but very unscrupulous as well. They have the edge on him in that way. Allen has principles and scruples where his opponents are without either. So he had better watch his step or some skunk like me (there are plenty) can be hired for a C note or less to bump him off. Now then about your sending me money. That's OK by me but I am not in need of anything so don't put yourself out. I didn't get the Little Blue Book catalog yet but I have an advertisement out of a magazine and I am going to try to send an order for 40 little blue books. I may not be permitted to have 'em but I'll try anyway. No harm in trying. If I can't have 'em, I'll get Royal Bengals and have a smoke of good weed on you.

You asked me about my school days. I'll try and explain briefly. I started to school at the age of 5 years and attended regularly until I was 11 years old. In that time I finished the 6th grade. I did not like school. I was pretty dumb but I kept up with the others in my classes. When I was 11 years old I was sent to the reform school. There I stayed nearly 2 years. During all of my time there I went to school but never learned a damn thing. In fact I was in the 5th grade of school when I left there. So you see that after 2 years in the Reform School I was farther back than when I started. From that day to this

I have never advanced any farther in school than I was before I went to my first reform school.

I may not have accomplished much in a scholarly way while there but I learned to become a first-class liar and hypocrite and the beginnings of degeneracy. I also learned how to sing hymns, say prayers and read the Bible. I learned so much about the Christian religion that I finally came to detest, despite and hate anything and everybody connected with it. I still do.

You also asked about my parents and my early upbringing. I had little of either. My father was no good and mother was very little better. Father pulled his freight when I was 7 or 8 years old, so you see I know a little about him and none of that good. Mother was too dumb to know anything good to teach me. There was little love lost. I first liked her and respected her. My feelings gradually turned from that to distrust, dislike, disgust, and from there it was very simple for my feelings to turn into positive hatred towards her.

Carl Panzram, 31614

Panzram's correspondence with Lesser appeared to have a calming effect. It brought out the curious contradiction of his concern for honest people in the midst of his dedicated hatred of humankind.[88] In October, Lesser, who was verbose in speech but restrained in his writing, discussed the prisoner's needs in his careful laconic way and sent him two dollars.

On Halloween night Panzram responded with perhaps the most ironical letter ever written by a multiple murderer.

I received your letter of Oct. 9. I wrote twice since then. Last Sunday I ordered 40 little books with the $2.00 which you sent me. But I have since then found out that it can't be done. They are not permitted here so I still have the money. Now I'll try to figure out some other way to spend it. I thought I would write you a letter today because I feel pretty good just now.

In fact, I feel pretty near human. For several different reasons—here are a few. Its so long since I have been beaten or kicked around, chained up or knocked down that I have almost forgotten how it feels but not quite. I still remember. Another reason is that I have just finished my supper and man, what a feed. I started with bacon and eggs, candied sweet potatoes, bread and butter, stewed prunes and 4 fresh pears. Thats a sample of the meals we get here every day, lately. After I finished throwing this feed into myself, I sat down to smoke and read the daily paper. In peace, quiet, and comfort.

Now perhaps you will know why this letter is a bit different from some of the others I have written to you. This is sure a queer old world. Here I am getting old after roaming all over the world, after serving over 20 years in jails and in some of 'em I got plenty of abuse for very little, in one of which, that's the last one in New York, I was sloughed up in Isolation for over 2 years and there treated worse than you and many other people would treat a mad dog. That treatment I received, not for what I had done, but for what others thought I might do. There I done nothing to deserve all of the abuse I got.

Now notice the contrast. I come here expecting to get more of the same kind of treatment but determined that this time I won't get it for nothing. This time I am hostile and don't care what the consequences may be. This time I figure I'll beat 'em to it. I make one attempt to escape. I fail but I don't get caught; immediately I begin getting all readied up to try again in another place. But before I can get properly organized I get into a small jam; this caused one to figure, judging by past performances in other prisons, that I am due to get another kicking around, so to forestall all that, I grab myself a 10-pound iron bar and go on the war-path. Before I have finished, I kill one man and try to kill a dozen more. After doing all of these things I walk into a cell fully expecting to be chained up and beaten to death. But what happens. The exact reverse of that.

No one lays a hand on me. No one abuses me in any way. This is how things have been for the past 3 or 4 months. I have been trying to figure it out and I have come to the conclusion that, if in the beginning I had been treated as I am now, then there wouldn't have been quite so many people in this world that have been robbed, raped, and killed, and perhaps also very probably I wouldn't be where I am today. Maybe I am wrong tho. I am too dumb to know what might have been, but I am not so dumb that I can't see a little way into the future. Not very far but far enough to see the end of

Carl Panzram, 31614

Lesser was encouraged by the relative balance and good feeling of Panzram's letter. He was particularly impressed by the convict's statement that if he had been treated better, he wouldn't have "robbed, raped and killed" as much. Lesser could still remember a younger Panzram, carrying the flag for the Oregon prison band, beginning an excellent behavior record in the days of the forward-looking Spud Murphy. Perhaps this was a good time for Lesser to write of rehabilitation, a message of determination and hope. Lesser believed that it was never too late, that anyone could be helped, anyone was capable of change, if you were unremittingly firm and kind to them. Had he not, after all, gained the friendship of a man who hated people and killed when he could, throttling with his hands or clubbing down whatever was human and alive that crossed his path?

Lesser wrote Panzram a "suppose" letter. Suppose, he wrote, that you later received a pardon, financial backing, moral support and a helping hand from people, would you reform and lead a productive life? It was difficult letter, and Henry Lesser spent much time and effort on it.

It took him some time to recover from the answer he received.

November 13, 1929

Your letter of Nov. 7 reached me this eve. What a kick I got out of reading it. You have it all doped out, eh! You have it all figured out that if I was given my freedom today, financial independence, moral support and a helping hand from powerful people and everything necessary that would help me to reform and lead a good clean Christian life, that's all that would be required. You figure that I would jump at it and be all reformed up the minute I hit the front gate. What a dream.

You're all wet. Wake up kid you're having a nightmare.

I can dream better dreams than that myself. If there was even the faintest possibility of your idea ever becoming a fact, then I would be right on the job. I would be the best little yes man you ever saw. You may not believe me, but if I cared to, I could be just as smooth a liar and hypocrite as any would-be Christian you ever saw or heard tell of and they are all experts. But it just so happens that I don't care to lie just now.

I am not going to try to deceive you and neither am I going to kid myself. I know myself and my own state of mind far better than you or anyone else knows me and the more I look deep into my own self, the less good I can see. You seem to think that all that is necessary for a person to do when he wants to change his mode of living is to just change and thats the end of it. All reformed up just like that. Thats how easy it is in theory.

But the reality is far different when you take into consideration all of the facts. The real truth of the matter is that I haven't the least desire to reform. Very much the reverse of that is the truth. I would not reform if the front gate was opened right now and if I was given a million dollars when I stepped out. I have no desire to do good or to be good. I am just as mean now as I can be, and the only reason I am no worse is because I lack the power and the proper opportunity for meanness. If I had the power and the opportunities, then I would soon show you what real meanness was. You overlook the fact that the law and a great many people have been trying their damnedest for 25 years to reform me. I am tired of having people try to reform me. What I want to do is to reform them and I think the best way to reform 'em is to put 'em out of their misery. It took me 36 years to be like I am now; then how do you figure that I could, if I wanted to, change from black to white in the twinkling of an eye?

Have you some kind of a secret formula, some mumbo-jumbo, or hocus-pocus that could cause this great change? If you know something like that, let me have it and I'll try it out on someone to see how it works. I have a good subject here that I would like to try it out on. He is nearly as bad a skunk as I am. Not quite, tho.[89]

Now then to answer some more of your questions. The little blue books are not allowed to anyone in here, but books from any other publishing company are permitted here. Why that is I don't know. It's a rule here, that's all I know about it. I have never read Jack Black's book, *You Can't Win*. *Harpers* or *Scribners* mags seem to be unpopular here. I haven't seen one of either since I've been here. There are lots of good magazines here but I don't get many good ones. But I guess that's because I don't love Jesus or maybe they want to lead me into the paths of uprighteousness by handing me such mags as *Argosy* and *Western Thrillers*. No there is nothing you can do for me unless your rich uncle should open his heart and his pocketbook. In that case you could if you would, have sent these two books, direct from the publisher to

Carl Panzram, 31614

What Carl Panzram thought he saw in his future was not to transpire with the swiftness he expected. Outside events were shaping to affect this course. They would bear heavily upon the question of whether the world, spinning on into subsequent decades, would ever hear about him.

XXVI

UNKNOWN TO Panzram, Henry Lesser at Dr. Karpman's suggestion mailed the prisoner's confession to a young psychiatrist who was, with his brothers, busily founding a dynastic mental health clinic in Topeka, Kansas.

From his professional beginning, Dr. Karl Menninger differed from most psychiatrists in his ability to write clear and unturgid prose. Born in the 1890s, Karl Menninger was of the same generation as Carl Panzram. When the convict was breaking rock at Fort Leavenworth in 1911, Menninger was a reporter on the Topeka *Daily Capital.* With his M.D. *cum laude* and a young wife, he left the University of Wisconsin for psychiatric studies. A man of towering energy and thorough training, he had already, by 1930, become a power among the Freudian "young Turks" of a medical world which still called psychiatrists "alienists." He had already sent off the final galleys of a book which was to become a perennial nonfiction best-seller, *The Human Mind.*

Menninger was fascinated by Freud's theories of Eros and Thanatos, the life and death instincts. He was doing research. Part of his work was to assemble clinical examples of people whose wish to destroy themselves had overcome the urge to live. This would later become a famous book, and Carl Panzram would be part of it. It was a time when Sigmund Freud's somewhat biblical and inherently dramatic concepts of human motivation, propelled by his genius and the gifted translations of Dr. Abraham A. Brill, had become a gushing stream of fascinating sexual interpretation of behavior which poured into the main river of American literature. The analyst's couch was becoming a commonplace. Scores of books were written with the Freudian superego, ego and id systems of the psyche as controlling personae. America's greatest dramatist, Eugene O'Neill, was undergoing psychoanalysis, and his newer plays were Greek drama in the color of Freud.

Karl Menninger was astonished at the brutality, insight and horrible impact of Panzram's confession. He was surprised to learn that Panzram was a convict in Leavenworth, that he had killed a civilian foreman and that he would soon be tried in a federal court sitting in Menninger's home town of Topeka.

Thus began a curious and persistent interest in Panzram by one of the great psychiatrists of this century. The fascination was to endure, along with that of the obscure guard Henry Lesser, for many decades, emerging again when Menninger was approaching eighty, in the different and fast-changing world of the 1970s.

XXVII

TWO DAYS before Panzram's Halloween letter to Henry Lesser, the Roaring Twenties, the Lawless Decade, the prosperous, mad postwar years in America, came to an end in the stock market crash on Black Tuesday, October 29, 1929.

The terrifying effects of this debacle, however, were little felt in the prison systems of the country or, at first, by much of the public. Most Americans were lulled into security and hope by the happy predictions of their leaders. Things were universally expected to improve, and except for an impressive number of suicides of brokers and business men who had been wiped out, the real bite of the Depression was yet to tighten upon the country.

In November, Henry Lesser could feel the desperation all around him in the nation's capital. The economy seemed to be falling apart and nobody was doing anything about it. On November 20, at President Herbert Hoover's call, the heads of the country's large corporations met in Washington to find ways of bolstering the nation's financial structure. This meeting was one of many futile measures.

Harry F. Sinclair was not invited, but it was an important day for him nonetheless. It was his last day in jail.

There was much hurry and bustle in the prison. When Sinclair's chauffeur rolled up before the jail in a new black limousine, trusties had already carried the financier's bags to the heavily barred front gate. Guards brought the bags outside, where the chauffeur, in shiny black leather puttees, smartly saluted the gratified guards, who returned his salute. When the prison doors swung open to let him go, Harry F. Sinclair, looking rested and majestic in expensive mufti and gray fedora, waved ironically to the press and photographers and strode to his car. The stock market crash had plunged the oil magnate into intense activity in a fight to hold together his empire. By the time of his departure from the jail, he was seeing people, including prison officials, by appointment. Every man on the guard force at the time of Sinclair's leaving received two twenty-dollar gold pieces from the famous inmate.

The big limousine sped Sinclair to the Washington Hotel and from there to his horse racing farm in Rancocas, New Jersey. An officer of the Sinclair Consolidated told the press that "Mr. Sinclair was railroaded to jail in violation of common sense and common fairness. He seeks the respect to which he is entitled as a man of honor and integrity."

Sinclair added to this statement: "My own absolute knowledge that I have committed no wrong gives me an unimpaired courage and absolute confidence of final vindication in the public esteem." And so, life went on.

A week later, Sinclair presided over the annual meeting of the board of directors of his company. The room was filled with flowers, telegrams and invited guests. When the ceremonies were over, they moved into a plain room and began to work on hard policy matters. The Washington prison, for Sinclair, had become a memory.

On December 5, Panzram was indicted for first-degree murder. The federal grand jury sitting in Kansas City, Kansas, and duly impaneled, sworn and charged, found on their oaths that

> on the 20th day of June A.D. 1929, at and upon the U. S. Military Reservation of Fort Leavenworth, Kansas, and within the confines of the United States Penitentiary at Fort Leavenworth, Kansas, and upon lands reserved and acquired for the exclusive jurisdiction thereof, and within Leavenworth County, Kansas, in the First Division of the District of Kansas and within the jurisdiction of this court, one CARL PANZRAM, then and there being, did then and there knowingly, willfully, unlawfully, purposely, feloniously, deliberately, premeditatedly, and of his malice aforethought, and with intent so to do, kill and murder one R. G. Warnke with a certain deadly weapon, to wit an iron bar about two feet long and about an inch or inch and a quarter in diameter, a further and better description being to the grand jurors unknown, which he the said CARL PANZRAM in his hand then and there had and held and with intent, as aforesaid, to kill and murder R. G. Warnke, strike at and upon the body of him the said R. G. Warnke with force, and then and there giving to him the said R G. Warnke mortal wounds of which said mortal wounds he the said R. G. Warnke, at the time and place aforesaid, did then

and there die; this the said CARL PANZRAM did, contrary to the form of the statute in such case made and provided and against the peace and dignity of the United States of America.

Inside the Washington, D. C., jail, Lesser read the news in the *Post* and waited to hear from Panzram. The convict's last letter had stung Lesser, who was in a turmoil of his own. He carried Sinclair's gold pieces in his blue trousers pocket, "waiting for the evil to wear off." The gossip of the guards about the munificence of Sinclair's style eluded the serious Lesser. And the obvious Christian analogy in convict gossip between gold pieces and Judas' thirty pieces of silver also had no effect.

Yet, although Lesser truly believed that no one had betrayed anyone, he felt as though he had. At one point he decided to send one of the gold pieces to Panzram, but thought better of it, and this increased his depression.

Panzram's trial would be coming up. Surely something could be done to help. Dr. Karl Menninger was reading his confession. Since Lesser had received Panzram's realistic and unusual reply, shutting the door upon rehabilitation, which was becoming such an important word in penological circles, Lesser began to think that the only defense possible for such a man as Panzram would be plea and proof of insanity. He convinced himself that something good would come from the trial.

Later, Lesser was able to forget about his rehabilitation letter to Panzram and the prisoner's disappointing answer. He would later say that he had only written Panzram "to get his reaction." In any case, he did not write Panzram for a month. Meanwhile, he had received two letters from his strange friend, which had brought him to the tasks in hand.

November 19, 1929

I received your letter of Nov. 7th which I answered the same day I got it. I had to cross out the last 2 or 3 lines of that letter because I wanted to enclose a small clipping of a magazine advertisement. But after writing the letter I found out a new rule here which I knew nothing about. Clippings are not permitted to be sent either in or out of here. It doesn't make any difference anyway so just forget it. The books I wanted to get were Schopenhauer's *Essays* and Kant's *Critique of Pure Reason*. They were a buck each in the ad I saw in the mag. I have the two bucks which you sent to me and I think I'll use them to get these two books later on. Not now, because I expect to go out for my trial very shortly. I figure it will be sometime in Dec.

Now then about that autobiography. I have no further interest in it. Its yours and whatever you do with it will make no difference to me. My only motive in writing it was to express myself and to state my beliefs fully and truthfully. I don't care what you or anybody else thinks, says or does about it. The question of what the outcome of it might be held my interest only so long as there was some little hope that I might profit by it to the extent that I might benefit by getting myself some good books that I have been wanting for a long time to read. But now that that possibility is out of order, I may as well forget about it. Besides its very unlikely that I'll LIVE long enough to be able to do very much reading of any kind. That will be about all for this time. Perhaps I'll feel more like a human being by this time next week, if so I'll write then but just now I feel more like a mad dog than

Carl Panzram, 31614

His next letter, despite the totally uncompromising character of its basic line, shows that Panzram sensed the effect that his previous letter had upon his guard friend. He let in some slivers of daylight.

November 28, 1929

I received your letter of Nov. 7. I wrote you two in answer and now this is the third one. In your last letter to me you asked me to seriously consider from all angles your proposition. That is, if I should be given my liberty with financial backing, what would I do with it? Could I and would I reform? In my other two letters I told you that I didn't believe I could reform even if I had the opportunity to and if I wanted to. I am of the same opinion still.

In the first place, I very much doubt that there is the remotest possibility of you or anyone else having power enough to get me my freedom. In the second place, I have no desire to reform under such conditions as would be required of me the way the laws of this country are today. In the third place, I do not care to live any longer if I must live in prison. I would far rather die and go to hell if that's where people like me go to after death. I have very thoroughly considered this matter and I assure you that what I now say is the truth.

My first reason for disagreeing with you is that I believe it is absolutely impossible for me to ever gain my freedom in a legal way because I have too much against me and too many people wish my death. I have confessed 21 different cold-blooded, premeditated murders, hundreds of cases of arson, burglaries, robberies, rapes and other crimes. The law has by this time looked 'em up and verified the truth of my various confessions. I am wanted in dozens of different states and other countries for every crime on the calendar, from petty larceny to murder. I expect to go on trial here next month for the last murder I committed. At that time I expect to be found guilty of murder in the first degree and then sentenced to be hanged by the neck until I am as dead as a dodo or the man I killed here last June. And you can take it from me, neither will ever be any deader than they are now.

That one reason should be sufficient answer to your question. But just in case you're not convinced yet that your dream is impossible of fulfillment, I'll give you my second reason and that is that I could not reform if I wanted to. It has taken me all my life so far, 38 years of it, for me to reach my present state of mind. In that time I have acquired some habits. It took me a lifetime to form these habits and I believe it would take more than another lifetime to break myself of these same habits even if I wanted to.

My philosophy of life is such that very few people ever get, and it is so deeply ingrained and burned into me that I don't believe I could ever change my beliefs. The things I have had done to me by others and the things I have done to them can never be forgotten or forgiven either by me or others. I can't forget and I won't forgive. I couldn't if I wanted to. The law is in the same fix. Those are two very good reasons why your proposition is not feasible. Its only a dream on your part, but I have no illusions as to its practicability.

My third reason for not agreeing with your suggestions is that I prefer death before spending more years in prison. My belief is that life without liberty is not worth having. If the law won't kill me, I shall kill myself. I fully realize that I am not fit to live among people in a civilized community. I have no desire to do so. If I had any choice in living any longer, the only way I would consent to do so would be to get clear out and away from all civilized people.

If I could get my freedom and a few hundred dollars worth of the necessarys of life such as clothing, medicines, tools, seeds, fishing and hunting tackle and some books and writing materials, and with those things a couple of dogs, and then clear out and go off to some faraway lonely island, then I would be contented. No one would trouble me and I would trouble no one else.

I know of just such a place, a small island off the San Blas Coast of Panama. I have been there before, years ago. The island has some hundreds of coconut trees on it and a spring of fresh water. The sea tortoises come there to lay their eggs. There are plenty of fish, some banana trees, some mango and lime trees. The soil will grow anything that's planted. This island is about 40 or 50 miles off the reefs directly east by north from a place called Peter's Island which is east of Chucumbally, which is on the mainland, and south of Povamella where the Panamanian Government has stationed their port of entry for traders on the San Blas Coast. I was a trader and skipper and owner of a small sloop down there in 1919 and 20 so I know what I am talking about. This island is owned by the San Blas Indians and they visit it once or twice a year to harvest the coconuts and gather in the eggs of the sea turtles, otherwise no one ever goes there. That's what I would like to do, and that's about the only way I would even think of living out my natural life. There I could live as I wanted to and I would not need to conform to the standards set by other people in civilization.

I am so set in my ways that I cannot adapt myself to the ways of other people, so that the only way for me to do would be to live by myself without any human companionship whatever. I sure would like to try it that way. That is about all for this time. Now you answer me a question. What do you think about it? I expect, tho, by the time you get around to answering this letter, I will have been tried, found guilty and sentenced to death or maybe I'll be already in my grave. So long—

Carl Panzram, 31614

Panzram's letters poormouthing any rehabilitation possibilities, together with the convict's constant suggestion that Henry Lesser abandon his job, the Sinclair gold pieces, the seeming impossibility of prison change in the D. C. jail, the Depression, and some problems of a personal nature all combined to cause Henry Lesser to consider leaving "the best job I ever had." His resolve was not weakened by Panzram's next letter, which arrived on the eve of the bleak Christmas of 1929.

December 20, 1929

I received your letter of December 7 several days ago but I delayed in answering it until now, because I wished to think matters over quite well before I reached the decision I have come to. I have been thinking for some time that our correspondence isn't worthwhile continuing. It does no one any harm but neither, on the other hand, does it do me any good. I have been writing to you for a year or more, and now after making a check-up I find that from you I received more promises than anything else. I can't spend your promises, so don't waste your and my time sending any more of them. You have written me several times that you enjoyed and may sometime in the future derive some benefit from my letters. Please bear in mind that I have no future. I may be brought to trial any day.

Just a few days ago I read in the K. C. paper that the Federal Grand Jury has indicted me for first degree murder and that the rider [prosecutor] had declared that he will demand the death penalty for me. O. K. by me. In any case I have the means at my disposal and the determination to use them to wind things up. I am all thru and ready to check out. Either one way or another. In the meantime there is very little that you or anybody else can do for me.

All that I want and that you could get for me if you wanted to is some more reading matter. If you have been and still are sincere in the promises which you have made me, then I believe its about time for you to fulfill them. If you're unable or unwilling to do the little I ask of you then don't waste your time and my time in politeness and diplomacy. The address of the publishing company that publishes the two books I referred to, namely, Kant's *Critique of Pure Reason* and Schopenhauer's *Essays,* for one buck each is,

Schulte's Bookstore
No. 80 Fourth Ave. and 10th St.
New York City

I should also like to have a subscription for 6 months to the *Saturday Evening Post.*

Also if you could possibly manage it I would like to have a three months subscription to a New York paper. Either the *Evening Journal* or the *Graphic.*

I believe that will keep me going as long as I'll be able to read.

You have been saying and thinking of changing your line of work for a long time. I think it's about time you done it instead of merely thinking about it.

I am not in a very good humor for the past week or so for reasons other than I have mentioned here, but they wouldn't interest you even if I told you. Otherwise everything is lovely. I am getting fat and greasy, lousy and lazy and I don't think it will be long now. I mean time, not my neck. I believe that my time is getting shorter but my neck will soon be longer. More truth than poetry, perhaps, but anyway my address is still

Carl Panzram, 31614

XXVIII

PANZRAM'S EXPECTATION of an immediate trial and an early execution went glimmering with the federal court's decision not to bring him to trial until April 1930. The delay may have been occasioned by the crowded calendar, the increasing number of indictments, or by other factors. In any case, Panzram's feeling deepened that he was going to have to fight in order to die. He was experienced in the matter of how to plead, and he proceeded to formulate a plan. By entering a plea of not guilty in a crime where his guilt was overwhelmingly obvious, he would increase his chances of a clear verdict and a death sentence. A second strategy would be to set up a conflict concerning his attorney. This would weaken the effectiveness of the defense. He would need to appear sane and responsible without altering his expressed convictions about the human race and about death.

He also sensed the chaos in Henry Lesser, and as he prepared the termination of his affairs, he wanted to do something for his young guard friend.

January 14, 1930

I received your last letter of December 7th. I answered it on Dec. 20th. Since then I haven't written until now. I have been waiting for you to write. Instead of you writing me a letter, I have received a daily newspaper. The N. Y. *Evening Journal* which I asked you for. Now I shall explain a few things to you that have been in my mind for some time but which I haven't said anything about. You know how suspicious I am of everyone. I never believe anything that anyone ever tells me. I always think the worst of everyone. Even when anyone does me a favor I always impute the worst motives for his doing so. I hate to believe anything good of anyone. It is hard for me to believe in such things as altruistic friendship. I can't believe in it myself and its practically impossible for me to believe that anyone else can.

But I have known you for some time now and I haven't ever yet known of you to be two-faced or selfish. You have always been quite frank with me in every way. You never have tried to fill me full of bull. You never flattered me or tried to gain anything in any way from me. YOU have been pretty decent to me and now I am beginning to believe that your only motive in writing to me is to be a friend to me and to do whatever good you're able to. I realize that you're not in a position to do a great lot for me. I don't expect it of you.

Time is getting very short and soon I'll be where I won't need anything from anyone. My troubles will soon be over. But before I leave this world entirely there are a few things I can do for you. I can give you a few ideas on things that I can do for you. I can give you a few ideas on things that someday may prove to be of great value to you. I am not asking you for anything in return for what I will give you. I would have given these inventions or ideas long before now but I have been waiting to see if you would keep the promises that you have made to me. Now that I see that you are sincere and really mean what you say, I will try to reciprocate by doing some favors for you.

You know that when I last saw you I told you that I had some ideas for new inventions. Some I showed you, others I held back. Those I am now going to tell you about. You can do as you like about them. You can be smart and make yourself a bundle of jack or you can be a boob and throw them away or give them away or let someone steal them from you. I know that these ideas of mine are very valuable if they are handled by the right man in the right way. One of my inventions which I told you of, and which you made use of, I have since told to another man here. He gave me $5.00 for it. He in turn has drawn up the plans of the 5-, 6- and 7-compartment cases. He has sent them out to his folks and they in turn have invested a little money in having a number of models made and they have applied for a patent on it. They will make money on it. You and I will make nothing. This simply because you haven't the imagination to see the possibilities, and me, because I haven't the opportunities.

Now then in these next letters of mine to you, I want you to get one permanent address and keep all of my letters for future reference. Let me know each and every letter you receive hereafter from

Carl Panzram, 31614

Henry Lesser sent to Panzram the formidable *Critique of Pure Reason,* by Immanuel Kant. Panzram acknowledged it on January 26, and went on with his ideas for his young friend. He was becoming apprehensive that his ideas might be stolen, but his desire to give something to Lesser overcame his suspicions.

I have been getting the *Evening Journal* of New York every day since the 11th of January. I am pretty well fixed for reading matter now. This is my third letter to you so far this month. I hope that you got the other two. In my last letter to you I explained an idea for an invention. It was nothing to get excited about. It wouldn't make you a millionaire if it should be successful. That one was only an idea which I have never worked out to a final conclusion. But in this letter I'll give you an idea that is not only plausible, but possible as well. Because I have experimented and proved conclusively that it can be and has been done, and what has been done before can be done again. I know that this idea is very valuable, but how, who, when and where, money can be made out of it, is more than I know. That's up to you. But I do know it can be done. I have done it.

I have discovered a new kind of food, or rather it is an extremely old kind of food but just a new way of utilizing it. This food is now in common use by all the people in the world. But it is used in only one way. That is, it is eaten raw in its natural state. The way it is eaten now it can only be eaten in that way while it is fresh and ripe. I have found out a way in which this food can be preserved indefinitely because it could be prepared, at its source and at very little cost. It grows only within the tropics where labor and land is cheap. Nowadays the food can be transported in any kind of a vessel.

It needs very little advertising because it is already known all over the world. To be eaten, it need not be cooked. It can be added to any or all of the breakfast foods that are now on the market, such as oatmeal, cornflakes, rice, hot-cakes, or it can be added to the flour in the baking of cakes or put in nearly any kind of a pudding or dessert.

Now I hope that you are able to see the large possibilities in this new idea of mine. I believe that you can sell the idea alone, but if you take my advice you will get busy and experiment until you have by positive proven tests got a good result, take that result and get a patent out in your own name. If you do this then you have something that should make you a millionaire many times over. Now you will want to know what it's all about. If you have done as I told you to do, to get from the Dept. of Agriculture some treatises and papers of the subject of dehydration of fruits and vegetables, then all you will need to do is to go to the nearest grocery store and buy a quarter's worth of ripe bananas. That's all you need. Dehydrate them until they are thoroughly dry and then grind the result into fine flour. Then eat it. You will find that it is very good. I have done this myself and I know. Did you ever eat oatmeal with chopped-up bananas in it?[90] That's something pretty good to eat but it is much better when it is fixed up as suggested by

Carl Panzram, 31614

February 2, 1930

The letter which you wrote on January 29th I received yesterday. In your letter you say that you received but two letters from me in January. You see if there hasn't been a mistake. Yes, there has been a mistake, but it wasn't made by either you or me. I wrote you three letters in January. Therefore one of my letters never reached you. How or where this mistake occurred I don't know. I can only suspicion. But I do know that the same mistake won't be made by me again. Hereafter, I shall take more precautions. I shall not write anything that the censor can take objection to.

I hope that you will understand without going more fully into explanations. Just remember that others as well as you or I can see a dollar as far and as quick as anyone else. I am really glad that, even if you did lose one of my letters, you got my last one of January 26th. In sending that one you got a very good idea, but whether or not you can do anything with it still remains to be seen. It's yours to do with as you like or are able. You owe me nothing. Of course, I gave you only the bare outline of the idea but if you handle it right, that's all you need. I am glad to hear that you have a powerful and intelligent friend in the Dept. of Agriculture who you believe to be honest. But you take my advice and don't put too much faith in someone else's honesty without first protecting your own interests. I also advise you that your future letters to me say nothing that might benefit someone else and to your own disadvantage. It is not necessary that I should know all that you have done or are doing.

In your letter to me you say that at the first available opportunity you intend to have sent to me the book, Schopenhauer's *Essays*. Please don't trouble about that and also about bothering to send me any money because now I am doing pretty well as far as reading matter. At least up until the 11th of April, and by that time I expect my trial will be all over. At least I hope so anyway.

When my trial is all thru, I expect I'll be thru too. At any rate I am sure that it won't be long after. In the meantime I shall from time to time give you some other ideas for you to work out if you care to bother with them. But first I want to make sure that you get them and not someone else. Even if you don't fully understand now, you will later on, so please have patience. Kant's *Critique* is pretty hard for me to read and understand but I am digging away at it and I enjoy and believe all that I am able to understand of it. In the letter that was lost I explained an altogether different invention to you but now there is no use in repeating it to you. But perhaps later on I'll be able to explain that one and some others that I have in mind.

In the meanwhile you can concentrate on the food product. That one is easy for you to work out and it is a very good one if you can handle it. I have others just as good or better. But first I want to make sure that you get all the letters that I write to you. Should you receive an unfavorable opinion of the food product, from the chemist of the Dept. of Agriculture, don't give up hope because neither he nor you know all that I have in my mind. So long and luck to you from

Carl Panzram, 31614

I received your last letter of Jan. 29th which I answered last Sunday, Feb. 2nd. Yesterday I received a package of literature from you which deals with patents. I wrote you three letters in January. One of 'em you didn't get. Why I don't know. I can only guess. Its useless to make any complaint about it. Just forget about it. The letter that was lost was a good one and I wanted you to get it. I wrote 2 double pages and I did not think when I wrote it that I put anything in it that was contrary to the rules there. But maybe I did. Anyway I won't write anything more like it or anything that some wise egg thinks he can make a dollar out of.

Several times since I have been here I have tried to explain to you about my mail privileges. I don't believe you have understood me. Surely if you stop and think a bit you will understand that, me in the position that I am now as a convict, I have no rights whatever except those that are given to me, or that I am able to take. And I asure you that I can take very, very little and anything I take I'll have to pay for and pay a hell of a big price for it too. So I don't take any chances.

I expect to have my trial sometime the latter part of this month or the first of the next. Then we will see what we will see. Either one way or another I'll be wound up and all thru. In the meantime I'll just slide along the easiest way I can. I won't write anything that I think would do anyone else any good or me any harm.

You, from your experience in the work you are doing, should surely know the inside workings of these kinds of places. There is no use in me trying to explain any further to you. The papers which you sent from the U. S. Patent Office were interesting reading, but I knew all of that before. I knew that there were such machines and patents in existence, but none that you sent me has my idea. I done the same as I have told you and I had no complication or expensive machinery to do it with. The only machinery I had was a small coffee grinder to grind the dried product into flour.

The only other things I used was sunshine and a few little odds and ends such as some pieces of wire, wooden boxes with glass covers and fresh air. You know I told you that I once worked in the United Fruit Company at their Costa Rica division. In that part of the world there are only 2 seasons, the rainy and the dry season. You know I am no chemist and I know nothing whatever about the finer points as they are explained in the papers you sent me. All that I do know is that I dried the food product, ground it into flour and ate it and found it good. What I done anyone else can do.

I have no doubt but what other people have had the same idea in mind. Some have developed the idea much farther than I have, but none have done anything worthwhile with it. The finished product is not on the market. That's where it belongs and not simply stored away in someone's mind or a shelf in a storeroom. Whether or no you can do this I don't know. That's up to you. I don't much like to write letters and I like it less when I take the trouble and time to write to you, and then you have someone else have the benefit of what I write to you and thereby depriving you who I am writing it for. It won't be long now when it will be the end of

Carl Panzram, 31614

Panzram's desire to be tried and convicted as a sane man surfaced again in his letter of February 16. He acknowledged a package of literature on patents which Lesser had sent him and then wrote with savage irony of his concern about insanity. His intensity would have been appreciated by H. L. Mencken.

I won't waste much time in writing this letter because I don't know if you will get it or not. Some of my others that I took considerable time and trouble to write to you, you never got at all. I wrote you three (3) letters in January and this is my third one this month, the other two I wrote on Feb. 2 and Feb. 9th. The last letter I got from you on Jan. 29th. But I did receive a package of literature in regards to patents from you.

My trial is soon coming up and in the meantime I am trying not to do anything, say or write anything which could be used as evidence to convict me of insanity. I know that there are some people who would like nothing better than to send me to the mad house. This I don't want because I would rather be dead. There are people here, as there are elsewhere, who are sincere in their belief that I am a lunatic, but there are others who know I am not insane but who want to have me declared mad. I don't want to give these people any more reasons to believe I am a bug. You know that one of the many different kinds of insanity is the invention bug. There are people in this world who are too stupid to invent anything new themselves and when they see someone else who has intelligence and ingenuity enough to discover a new idea, they at once say he is crazy, but they themselves are not unwilling to steal the same idea and profit by it. I have other reasons also, why at this time and place I don't care to write a great deal. First I shall wait until my trial is over with. Whatever the outcome may be, then it is time enough to continue explaining some of my other ideas to you. In the meantime, continue to have patience as I do,

Carl Panzram, 31614

It was odd that the irascible convict would find himself counseling his guard friend Lesser to "have patience as I do." Panzram may have sensed the growing disquietude in Lesser. The value of Panzram's invention ideas was expressed carefully in a situation of uncertainty. Neither Lesser nor Panzram could be certain that a letter would be received. In capital cases in those days the warden routinely read the mail of the incarcerated defendant and saved for the prosecution anything which could be used as evidence.

Actually, Lesser had already accepted an offer from the newly formed Federal Bureau of Prisons for employment and was to begin with a training course at the federal penitentiary in Atlanta. He felt there was much to learn and more to be done in the improvement of corrections and, through conversations with zealous Bureau officials, he had become infected with the missionary zeal of a new agency, being formed with new guidelines and with a determination to clean up and regularize the chaotic, corrupt and idleness-ridden federal prisons.[91]

Panzram's reading program suffered a setback in March. He, like many another, lost a struggle with Immanuel Kant.

March 9, 1930

I expect that I'll get the *Sat. Eve. Post* soon. I'll be glad to get it. Because I like to read and all that I have to read nowadays is the newspaper which you had sent to me and the one I ordered with the 2 bucks you sent to me. I don't get any books or magazines anymore. I was getting both for awhile, but then towards the last I couldn't get the kind I wanted so I refused to accept the ones that was offered to me, so now I get none at all. The book which you sent me, Kant's *Critique,* I read for about a month but it is too deep for me to understand. The most of it went over my head. Finally I got so disgusted and discouraged that I went into a tantrum. In a mad rage, I tore it up into 10,000 pieces and fired it out of my door. That left me with my two papers only and those I haven't been reading very much because for the past month I have been pretty hostile.

I am always mad anyway like a mad dog but sometimes I get a little more peeved than at other times when most anything is liable to happen to me or anyone else who may be near me. As you know I am confined in the isolation here, but it's all right so far, no one has bothered me or abused me. There are men here who would talk to me if I would listen to them and if I cared to speak to them, but I won't do either one. There is no one here that I care to talk to or have talk to me. For awhile here there was one man that I used to talk to and to listen to occasionally, but I finally broke off diplomatic relations with him and I agreed to disagree. Then lately there has been another man here who tried to be diplomatic and civil to me for the past week or 10 days. From all outward appearances he seems to be not only willing but anxious to talk to me and to have me speak to him. But you know how I am, I don't believe anyone means right by me. I believe bad of everyone and good of no one.

I understand now that I will not be tried in K. C., Kansas, this month. I'll be put on trial early next month. That is providing that I consent to wait that long. I have waited for 8 months and I am pretty tired of waiting. The longer I have waited, the madder I have got until now I am so hot that I am liable to explode and blow myself completely out of not only the prison, but out of this world also.

While awaiting trial Panzram had resumed writing his views of crime and criminals. One of the frequent visitors to Isolation at this time was the distinguished criminologist Austin H. MacCormick.[92] A disciple of Thomas Mott Osborne, MacCormick had been a strong force in the National Society for Penal Information, whose scathing investigations of American prisons had provided a cornerstone for prison reform.

Now a high official in the new, groping Federal Bureau of Prisons, MacCormick made periodic tours of the federal bastilles. He was a trim, self-contained man and a natty dresser whose hard-worsted suits drew the admiration of convicts. He may at times have felt more welcome among the prisoners than the officials, who felt their power oozing away to the Bureau in Washington. He discussed prison improvements with Panzram, and noted the sharpness of the convict's mind and also his preoccupation with death.

Panzram had ideas about the improvement of prison morale and some concern about prison industry. He was interested to the point of writing extensively on the subject. What happened to these writings, in common with authenticated instances of entire book manuscripts created behind bars, is one of the mysteries known only to the voluminous files of the Federal Bureau of Prisons.[93]

Panzram's letter reveals a glimmer of his existence in

the Isolation section. His social life was nonexistent, and it is notable that even the occupants of Isolation, a temple of loneliness, did not find it possible to communicate effectively with Carl Panzram.

He spoke almost daily to one man, the guard Red Ballard, a young, peremptory but basically humane individual, who had been assigned special watch duties over Panzram. The man he"agreed to disagree with" was Ono Manuel, who had killed a guard years before, was given life imprisonment, had tried and failed to raise canaries and had been transferred from Isolation into the regular prison population. The prisoner who was "anxious to talk to me and have me speak to him" was Robert Stroud, the "canary doctor."

Stroud's reasons for better contact with Panzram were motivated, as his writings show, by neither friendliness nor loneliness. Stroud was already convinced that Panzram would receive a sentence of execution. He was concerned, in common with other long-term convicts, that a hanging might actually occur for the first time since 1888 in Kansas. He had come within eight days of execution in 1920. President Woodrow Wilson had commuted his sentence under pressure from his mother, Elizabeth Stroud, and from the President's wife, Elizabeth Bolling Wilson, who for a time became virtually acting president after her husband was stricken with paralysis. In the cell next to Stroud, and across the hall from Panzram, was John Aday, a frightening Apache Indian in his eleventh year in Isolation. Aday had had a sentence of death pronounced upon him, only to receive a new trial and a sentence of life imprisonment in solitary confinement.

Stroud was determined to help Panzram do away with

himself and cheat the executioner. He was planning to provide the burly convict with the means to do so, and he made pleasant overtures in a whispered sentence or two as he was ushered into the exercise yard with cages of twittering birds in his hands, to give them an airing.

Panzram, however, was more alienated from the other prisoners than the cool, paternally egocentric Stroud. Panzram was, paradoxically, more a citizen of the world, however much he wished to destroy its occupants. He had traveled more widely than Stroud, whose entire life from the age of eighteen had been spent in prison, the last eleven years of it in solitary confinement. He was only two years older than Panzram. In a sense like the New Yorker who never leaves New York, Stroud was a loyal provincial.

On March 23, Panzram wrote Lesser that he would be tried in April and suggested that Lesser subscribe to a Topeka paper in order to learn more details about his case than could be told in their restricted correspondence.

The only news that I have which might interest you is that the date of April 15th, 1930, has been set aside as the time I'll be tried and the place set as Topeka, Kansas, in the U. S. Federal Court under the jurisdiction of Judge Hopkins and Judge Pollock.

Why there should be 2 judges I don't know, or why the place chosen for the trial should be Topeka, I don't know either and care less. The only part that interests me is what the result will be and I already know what that will be.

It might pay you to get a subscription for your own use of a Topeka or a Leavenworth paper for the month of April next. In that way you'll learn more about my case than I could tell you in my letters. But in reading the papers you must remember to use your own judgment about what is printed about me because the papers are only interested in printing what they think their subscribers would like to read. The truth has very little appeal to them.

Both of my papers will run out on the 11th of April, but I don't want the subscriptions renewed, neither of them. What little time I'll have left after the 11th of next month, I won't care to spend in reading a lot of lies and hot air that the papers will publish about me.

Carl Panzram, 31614

On March 30, Panzram wrote to Lesser and carefully repeated the dates of his letters and the dates of answers received. The prisoner was growing careful, knowing that some letters did not get to Lesser, and not wishing to accumulate evidence against himself as mentally unbalanced.

You asked me in your last letter to continue to write down my ideas because you would like to get them. I am not doing any writing nowadays, simply because I don't care to. There are a good many things I would like to write down, some of which I believe to be of considerable value, and all of which I believe to be truthful and interesting, but at the present time under the existing circumstances it would be worse than useless for me to do any writing. Should conditions be changed in such a way that what I write wouldn't harm me but do me good and harm my enemies, then I would be only too glad to express myself in writing.

You also asked me if there was anything you could do for me. Yes, there is. You can, if you will, subscribe for the *Christian Science Monitor,* a Boston newspaper, for me by the month, one month at a time, as long as I am alive to read it, which I believe will not be over 3 months at most and probably 2 months but possibly only one month.

The *Monitor* is a pretty good paper because it does not print a lot of bull or lies and no criminal news. What it does print can be depended on to be pretty near true and the most of what it does print is on a subject which interests me, world affairs. This paper doesn't interest most people but it does me. I know your bank roll isn't very fat, but this won't break you, I guess. How about that silk thread you were going to send me? When you do send it be sure that it is the rayon or imitation kind, like the bit I sent to you.

I don't know if you got all my other letters or not, but I believe not, but I think you'll get this one all right because no one can take exception to anything I have written here. Now I'll ring off in this one before I do write something that's not according to the laws of John L. Sullivan or some other all-powerful God. So long,

Carl Panzram, 31614

Panzram had written many times that "might makes right," but he had become careful. He mentioned John L. Sullivan and let the implication work.

Writing two short letters early in April, Panzram informed Lesser of progress on the upcoming trial and the name of the assigned judge, Richard J. Hopkins. Upon receiving an immediate answer from Lesser that all of Panzram's letters had not been received, the convict responded immediately.

I suspected that all along.

The officials here know who and what you are, and knowing that, they also know that you are not the type of man to do anything wrong in corresponding with me.

As for me, I couldn't if I wanted to. Still my letters are stopped and no reason given me. I never know when a letter of mine will be held up by the censor here. The censor in this case is the warden here. He has the power to do just as he pleases with my mail and it seems to please him to stop some of my letters occasionally.

I can't stop him from doing this but what I can do and will do is to stop writing letters.

I won't write to you any more under the circumstances as they are now.

When, if ever a change is made, then I will consider renewing our correspondence. I am

Carl Panzram, 31614

On March 26, Panzram's frustrations were increased by another unwelcome and unsolicited move on the part of the federal judiciary. Guard Ballard poked a letter through Panzram's bars from United State District Judge Richard J. Hopkins, which brushed aside Panzram's request to act as his own lawyer. The glowering convict's profanity echoed in the cell tier and mixed with the sound of Robert Stroud's canaries. Judge Hopkins had appointed as defense counsel one of the best-known lawyers in Kansas, Captain Ralph T. O'Neil.

Ballard was surprised at Panzram's rage upon receiving such distinguished help, but he complied with Panzram's request for pencil and paper.

Now cold and grim, Panzram wrote a letter to Judge Hopkins of a kind which that judge had never before encountered:

To Judge Hopkins:

You have acted without my consent. I do not want a lawyer. I intend to plead not guilty; I intend to demand a jury trial; I intend to act as my own counsel; I refuse to accept the services of any counsel which the court may appoint to defend me; I do not intend to call any witnesses in my defense; I do not intend to cross-examine or challenge any of the witnesses or evidence of the prosecution; I do not intend to take the witness stand in my own defense; I do not intend to cross-examine or challenge any of the men or women of the jury; I do not intend to plead for either pity or sympathy; I demand justice.

My conception of justice is that I be found guilty of murder in the first degree and then sentenced to death, and that sentence carried out.

Regardless of what the outcome and the sentence of this trial may be, I refuse to appear for a new trial.

Carl Panzram

Word of Panzram's letter leaked to the press. It must have created a jarring effect in the United States Attorney's office as Hopkins disclosed the contents to the prosecutor, Dan Cowie, and to defense lawyer O'Neil.

Panzram had learned by then from newspapers and probably from Robert Stroud that in Kansas state law the ultimate penalty was life imprisonment. (Capital punishment had been abolished in that state in 1907 and was not restored until 1935.)[94] There had been no execution on Kansas soil for more than four decades, since a federal prisoner from Indian Territory had been hanged in Wichita in 1888. But if a capital crime were committed on federal property within the state of Kansas, then federal, not state, courts held jurisdiction, and the death sentence could be pronounced and carried out, provided that the execution took place on federal property. Leavenworth prison was federal all the way.

Knowing the formidable opposition to an actual execution and knowing the commutations and changes of sentence in past federal cases, Panzram had planned his procedure with care. In sum and clearly stated, Panzram was combining with the federal prosecutor to secure a verdict of first-degree homicidal guilt from a jury and a sentence of execution from a federal judge. This introduced some static into the clear music of the "adversary system" upon which the nation's courts are based. Although the indictment read *United States v. Carl Panzram,* the true relationship under the palimpsest of reality was the *United States and Carl Panzram v. Panzram's Continued Existence.*

To Panzram's chagrin, however, the effect of this situation was to raise further doubts in the minds of concerned Kansans who had not allowed a *state* hanging since 1872.

The legal technicality that Leavenworth was federal property did not remove this formidable objection to the legal infliction of death in Kansas.

Although he had been indicted by the federal grand jury on December 5, Panzram was not served by Federal Marshal MacIvor until March 26 of the year following. The grim, husky marshal, who was to face a problem of major concern to both the state and Panzram for many months, was surprised to see the relief on the convict's face as he signed a receipt for the summons.

Another visitor, who fared less well, was Panzram's court-appointed counsel, Ralph O'Neil. O'Neil was a big, hearty man in his forties, prematurely gray, who was to become one of the national leaders of the American Legion. He was a well-trained, serious and capable lawyer, and he took his appointment to defend Panzram with gravity. Panzram saw him, but refused to answer questions or to volunteer any statements. O'Neil returned to Topeka in frustration and thought about his client.

Panzram's letter to Judge Hopkins and his refusal to cooperate in his own defense made O'Neil feel unprofessional and miserable. To his relief, he was able now to question the prisoner's sanity. This might be the best legal defense.

O'Neil knew that in any trial for murder, two questions immediately arose. Was the defendant competent to stand trial? And had the defendant been sane at the time of the crime?

In order to stand trial at all, Carl Panzram would have to meet two tests. He must be able to understand the charges against him; and he must be able "to assist in his own defense."

If he passed these tests, a trial could be held. The next problem would center around Panzram's mental condition at the time of the killing of Warnke, bringing into play the McNaughton rule,[95] which was in force and effect without challenge in that day. Did Carl Panzram know he was committing a wrongful act in killing R. G. Warnke? Did he appreciate the nature of it, the gravity of taking a human life? This would be for the jury to decide.

O'Neil ruminated on these legal matters. His assurance returned. He would rely upon the insanity defense, confident that Panzram showed convincing evidence of incompetence. This included the convict's preoccupation with death.

It was not easy in that day (or perhaps in any other) to conceive of a consistent and logical desire to die, except in martyrdom, self-sacrifice, unendurable pain or other circumstance *in extremis*. Panzram, it seemed, confounded everyone with his desire to leave this world.

Returning to Topeka, O'Neil called his friend "Dr. Karl," as Menninger was known among his widening circle. The attorney was surprised to learn that Menninger was not only familiar with Panzram's background but had intended to discuss the matter with O'Neil.

Menninger agreed to examine Panzram. Both he and O'Neil felt that a Sanity Commission should be appointed by the judge to look into the question of whether or not the irascible convict was capable of assisting in his own defense.

But another question still slept untouched: defense against what? Against a trial for murder, when the defendant wished to be executed? Could an individual logically defend himself in favor of his own death?[96]

Attorney O'Neil made explorations with the judge concerning the feasibility of appointment of a Sanity Commission. Judge Hopkins took the matter under advisement. The prosecution did not oppose the idea. O'Neil advanced a formal written notion to be made to the court. The judge had the alienists notified to be available on April 15, the day of Panzram's trial.

XXIX

At this time—April 14, 1930—Carl Panzram had access to newspapers. If he had read them at about the time a Sanity Commission was being assembled to examine him on the morrow for evidence of irrationality, he could have scanned the following items concerning the rationality of the world around him.

President Herbert Hoover, after having issued further assurances of early prosperity for the disintegrating economy, tossed out the first baseball in the opening game of the Senators. In March he had announced the end of unemployment in sixty days. It was April. Millions were jobless and thousands were joining their ranks each day. It was only the beginning.

In Washington, Senator Capper of Kansas termed the London Naval Parley of the great powers then in session

> another milestone on the path to peace, parity and profit. Three great naval powers, The United States in the western

Hemisphere, Great Britain in Europe and Japan in the Far East, are writing an agreement that they will end the fatal and destructive race for supremacy among themselves. The agreement will apply not only to battleships but also to cruisers and submarines.

London revealed it had twenty murders in the previous year and all were solved. Chicago had more than 500 murders during the prior three years and virtually no one was arrested; or, if arrested, prosecuted; or, if prosecuted, found guilty.

The prohibition of alcohol continued to be the law of the land.

In 1930, Congress passed laws mounting into the thousands.

In Austria, an obscure army veteran was organizing brown-shirted men, and in three years he was to be democratically installed chancellor of Germany.

The question of world sanity was not at issue, but that of Carl Panzram was. Early on the morning of April 15, he was taken by automobile, in a heavy rain and lightning storm, to Topeka.

He was attired in a dark suit, white shirt and tie, and was manacled and leg-ironed. In the Topeka courthouse building, Panzram was taken into a small room where he sat under federal guard. At 8:30 A.M., O'Neil, Panzram's defense attorney, appeared in the company of Dr. Karl Menninger, a large, imposing man with glasses. They took off heavy slickers dripping with rain.

Panzram sat stiffly, ignoring O'Neil. O'Neil introduced Dr. Menninger. Panzram scrutinized him carefully.

Menninger's fifty-minute examination of Panzram, in chains, with guards poised to spring to the psychiatrist's protection on a second's notice, was one which Menninger would never forget. The doctor saw deep into a human psyche in ways he had not seen before. When Panzram rose, rattling his chains to threaten him, Menninger saw kill-hunger in the eye of a multiple murderer glaring at him four feet away. He had studied the evolution of Panzram's personality. Deeply moved, Menninger later wrote:

> All of this sounded like a mighty bluff, to be sure, but it was in keeping with a life story which the police had thought was a bluff or a fantasy until they checked up and found that every word he said was true.
>
> He had been hurt so much that he no longer had any compunction about hurting anybody and everybody and virtually begged for death to put him out of the misery of his feelings of vengeance.
>
> I recall vividly his violent feeling about psychiatrists. He said, "I want to be hanged and I don't want any interference by you or your filthy kind. You know —— well I am no more insane than you are. I just know more about the world and the essential evil nature of man and don't play the hypocrite. I am proud of having killed off a few and regret that I didn't kill more. I absolutely refuse to permit you to get up and testify about my mental condition and blab a lot of stuff about insanity and irresponsibility. I am saying I *am* responsible and I *am* guilty and the sooner they hang me the better it will be and gladder I will be. So don't you go trying to interfere with it."
>
> The same psychological factors later discovered in the psychoanalytic investigation of [this prisoner] were recognized in himself by this extraordinary fellow and set down by him in these comments about his own psychology, the psychology of mankind and of criminals in particular. They are, in short, that hate breeds hate, that the injustices per-

> petrated upon a child arouse in him unendurable reactions of retaliation which the child must repress and postpone but which sooner or later come out in some form or another, that the wages of sin is death, that murder breeds suicide, that to kill is only to be killed, that there is no real atonemen but suffering, and that bitter suffering bears no fruit.[97]

Carl Panzram wrote nothing that is known concerning his reaction to Dr. Menninger, who did not testify at Panzram's trial. In one of his letters, however, Menninger states that he reported his impressions to the judge. In any case, the only report that would be legally decisive was necessarily that of the Sanity Commission.

XXX

NEWS OF the unusual trial had gotten about, and there were no empty seats in the federal courtroom when it went into session, with Judge Richard J. Hopkins presiding, at 9:30 A.M., an hour after Dr. Menninger had seen Panzram.

Carl Panzram limped into the courtroom, looked long at the prospective jurors and sat down, his gaze still intent upon their faces. Reporters remarked that Panzram, unmanacled and clad in a dark suit, with his huge shoulders and large, round, half-bald head, looked more like a magistrate than the dry, clerical Hopkins.

Twelve Kansas farmers were picked, and Judge Hopkins began to explain the defendant's constitutional rights, including his right to an attorney. Ralph O'Neil was standing at the counsel table.

"I won't cooperate with any attorney," Panzram interrupted. "You can have him, let him go ahead and do what he wants to." The spectators murmured. Panzram kept his eyes on the judge, who resumed his discourse concerning rights.

"If you want to know how I plead," Panzram interrupted again, "I plead not guilty. Now go ahead and prove it."

The young prosecutor, Dan Cowie, assembled his papers and began to plead his case. He had a clear field to run in, and his sprint was fast. He introduced three inmates, eyewitnesses to the murder. He identified, through eyewitnesses, the heavy iron bar which lay on the court's exhibit table.

Through federal prison investigator J. R. Burger's interview of Panzram in his cell, and through an inmate, Jack Shapiro, he established premeditation and plan; to this incriminating evidence he forged overwhelming proof that Warnke's death, according to testimony by the examining prison physician, was caused by blows from this same iron bar; and through the testimony of Fred Morrison, who had been recently appointed deputy warden, the prosecutor made it clear that Panzram was known as a "tough character to handle."

Throughout these rapid proceedings, Panzram maintained a massive silence. Attorney O'Neil went through a brief cross-examination of the prosecution's witnesses. The government rested its case in less than an hour.

Judge Hopkins immediately called for the defense to put its case. Ralph O'Neil rose quickly and moved that the court appoint a Sanity Commission to examine Panzram. The convict half stood, scowling. He watched the judge. Judge Hopkins asked if the prosecution had any objection.

Cowie had none. Judge Hopkins appointed three alienists to examine the defendant and then adjourned the court until four in the afternoon. Panzram, still scowling, shrugged and sat down. The bewildered jury filed out, and the spectators, looking forlorn, stood up and peered out into the pouring rain. Word soon went among them that there would be a few seats available in a large office where the Sanity Commission would convene at two in the afternoon. But many left under the impression that there would be no more court that day.

But court there was—probably the swiftest capital case which included a sanity hearing in the history of the federal judiciary.

The Sanity Commission—three pale, white-faced and obviously shaken physicians—submitted its report in a sealed letter. Dr. M. L. Perry, director of the Topeka State Hospital for the Insane, handed the letter to the court clerk.

The clerk handed the contents of the envelope to Judge Hopkins. The judge read the report, gazed briefly at the angry-looking Panzram and ordered the court to reconvene. It was 4:20 P.M. and the jury filed in quickly.

Judge Hopkins announced that the Sanity Commission had found Panzram to be of unsound mind—and he paused as a deep silence fell upon the courtoom—but that Panzram "knew what he was doing," which meant, the judge explained briskly, that the defendant was able to understand the nature of the charge against him and was capable of assisting in his own defense, in such ways as he wished. The court, therefore, ordered the defense to proceed.

Visibly stunned, Ralph O'Neil pulled himself together, and glanced quickly at Panzram. The defendant's scowl had vanished. He looked satisfied and resumed his contemplation of the jury.

There were no witnesses for the defense. Ralph O'Neil asked the burly defendant to take the stand, make a statement to the jury, say anything in his own defense.

"You and the judge wouldn't let me be my lawyer, so go ahead. I have nothing to say." Panzram's tone was as careful and cold as that of the prosecutor.

Thus the defense subsided into silence and uneasily rested its case. Judge Hopkins then instructed the jury with great and explicit concern about the care they should take in weighing the evidence. He severely informed them to keep in mind that the defendant was innocent until proved guilty beyond the peradventure of a doubt.

The jury returned in forty-five minutes with a sealed verdict. Judge Hopkins adjourned his court until the following morning. Carl Panzram was manacled and spirited from the court to the Shawnee County Jail, where he spent his first night outside of a penitentiary since September 1928.

What had happened in the Sanity Commission? These proceedings proved to be available only through the reports of the press.

> The commission . . . heard the hard-boiled giant tell of the fun which he received killing a man. "And there isn't a man in this room I wouldn't kill," the cruel-visaged, steel-eyed man . . . told the commission.
>
> "I'm mad—plenty mad right now. I don't believe there is any good in any man. I'd like to have the opportunity to go away, gain power and brains and then I'd like to kill off the rest of the world," the convict said.

Dr. Perry asked the giant if he believed himself better than the rest of mankind. "Hell, no," was the reply. "I've checked up on myself lately and know that I'm probably worse than the rest of you. I have no desire to live. If you would hang me my troubles would be over and I would be better off."

"But don't you fear hell-fire?" a member of the commission inquired.

"You haven't been able to prove to me that there is such a thing," Panzram answered.

The man boasted in court of killing 21 persons and vowed that, were his parents living, he would kill them "for bringing me into the world."

"There are just two things in this world that count as powerful—money and knowledge. If I could get enough money I could buy brains because brains are for sale.

"I would get brainy chemists and I would have them prepare me a lot of poison gas and germs. With these I would be able to exterminate a great mass of human beings. Then I would kill myself.

"Society should build me a great monument because I have never propagated my kind."

Most of the two hours conversation of questioning by the commission was punctuated with vulgar remarks and sordid ideals expressed by the convict.

Panzram was heavily guarded to protect members of the commission who sat in the room with Panzram while he was allowed to smoke and sit unshackled while answering the questions.

Panzram seemed utterly unconscious of the staring crowd which was assembled in the office in which the hearing was being conducted. A queer philosophy of life . . . [which] seemed to have resulted from a hopeless aspect

> and which has been soured by solitary confinement bringing hours upon end of brooding was unraveled by the defendant.
>
> At times the man presented an almost forlorn picture, sitting as he was all alone in the midst of a group of prosecutors and curious spectators, careful not to get "too close" while his guards never let their gaze leave his figure.
>
> A man alone—against civilization's power and resources—the crowd could but respect the lone giant's magnificent courage—a courage which at no time has faltered under the strain to which it has been subjected, the courage deserving of better direction and use.[98]

The court convened again the next morning, and the judge, having been given no alternative by the hard, rural jury, looked down at the defendant and pronounced him guilty—with no mention of the life-saving phrase "without capital punishment." Panzram had nothing to say concerning the sentence. Hopkins then ordered that he be "remanded to the care of the warden at the federal penitentiary at Leavenworth, there to be confined until the fifth day of September when, between the hours of six and nine o'clock in the morning, you shall be taken to some suitable place within the confines of the penitentiary and hanged by the neck until dead."

In the words of the press, "the crowded courtroom had held its breath while the fatal words of the court were enunciated. A pin could be heard to drop as several hundred Kansans gasped with curiosity and wonder as a man was sentenced to be hanged in a state where capital punishment had been long since abolished."

Panzram stood impassively, a heavy, glowering man of thirty-eight, his handsomeness gone to bearlike fat, his hair half-gone and his heavy black moustache now gray-streaked and huge, turned down, covering his mouth. His huge hands and heavy, muscled wrists worked a little. Only his unblinking slate eyes showed awareness of the proceedings.

The judge then announced the ninety-day interval to allow for any bill of objection and appeal. Before the defense attorney could speak, Panzram said swiftly, "I don't want any attorney to file for a new trial or appeal anything. I am satisfied with the verdict."

XXXI

Carl Panzram was soon back in his solitary-confinement cell. He was cheerful and relaxed. He'd had a trip, and a United States Court had guaranteed him fulfillment of his desire to die. He hastened to inform Henry Lesser of the proceedings.

April 17, 1930

I have known you for nearly 2 years. During that time we have been in correspondence with each other continuously with only a few brief interruptions. But now circumstances are such that I believe the time has come for our correspondence to end.

Therefore, I am writing this letter which I now believe will be the last letter I shall ever write to you or anyone else. I shall endeavor to explain to you a number of things that I believe you would like to know, and these explanations are the last I intend to make to you or anyone else. Ten months ago I killed a man here in this prison, yesterday I was taken into court, given a legal trial, found guilty of the crime charged against me and then sentenced to death. This execution to take place here at this prison on September 5th, 1930, between the hours of 6 A.M. and 9 A.M.

With my trial and the sentence of the court I am perfectly contented, altho I have believed all along and I still believe that it was the intention of the court and the majority of those connected with it to give me the full benefit of the law, but not a fair and impartial trial. They succeeded in giving me a legal trial and between these two there is some difference, but this difference is in my favor.[99] I prefer to have things just as they are now. I believe that the intention of the people who tried me was to perpetrate a travesty of justice, not to give me a fair and impartial trial but to give me a legal trial. The actual results accomplished are that I was not only given what the people wanted to give me, but what I also wanted them to give me. They gave me justice. This is the one and only case that I actually know of where law and justice were synonymous. I believe that I know what justice is, and justice is what I have been wanting and trying to get all of my life but what I have never got until now, and I don't get that until the 5th of next September.

There are a number of other things that I also wanted to tell you. During my time in this prison I have received very fair treatment in every way. I have been treated far better than I have treated others and far better than I deserved to be and also better than I would mete out to others if I had the power which they have, if I was in their place and they were in my position. I don't deserve very many of the good things of this world. I expect very little and I ask for very little.

Among the things that I think that I am entitled to and that I would like to have is enough reading matter to occupy my mind and my time for the balance of my life which is very short. At the present time all of the reading matter I have is only one magazine, and that one is the *Saturday Evening Post,* which you were good enough to have sent to me. This isn't enough for me. I want more. I realize that I can't have everything I want, but I want very little and that little I want to choose my own self.

I do not want to read what others want me to read. Now this is what I want you to do if you will. I want to have you choose from the following list a number of magazines and one paper. The daily *Christian Science Monitor* which I would enjoy reading, that is the first 4 pages of it and the editorial page. The balance of the paper I think is all rubbish and not worth reading. That's the only newspaper I care to read. Among the magazines I would like to read are the *Mercury,* the *Forum, Time,* the *Atlantic Monthly, Collier's Weekly, Liberty,* the *Pathfinder,* and the *Psychiatrist's Review.* I don't want all of these because I couldn't read them all and it would be too much expense for you to go to. I wish you would subscribe for a few of these for 3 months for me. That's all I want from you. I believe that you will receive this letter and if you do I want you to do this, my last request of you, and I want you to do it now and not wait until I am dead and then send me reading matter. I want to read now and not sometime next year.

If you get this letter you need not answer it, except by subscribing for some reading matter for me. That will be sufficient.

You are one of the very few men in this world that I know and who I do not wish to harm and do not wish you any bad luck, but I do wish you all the good luck that you are entitled to, and it is my opinion that you deserve quite a bit of good luck. That is all that I care to tell you now. This will be the end of this letter and in 89 days from today will be the end of me.

Copperjohn 2nd
Carl Panzram

Henry Lesser had learned of Panzram's conviction and death sentence before the prisoner's letter arrived. In the Washington, D. C., jail it was discussed by both staff and inmates. Lesser's guard friends avoided mentioning the matter; some of the others made clear their pleasurable expectations and the hope that they might arrange some official trip to watch the hanging. Lesser said nothing. He had expected "some good" to come from the trial; he had expected a legal finding of insanity.

He also wondered about Dr. Menninger, who had been reading Panzram's confession. But he did not write to the psychiatrist nor did he receive letters from him.

Panzram's letter terminating their correspondence, although long and unusually friendly, depressed the young guard. Lesser had been invited by Austin MacCormick to enter the Federal Bureau of Prisons system, beginning with an in-service training course in the federal penitentiary at Atlanta. He had accepted. He was due to leave "the best job I ever had" in the Washington, D. C., jail for a new job in Atlanta on May 13. He had decided to continue in correctional work despite Panzram's repeated urgings to leave it and despite his own discouragements at the thankless uphill nature of prison work for a liberal reformer. These problems were balanced by the fascination of new theories, the chance for more education, the leftward trend of the country and the fire of the zealots in the new Bureau of Prisons. Finally, Lesser's move was set off by something in the back of his mind, an illogical fantasy, a hope. Someday, Lesser wanted to become warden of the Washington, D. C., jail. He wanted to show what the new penology could do for "offenders" and how much better the jail would be then than it was under men like the continuing incumbent, the now Colonel W. L. Peak.

Lesser, however, had learned something about himself and about the irrational guilt feelings caused by the two twenty-dollar gold pieces that were Harry Sinclair's gift. He had discovered that a prison searches out the flaws in every man it reaches, whether convict or staff; and he had found in himself a weakness. He was like the latent sadist who, to his surprise, finds something familiar in the handle of a whip.

A fortnight before Panzram's letter arrived, however, Lesser put the whole problem about the two twenty-dollar gold pieces to rest. He spent them.

Now preoccupied with penology and reluctant to tell Panzram about his decision to go deeper into prison work, Lesser was relieved by the prisoner's insistence that he not write, but merely send reading material.

Panzram's request was a stiff one for Lesser's slender budget, but he hastened to comply. He arranged for half-year subscriptions, subject to cancellation, to the *Christian Science Monitor, Saturday Evening Post,* the *Forum, Time,* the *Pathfinder* and *The American Mercury.* Then he began to wind up his affairs preparatory to leaving for his new job in Georgia.

XXXII

JUDGE HOPKINS' imposition of the death sentence on Carl Panzram, to be carried out on September 5, 1930, on the federal ground of Leavenworth, made the deeply sequestered convict a matter of concern to a growing number of people. Status is conferred upon the condemned.

The United States marshal's office realized that theirs would be the responsibility for learning how legally to hang a man. They needed to check current methods in this ancient area of expertise,[100] and in the way of officials seeking advice, they wrote to Washington. They prepared to get started on their project during the summer.

The prison authorities, who held legal custody of Panzram, were obliged to protect his safety until execution. They shared with the United States marshal the responsibility for making mechanical arrangements for the execution, including the building of the scaffold itself. The result of these official duties was an even tenderer solicitude for Panzram: one more guard was added to the Isolation shift to keep the condemned man under constant scrutiny around the clock.

Inside the Isolation building some prisoners watched Panzram as carefully as did the officials. Prison minds were working, and the busiest was that of the segregated convict, bird doctor Robert F. Stroud.

Outside the prison walls anti-capital punishment groups were becoming aware of the anomaly of Panzram's death sentence in the state where executions were illegal. Plans were made to secure a presidential commutation of Panzram's execution order. An important part of such a plan was to secure the signature of the doomed defendant upon a petition.

In May, a small delegation of earnest Kansans appeared in the visiting room of the Isolation building. They requested that Carl Panzram sign a petition for the commutation of his death sentence by the only man who could so commute in a federal case: President Herbert Hoover.

Since Panzram was not allowed outside his cell, the delegation came to him. Behind bars and mesh, he saw them and heard the crackle of a large petition paper. He listened carefully to what they wanted. His face darkened, and in a sudden rage he roared curses upon the dumbfounded committee. When he learned that the committee was part of a national organization, Panzram wrote a statement to them. What follows is possibly the most lucid presentation ever written of a hopelessly immured and behaviorally bankrupt convict's logic for dying.

May 23, 1930

Society for the Abolishment of
Capital Punishment,
National Headquarters,
Washington, D. C.

I, Carl Panzram, No. 31614 of the U. S. Penitentiary at Leavenworth, Kansas, am writing this statement of my own free will, without any advice or suggestions from anyone.

In the year 1928 at Washington, D. C., I was charged with and tried for the crimes of burglary and grand larceny. Although I was guilty of both these crimes, I stood trial and pleaded not guilty, but the jury found me guilty on both charges and the judge at once sentenced me to the term of 25 years.

On February 1st, 1929, I began serving this sentence at the U. S. Penitentiary at Leavenworth, Kansas. On June 20, 1929, I murdered one man, a civilian employee of the prison, by the name of Warnke, and at the same time and place I also attempted to murder a dozen other men, both guards and convicts. The only reason I did not kill them also was because I couldn't catch them.

For this crime I was indicted by a U. S. Grand Jury and on April 15 and 16 I was tried in the U. S. Court at Topeka, Kansas. This court was called and sat under the jurisdiction of Judge Hopkins.

At this trial I pleaded not guilty and was at once put on trial for the crime of murder in the first degree. So far as I know, I was given a legal trial and was not deprived of any of my constitutional rights. The jury found me guilty as charged in the indictment. The judge thereupon pronounced sentence on me, and the sentence was that I should be hanged by the neck until I am dead. This sentence to take effect between the hours of 6 A.M. and 9 A.M. at the U. S. Penitentiary at Leavenworth, Kansas, on September 5, 1930.

The findings of the court and the sentence of the judge meet with my approval, and I am perfectly satisfied to have the sentence carried out without any further interference from anyone. I do not wish to have another trial and I do not wish to have that sentence changed in any way.

If I am given another trial or if the death sentence should be commuted to life imprisonment, either in a penitentiary or an insane asylum, it will be against my will.

Now then, I come to the reason why I have written this letter.

I have been informed that your organization, or at any rate some of the members of it, have made or are making an attempt to change my sentence to life imprisonment in solitary confinement in a prison or in an insane asylum.

This you are doing without my consent and absolutely against my will.

I shall never willingly grant you my permission to have this done for me.

For your information and guidance, I am going to inform you of some facts which I believe you are unaware of at this time.

I believe that your reasons for trying to set aside the sentence of death in my case are that you think this penalty is not a humane form of justice. You are sincere in your beliefs that this is a barbaric and inhuman form of punishment.

Another one of your reasons is that you are laboring under the delusion that I am insane and therefore not responsible for my acts.

Now, I am going to attempt to show you that this sentence of death is absolutely just and also that it will be carried out in a very humane manner, and I shall also try to convince you that I am in full possession of my faculties and that I am now and always have been perfectly sane and I am therefore fully responsible for everything I have ever done.

First, I shall try to convince you that I am quite sane at this time. I believe that any person who is sober and sane and who is not blind and who is able to read and understand the English language as I am here writing, he or she should be convinced without any further argument that I am perfectly sane in every way and therefore responsible for my acts.

I am at this time 38 years old, a big, powerful man, strong in both body and mind. My physical fitness is not good as it once was, but my mental faculties are unimpaired in any way. I have never used drugs of any kind at any time. I am and always have been a very moderate drinker of liquor. Practically a total abstainer. I have never had any disease of any kind which would have a tendency to weaken my intellect. I have never been addicted to any habits of sexual excesses of any kind over which I didn't have complete control of myself.

So far as I know, none of my relatives or ancestors have ever been in any kind of an institution for mental defectives.

I, for my own part, have been examined on numerous occasions by various duly qualified, capable and impartial doctors as to my sanity, and so far as I know, I have never been pronounced to be insane or incapable or irresponsible for my acts.

I have never spent one single day of my life in any institution for the insane.

But I have spent 22 years of my life in various penal institutions.

I started doing time when I was 11 years old and have been doing practically nothing else since then. What time I haven't been in jail I have spent either getting out or getting in again.

During this time I have been into every kind of a penal institution there is in this country and some in other countries.

Therefore I consider myself pretty well qualified to know what the conditions of prisoners, prisons, policemen, courts, prison guards, prison officials and the existing conditions of penal institutions are today, here and now.

Knowing the real facts as I do from practical experience and also knowing that there is only one chance in a thousand of my ever getting my freedom, and also knowing that I, like all other men, must some day die, I have deliberately and intentionally made my choice.

I choose to die here and now by being hanged by the neck until I am dead.

I prefer that I die that way, and if I have a soul and if that soul should burn in hell for a million years, still I prefer that to a lingering, agonizing death in some prison dungeon or a padded cell in a mad house.

Now, I want to know, if this isn't good logic and reason, then what the hell is it?

Now then, I shall give you my second reason why this sentence should be carried out. I do not believe that being hanged by the neck until dead is a barbaric or inhuman punishment. I look forward to that as real pleasure and a big relief to me. I do not feel bad or unhappy about it in any way. Every day since I received that sentence I have felt pretty good. I feel good right now and I believe that when my last hour comes I will dance out of my dungeon and on to the scaffold with a smile on my face and happiness in my heart.

Another reason why I believe that this sentence should be carried out is because I believe it is justice, and I am quite sincere when I say that this is the first and only time in all my life of battling with the law that I ever did get justice from the law.

Now, you who do not know me or my wishes, you decide without consulting me in any way; you start to try to revoke the judgment of a legally constituted court and the sentence that was pronounced on me.

One other thing I am going to tell you before I stop this letter, and that is this: the only thanks you or your kind will ever get from me for your efforts on my behalf is that I wish you all had one neck and that I had my hands on it. I would sure put you out of your misery, just the same as I have done with numbers of other people.

I have no desire whatever to reform myself. My only desire is to reform people who try to reform me, and I believe that the only way to reform people is to kill 'em.

My motto is: "Rob 'em all, rape 'em all and kill 'em all." I am,

Very truly yours,
COPPER JOHN II
Carl Panzram

Why did he call himself Copper John II? This was the second time he had signed himself this way. Copper John had been in Panzram's mind for years. In an earlier writing he explained, and in doing so symbolized, his ultimate desire to turn his back on everything.

In one of the large prisons of this country [Auburn, New York] on top of one of the front buildings is the statue of a man made of copper. This statue is known as Copper John.

The cons have made up a piece of poetry about this Copper John and the cons themselves. The first line of it is:

If Copper John could only turn his face
And see the muzzlers and guzzlers in this place

From there it goes on to tell just what he would see. The meanness, degeneracy, unprinciple, treachery, brutality, and every kind of roguery and filth there is that is confined behind the stone walls and iron bars that Copper John has turned his back on.

It is well understood in the underworld that the worst insulting name that anyone can call another is that he is a muzzler and guzzler. This means that the man is lost to all decency and is beyond all redemption. He is the most low-down specimen that is on earth of the whole human race.

During my last term in prison I was given the nickname or monicker of Copper John and was known as a first-class muzzler and guzzler. When I was given the rep I wasn't altogether entitled to it but am now. I plead guilty. I fully deserve it now. I am as rotten as I know how to be and the only reason I am not worse is because my opportunities and abilities are limited.

Not satisfied yet, Panzram on May 30 addressed a letter to President Hoover to make absolutely sure that no one had misrepresented his position.

President Herbert Hoover
c/o Attorney General Mitchell
Washington, D. C.

I am writing this letter to notify you that I have been tried in the U. S. Court for the crime of murder in the first degree; I was found guilty and sentenced to be hanged by the neck until I am dead.

I hereby notify you that I am perfectly satisfied with my trial and the sentence. I do not want another trial.

Neither do I want to have that sentence changed in any way.

The only way this sentence can be changed is by the direct action of the President of the United States. I believe that I am within my constitutional rights when I refuse to accept a pardon or a commutation from the death penalty to a sentence of life imprisonment, either in a prison or an insane asylum.

I absolutely refuse to accept either a pardon or a commutation should either one or the other be offered to me.

Carl Panzram

Having prepared these letters to insure his ultimate position, Panzram talked to guards and a prison doctor who came to look him over. There is also evidence that he achieved communication with other prisoners. According to Stroud, what discussion there was centered on one enterprising topic: how to cheat the hangman. Panzram may have been told that the efforts of the Kansas committees would be futile, and that if the President wished to commute his sentence he had the power to do so irrespective of any representations by Panzram or anyone else. Panzram decided not to send the letters but instead to save them for Henry Lesser, who would want to know about the convict's logic and decision. Lesser eventually did receive the letters and saved them for readers today.

XXXIII

INSIDE THE WALLS of Leavenworth, skeptical officials and cynical convicts, who had considered Panzram's effort a colossal bluff, the gamble of a madman, now accepted with reluctance the gathering evidence that here was a man who was dedicated to one proposition.

There were exceptions, however. One of the total skeptics, shut in his cell with the abounding, musical, odoriferous and busy life of more than two hundred chirping canaries, was Robert Stroud. He had been watching the behavior of birds for ten years and of jailbirds for twenty-two years.

His account of "Panzeran" in his enormous prison manuscript, written fifteen years later, dismisses Panzram's murders as fictional and his desire to die as a pose. Despite his desperate outlook, Stroud was a tenacious liver of life. In common with most persons, he was unable to accept the idea of a sustained desire for one's own death. Not knowing Panzram, Stroud believed that Panzram's hunger for his own execution had to be a bluff.

Stroud had followed the history of John Aday, the half-Apache Indian who had raped and killed an Indian girl and later had murdered an inmate in Leavenworth in 1920. John Aday, like Panzram, had ignored the attorney appointed to defend him and had said that he wanted to be found guilty and executed from the center chandelier in the courtroom. In 1921, a year after Stroud's life had been spared by commutation, Aday was sentenced to death, and a gallows was built. Then he was allowed a second trial on a technicality. At this time, the Indian announced that he was ready to plead guilty to first-degree murder. He was then given a second life sentence and placed in the Isolation section. He thanked the judge for relieving him of the anxiety of an execution. Stroud had never had any use for Aday, but he had contributed a few dollars and written to people trying to prevent Aday's execution. Stroud and Ono Manuel, another gallows escapee, had both prepared themselves when under execution dates to commit suicide. To prisoners and public alike, the precedent was not to be broken: there must be no hangings in Kansas.

On June 5, Panzram broke his self-imposed silence and wrote at length to Henry Lesser. He did not try to send the letters, but saved them to be forwarded to the guard after his death. These letters reveal that Panzram was still expecting his execution in ninety days.

I am writing this letter today, June 5th, but I don't expect to have it mailed to you until September 6, 1930, because on that day I will be dead and buried.

There are a good many things I would like to say or write

to you, but because I don't know whether or not you'll ever get this letter, I cut it kind of short.

First, I want to tell you that up to now I have been getting the reading matter which you were good enough to subscribe to for me. There is nothing I can do for you to repay you for the many favors you have done for me, excepting to thank you and wish you good luck. I would like to be able to truthfully tell you that I do thank you, but this I cannot do, simply because there is no such thing as gratitude left in me.

There was at one time, but that time is long gone. Gratitude is one of the many things that have been kicked out of me. I can and do truthfully wish you good luck. All that you deserve and I am of the opinion that you are one of the very few men I have ever known that really deserves good luck in this world. You deserve what I have missed in life—happiness, peace and contentment.

As for me, I'll soon be at peace. I have never had the good fortune to find it in life, so I expect to find it in death. I hope so and believe so.

To some people my death will seem to come in a horrible form, but to me it seems a very easy way to die. I look forward to it as a pleasure and relief.

It is a far easier death than I have dealt out to some of the people I have killed. I couldn't and don't ask for any easier way to die.

This will probably be the last I'll ever write to anyone, because in just 90 days more I'll be hanged by the neck until I am dead. But I feel fine and am feeling better every day as the time grows shorter.

I intend to leave this world as I have lived in it. I expect to be a rebel right up to my last moment on earth. With my last breath I intend to curse the world and all mankind. I intend to spit in the warden's eye or whoever places the rope around my neck when I am standing on the scaffold. I always did want to spit in a copper's eye and also a preacher or priest. That will be all the thanks they'll get from me. I don't know which I despise and detest the most, a copper or a buck. I guess the soul-saver takes the palm. I have met only one priest that I felt I could respect, but I have known quite a number of coppers I could, did and still do respect. You are one of them. I never have liked any of them, but I did respect 'em, when they have deserved it—and some do—not many, but some anyway.

Enclosed in this letter I am sending you a number of different letters and articles that I have written since my trial.

Within the legal papers, journal entries and the certified copy of my indictment, you will find the names and addresses of all or nearly all of the men who had anything to do with my trial. Among them you will find the names of the doctors who were appointed and sat as a commission to inquire as to my sanity and who pronounced me to be insane, or of unsound mind, as you will see, according to the Clerk of the U. S. Courts certified copy of the journal entries. I believe this verdict was unfair and I also believe that if you would send each or all of them a copy of the book of my life story, which I wrote and gave to you, they would be quite convinced that their verdict of insanity against me was and is unsound and not my mind that is unsound.

By the time you or they get this letter I'll be very, very dead, so it won't make any difference to me, but it may to someone else sometime.

Carl Panzram, 31614

Later in June, Panzram's increasing fears that he might not be executed turned his mind to thoughts of self-destruction.

Stroud began long disquisitions to the guard Red Ballard, to the orderlies and to Ono Manuel in a loud clear voice, hoping that the information would reach Carl Panzram. He talked about how simple and painless it was to end it all: press two fingers into the groin until the throb of the femoral artery can be felt, work the fingers back and forth until the artery is brought against the skin, and cut it with a long, sharp thumbnail or a chip of razor blade. Death would come in ten minutes. This artery, Stroud explained in loud tones, is the only one which can be easily reached, yet cannot be tied off. He also spoke of making a paper quill, opening a large vein anywhere, inserting the quill and blowing a bubble or two into the vein. Or, he added, simple tap water would do it.

Ballard said nothing. He closed the wooden door to Panzram's cell and cautioned Stroud to lower his voice. Ballard placed his chair in front of Panzram's door and closed the wooden door whenever he left. This caused maximum watch and minimum communication.

What happened during the following two weeks in June 1930 can only be surmised. But on June 20, Panzram wrote his next-to-last letter to Lesser, setting it aside with the others in his cell. It was the only letter Panzram never signed.

The other half of this letter I wrote 20 days ago. Since then conditions have been changed a bit. Not very much, but just enough for me to commit suicide tonight instead of waiting until September 5th to be legally hung.

So if I succeed in my effort at suicide tonight, then this will sure be the last I'll ever say or write on this earth.

The choice is mine and I fully realize just what I am doing.

I would like to have it known just why I do this. I had no choice about coming into this world and nearly all of my 38 years in it I have had very little to say and do about how I should live my life. People have driven me into doing everything I have ever done. Now the time has come when I refuse to be driven any farther.

Tonight I die and tomorrow I go to a grave. Farther than that, no man can drive me, I am sure glad to leave this lousy world and the lousier people in this world; but of all the lousy people in this world, I believe that I am the lousiest of 'em all.

Today I am dirty, but tomorrow I'll be just

DIRT

Panzram then sat waiting patiently for Guard Ballard, whom he tolerated, to go off shift. Then he plugged up the lock in his cell with wood and cloth, forced himself to eat a poisonous plate of beans which he had hidden and allowed to rot, and then cut a deep six-inch gash in his leg.

The night guard heard the violent retching of Panzram's nausea and saw in the yellow tier light the faint glisten of red upon the floor. He called for help and tried to open the cell without success.

More help came, and guards forced open the cell

door. Hospital trusties administered first aid to the cut, bound it tightly, pumped out Panzram's stomach and laid him back upon prison cot.

His attempt to destroy himself was singularly clumsy for someone otherwise as capable as Panzram. Guards found a sharpened bloody button in his cell. Did the strange prisoner make the attempt as a concession to the "con code"—and to the need to stop the precedent of a legal execution in Kansas?

Perhaps a deeper meaning lay in the date he chose, June 20, 1930. Panzram had killed R. G. Warnke, the laundry foreman, on June 20, 1929.

XXXIV

In the summer of 1930, the optimistic voices of apostles of free enterprise and a bright future faltered and finally went unheard in the hard, dry winds of economic stagnation, unemployment and drought. In the Plains states, the "Dust Bowl" became unlivable, and thousands of the poor were driven westward. By July, over a thousand banks had crumbled. Hemlines dropped. The voice of H. L. Mencken was no longer stentorian. Herbert Hoover's years of capable public service were forgotten in the rising misery: he was the helpless relic of a vanished age. Covarrubias, one of the great caricaturists, was even then preparing a pen and ink drawing of Hoover which was perhaps the most savage sketch ever inked.

Chicago's grotesque mayor, Big Bill Thompson, was finally thrown out of office. The gangster Al Capone drove in his armored car to the "feds," tried to make a deal with an offer of four million dollars and was turned down. But the gangs flourished like yeast in the mash of Prohibition. Bonnie and Clyde types were swiftly becoming unheroic, and J. Edgar Hoover's G-men were to be the national heroes for years to come.

The Depression was finally beginning to bite through the tough hide of the American prison system. Men committed misdemeanors and felonies, each after his fashion and need, simply to get food, a roof over his head and the magnetic companionship of shared immured misery.

In attempting to promote a forward-looking prison-industries program for their corrosively idle penitentiaries, the Federal Bureau of Prisons ran into desperate opposition from merchants and labor unions, each seeking to remain busy. But the young penologists and efficiency experts were determined and capable, and their empowering laws had already been passed. They had been enacted at a time of prosperity but they were still laws, and they led the country into a new era of physically and socially improved, although bureaucratized and politically harassed, prison regimes.

Henry Lesser was now training at Atlanta prison. He soon discovered that the prison officials did not necessarily follow with slavish concern the new philosophy and directives from Washington about "treatment." Lesser was deeply moved by the lectures of Professor Jesse O. Stutsman and others, even as he watched with loathing the actual treatment of men by officials who kept their hats on the backs of their heads, relaxed with their feet on the penal office desks and continued their former patterns of custody and punishment.

Lesser met two former Washington, D. C., jail inmates

in the yard. He called them "brothers," shook hands with them—and was promptly hauled before the tired warden for a cold reprimand. The chafing young guard went back to his class notes and threw them on the floor.

He saw but could not express the hypocrisy of the tougher prison officials, who seemed inevitably to survive. More decent types were like the fat men in the old war parades—they weren't around. Occasionally a few did persevere, employing good heart and talent effectively against politicians; but these politicians knew how to evoke a certain crude response from the public—the attack of a brutish, vengeful and kill-prone herd of animals.[101]

Lesser saw that sociological needs governed the penal road to survival and accounted for the grotesque cultural lag in the evolution of prisons. The pronouncements of penal authorities sounded despairingly like those of 1878 and were no more relevant.

Leavenworth baked in another hot summer. But the prison was relatively quiet; better food and somewhat improved conditions contrasted favorably with the worsening Depression on the outside. There would be no major action for a year.

On July 16, Panzram's legal limit for an appeal from execution expired. One more hazard between the convict and his date with the rope had been removed. He still had other convicts and their needs to contend with; and a presidential commutation was possible at any time up to the springing of the trap.

One day, Panzram was reading the *Christian Science Monitor* when the hard yet cordial face of Austin MacCormick, second in command of the Federal Bureau of

Prisons for a brief time, appeared outside his cell. After an extended visit, Panzram gave MacCormick his letters and documents and asked the prison official to deliver them to Lesser. MacCormick agreed and was as good as his word. Lesser received the Panzram material by mail from Washington, D. C.

Lesser read MacCormick's covering letter, informing him of his visit with Panzram and of the convict's unsuccessful suicide attempt. When Lesser read Panzram's June letters and MacCormick's account of what had followed, he felt powerless and his depression returned. For perhaps the first time, Lesser's sense of the omnipotence of "doing good" was shattered. Were there some situations in the human lot so utterly dead-end that oblivion was an easement? But Lesser faced out his depression, forced his mind to work and grimly wrote Panzram a letter which, Lesser thought, was one of the longest and most responsible missives he had written. But it was flawed with self-interest, however reasonable. It was to evoke a curious response.

Henry P. Lesser, Guard
Atlanta Penitentiary
Atlanta, Georgia
August 4th, 1930

Mr. Carl Panzram, #31614
P. O. Box #7
Leavenworth, Kan.

Dear Carl:

I want to thank you very sincerely for the letters which you asked Austin MacCormick, Assistant Director of Bureau of Prisons to hand over to me. He informed me of your attempt at suicide. I believe that you are under the impression that Mr. MacCormick did not receive the material which you sent him some time back dealing with your views on crime and criminals. I know for a fact that he received it, and I am sure that he must have acknowledged it, although you may not have received the acknowledgment.

You asked me to submit a copy of your autobiography to the psychiatrists who declared you to be of unsound mind although aware of the difference between right and wrong, which made you legally responsible for your act.

I have already sent Dr. Karl Menninger, whom you have already met, a copy of your story. You say that you would like to write me about certain things. If you still care to, I will be more than glad to hear from you. I see no reason why your letters will not reach me, even though you send them directly to me. It seems that your life story will be published shortly just as it was written, so that society will know your side of it. I am telling you this because you always seemed to be anxious to have your version of things explained by yourself.

If, as you have written me on numerous occasions, you are desirous that I receive the financial rewards, if any, as a result of the publication of the work, I would like to have you state so again in your next letter. I want you to know that I will make whatever disposition of the money you care me to make. Your letter to the Society for the Abolishment of Capital Punishment was as you thought—very logical. I do not see how they could take any other view of it. I will now close this letter with the expectation of hearing from you shortly. If there is anything that I can do, please do not hesitate to notify me. I want to thank you very much for your kind expressions of good will and confidence in my desires in the past to do all that I possibly could for you. With kindest personal regards, I remain,

Affectionately,
Henry P. Lesser

Only surmise is possible concerning Panzram's state of mind when he received Henry Lesser's letter of August 4. His response was scrawled on the back of Lesser's letter and was forwarded to him immediately.

H. P. Lesser, SCREW
Atlanta Penitentiary
Atlanta, Ga.

I've read this letter and in reply write that there is nothing more that you can do for me. Also that as far as any financial [illegible word] publication and sale of my autobiography are to go to you to do with as you see fit.

Signed
CARL PANZRAM, 31614

It was the first and last time that Carl Panzram had ever addressed his friend as "screw." He had put the word in capitals. The note was in effect a holographic will which would remind Henry Lesser, during every day of the next forty years of his life, who he was, what he wanted, and at the same time what his mission had to be so long as Panzram's confession remained unknown to the world.

XXXV

UNEASY at their lack of experience, officials at Leavenworth and the United States marshal's office carefully studied the material from Washington and from their own files on the problem of how to hang a man.

The first question at issue was: Who would do it? This question had to be answered early because whoever would do it would know how to do it, and would be of considerable help in solving other questions, such as with what, and where. The names of hangmen remain carefully anonymous for a number of important reasons (not the least of which is their safety). But whatever his name, a reliable hangman was soon located in an adjacent state and retained.

A well-thumbed scaffold blueprint with specifications was found in the Leavenworth files. At least three scaffolds had been built in Leavenworth, but none had been used. Warden White must have been surprised by the volume of detail work involved in doing the job right. Directives flowed in from the Bureau in Washington—but as harassed Deputy Warden Zerbst muttered to Red Ballard through the Isolation gate, directives were always flowing in from the Bureau in Washington.

There were several unofficial visits from the hangman as Warden White and Deputy Zerbst were informed of various technical requirements of the execution. There was a discreet discussion of fee.

The hangman asked and received permission to cure a new thirteen-foot length of rope by suspending it in the prison armory with a heavy concrete weight attached. Each day, guards saw the concrete sag slowly toward the floor until, at last, there was as little give in the five golden strands of Italian hemp as in an iron bar of similar diameter.

Working from Panzram's body measurements and an estimated weight of 212 pounds, the hangman calculated that a drop of 7 feet, 8 inches would suffice. He explained to the discomfited officials that drops were designed to produce a force of 2,400 pounds on the prisoner's neck as the rope snapped to full length. However, he explained, some modification of this figure was necessary, depending on the hangman's professional judgment of the prisoner's muscular development. Too long a drop had been known to tear a man's head off; too short a one would cause too lingering a death. The hangman checked his figures and made several small corrections on the government blueprint, which was then handed to Leavenworth's carpenters.

The gallows site was where it had been in past execution attempts in Leavenworth—in the small walled-in exercise yard attached to the Isolation building. Removed from the prison population, it was the safest, most controlled and most private place in the Leavenworth compound.

Panzram continued to read in his cell. As the solid sound of hammering floated into Isolation in the balmy late summer, he cocked an ear and listened, in the same way Stroud listened to his canaries.

The scaffold must have disturbed Stroud. Ten years before, he had seen his own gallows built and had lived to see it torn down. The new gallows, gleaming with fresh wood, looked exactly the same as the one he remembered. He avoided the area as he moved silently around the exercise yard and returned to his twittering birds. Stroud's restiveness increased as time grew short. He remained convinced that Panzram wished to cheat the hangman and that the brawny, overweight convict was a fool who had muffed his chance at suicide. On a second chance, he might succeed. Two weeks before the execution, Stroud saw his opportunity. He wrote his earlier instructions on a slip of paper, broke a new Gillette blade in two and wrapped the paper around the top halves of the broken blade. Having found an old tube of watercolor gray, he painted the package the same color as the concrete floor. He then persuaded a new short-term prisoner, who had been made an orderly in the Isolation section, to throw the tiny packet into Panzram's cell the first time the guard, Red Ballard, turned his head. The orderly agreed, saying he would do it when he brought Panzram's food tray. The cost was a pair of earphones, which inmates had to purchase themselves, for the radio system in the prison.

The packet was dropped into Panzram's cell without

incident and the transaction of the earphones followed. Stroud waited patiently for Panzram's second attempt.

September 4, the day before Panzram's scheduled execution, Ballard was looking in on the prisoner when Panzram signaled him. He handed Ballard two gleaming shards of the blade. The camouflaged wrapping was gone.

The two men, the guard and the condemned, stood still, saying nothing. Ballard took the blade.

"Where did you get these?" Ballard demanded.

"None of your damned business," said Panzram.

The rest of the day passed without incident. In the afternoon, Warden White and a select group of officers met with the hangman to rehearse their roles.

Solid outer doors on the Isolation cells were shut as a volunteer guard allowed Ballard and the hangman to practice adjusting the leather harness which would be fastened on Panzram the following morning. The harness, resembling a corset, was buckled around the guard's waist. Thick straps pinioned the elbows at the side, and the wrists were strapped in front. The operation was performed several times until it could be done in less than half a minute. Satisfied, White suggested they proceed to the scaffold where Ballard and the United States marshal, Donald MacIvor, were shown how to position a man on the set of chalk marks over the double oak door.

Ballard was given instructions on fastening a final leg strap just below the knees while the hangman went through motions of adjusting the noose and black hood. "Step off the trap quickly," instructed the hangman. He kicked an iron pin and there was a loud thud as a sandbag dropped through the banging doors.

Several newspaper reporters, including Mark Dunlap and Jack Charvat of the Topeka *Daily Capital*, had arrived at the prison for orientation. The following morning they would be allowed in the exercise yard to cover the hanging itself.

As the blue-shirted guard detail marched out of Isolation, the two newsmen wrangled permission from Zerbst to see Panzram. Zerbst warned them that Panzram probably wouldn't talk, but he ordered Ballard to let them in. Panzram ignored their questions and continued to read magazine stories as he lay on a mattress smoking a cigaret.

"Aw, he just wants to die so why don't you leave him alone?" said Ballard, irritated.

Charvat wasn't easily put off. He had orders to write a feature story on the man awaiting execution.

"How did he feel about the rehearsal?" Charvat asked Ballard.

The guard's angry reply was interrupted by Panzram's voice behind the wire mesh. "Don't bother me with that stuff. My part of the performance isn't ready yet, but I'll prance up those thirteen steps like a blooded stallion. Are you sure the scaffold is strong enough to hold me?"

The reporter scribbled hurriedly, tossing another question loudly to Ballard.

"Does Panzram have any regrets?"

"Yeah," came the voice. "I regret I won't be able to read the end of this magazine story. It's continued next issue."

There were no more questions. The reporters looked around at the long double row of cages and at the dingy lights burning in the afternoon, and left.

On the evening of September 4, Dr. Bennett, the second

prison physician, asked the trusty night nurse to pack the doctor's bag for Justin K. Fuller, M.D., of the United States Public Health Service, and to be sure to include the stethoscope.

"Any medicines you want, I'll need the key."

"No medicine is going to help," the doctor snapped.

The trusty, one of the few trained male nurses to be sentenced to Leavenworth in that day, wrote several doggerel verses about the situation. The doctor's purpose was:

Not to improve his blood or bone
Nor yet prolong his breath
But only for to certify
His true authentic death.

In Atlanta, Georgia, Henry Lesser was passed through the gate of the federal penitentiary at high noon on September 5, 1930. He had a newspaper pressed tight under his arm. He knew the meaning of the date, and thoughts of Panzram weighed heavy on his mind. Lesser had half-expected a letter, but none had arrived.

His hand shook a little as he forced himself to open the paper. Lesser was nearsighted and he spread the Atlanta *Journal* on his desk. Buried on an inside page, he found a United Press story, datelined the Federal Penitentiary, Leavenworth, Kansas. It began: "Showing contempt for life until the end, Carl Panzram, who proudly referred to himself as 'the most criminal man in the world,' died on the gallows here today for the murder of a prison foreman. The trap was sprung at 6:01 A.M. He was declared dead at 6:20 A.M."

"All night long that last night," Robert Stroud wrote of Panzram, "he walked the floor of his cell, singing a pornographic little song that he had composed himself. It was not much of a song, either from the point of view of melody or lyrics, but it undoubtedly expressed, in not too polite terms, the deepest craving of his heart. The principal theme was 'Oh, how I love my roundeye!' "

At Leavenworth, the lights of Isolation had burned into a pale gray dawn on September 5. When Panzram heard the distant rattle of footsteps it was not quite six o'clock. Guard Ballard went over to the steel door leading to an outer corridor and peered through the small, barred window. Warden White's voice was heard and the guard turned a brass key in the lock.

The door swung open. White entered Isolation at the head of a procession of some twenty persons, including guards and newspaper reporters. Immediately behind the warden was Marshal MacIvor and the tall government hangman, carrying the leather harness over one arm. White stopped in front of Panzram's cell as Ballard remembered to hurry down the line and close the wooden doors on Stroud, Ono Manuel and John Aday. The spectators pressed themselves discreetly against the opposite wall as Panzram faced them, searching through the wire mesh with hostile eyes. He saw two men in clerical garb on the fringes of the crowd and at once began to roar at White.

"Are there any Bible-backed cocksuckers in here?"

"I thought you might change your mind," White apologized. "These gentlemen came a long way to offer you comfort."

"Get 'em out," shouted Panzram. "I don't mind being

hanged, but I don't need any Bible-backed hypocrites around me! Run 'em out, Warden, or you're going to have one hell of a time getting me out of this cell. Every man I get a hand on is going to a hospital!"

White knew Panzram was within a condemned man's traditional rights regarding witnesses of his own execution. The disappointed clergymen were escorted out.

"All right," said Panzram, "Let's get going. What are we stalling around for?"

White motioned the guards and newsmen to proceed to the exercise yard as Ballard opened Panzram's cell. Panzram helped his escorts fasten the leather corset.

"Anything you want to say?" asked the hangman, fumbling with a strap.

Panzram snapped impatiently, "Yes, hurry it up, you Hoosier bastard! I could hang a dozen men while you're fooling around!"

In the yard the newsmen took hurried notes. The scaffold looked strange and somehow unexpected. Dew glistened on boards that had the raw, temporary look of a structure erected for a county fair. It was not as one might have imagined it to be.

In less than a minute the back door of Isolation opened and Panzram emerged between Ballard and the hangman. Panzram was almost running ahead, half dragging his taller escorts. White and the marshal hurried behind, trailed by officers trying to look dignified as they ran.

In confusion, the spectators parted into two lines as the procession raced pell-mell in their direction. Panzram's face was rigid and looked straight ahead, his eyes fixed on the rope. Only at the foot of the stairs did he seem to notice the transfixed onlookers. He paused, looked slowly around and spat twice. Then his face was forward again. Everyone's nostrils inhaled the sweet smell of new oak and hemp and everyone's eyes followed him up the thirteen steps which he felt with his feet. He hurried up the gallows, as toward a gate, pulling Ballard and the hangman with him.

Records of official entry regarding the death of Carl Panzram are brief. Dr. Justin K. Fuller, one of two doctors in attendance, stepped forward to the stretched body underneath the gallows, placed a stethoscope gently to the chest and palpated the neck. Later he dictated his report to a prison clerk.

MEDICAL CERTIFICATE OF DEATH,
CARL PANZRAM

I hereby certify that I examined the body of Carl Panzram, in accordance with the directions of the Surgeon General of the U. S. Public Health Service and the Attorney General, at U. S. Penitentiary, Leavenworth, Kansas, on September 5, 1930, and pronounced him dead at 6:18 A.M.

I found the cause of death to be:
Dislocation cervical vertebra,
Strangulation,
Legal execution.

Reporters who had witnessed this event were surprised by its swiftness, and their accounts were in conflict as to time and exact detail. There was uncertainty as to whether Panzram had been able to spit on the executioner as he had promised he would. The reporters' notebooks had hung limp during the swift adjustment of rope, the exploding sound of the opening doors and the swift downward stroke of the body. Later, they recalled the mist which had settled on the yard and the indistinct figures of guards watching from a tower on the wall. The prison had been quiet; the first bell was not scheduled to ring for an hour. Reporters had left the same way they came in and were relieved to find themselves outside the walls.

United States Marshal MacIvor visited briefly with Zerbst and Morrison and then also left. He picked up a copy of the surgeon's report to complete his own paperwork. In Topeka he made a return on the writ of execution which had been handed to him after Panzram's trial in April. The writ certified that Panzram had been duly executed according to the instructions of the federal court, claiming a fee and cost of $111.28. F. I. Campbell, clerk of the court, inspected these documents and closed the Panzram file. Later it was forwarded to Washington for permanent storage in the archives of the Department of Justice.

Burial arrangements had been made while the final paperwork continued. Panzram's body was removed to the Leavenworth mortuary as prison officials ascertained that no relatives had made claim to it. Warden White signed an order authorizing a grave at government expense. This was dug in the Leavenworth Cemetery—"Peckerwood Hill" to inmates—on a slope directly west of the prison. After an autopsy, Panzram's body was delivered and interred without ceremony, except for the placement by trusties of a standard concrete marker inscribed with the prisoner's number, 31614. An entry was marked in the official cemetery record as Panzram's body became the permanent property of the federal government.

It became the chore of John J. McConlouge, the polite record clerk of Leavenworth, to inform the various jurisdictions around the country who had filed detainers upon Carl Panzram that the United States had claimed the convict in a manner that forever released all holds.

One of McConlouge's missives duly arrived at Oregon State Penitentiary in Salem.

September 11, 1930
Re: Carl Panzram #31614

Dear Sir:

Our records revealed the subject was wanted by your department at the expiration of his sentence.

I regret to inform you that this subject died by a legal execution (by hanging) September 5, 1930.

J. S. Murray, the gray veteran clerk of Oregon's prison, was startled to learn of Panzram's demise and the manner of it. He felt that old Charles A. "Spud" Murphy, the former warden who had so daringly attempted to change the prison pattern, should hear the news. He called Murphy, then an engineer for the Portland school system. He read the letter to Murphy. Murphy was puzzled by the phrasing.

"Is that what the letter says, '*I regret to inform you*' that he died by execution? Why 'regret'?"

"Just being polite, Spud. Because *we* wanted him. Panzram still owes us fourteen years. What should that clerk write—'*I am glad to inform you*' that he was executed?"

"No sir, they couldn't say that either, could they? I remember Panzram. Dangerous man. Wasn't he the one that used to carry the flag in front of the prison band?"

EPILOGUE

AFTER THE execution, Henry Lesser gathered up the manuscript of Carl Panzram's confession and put it away with typed copies. It remained in his rooms, a presence labeled "My Friend P."

Lesser finished his correctional training and became a busy parole officer in Virginia. The economically shatttered country voted Herbert Hoover out and Franklin D. Roosevelt in. Under these violent impacts, the new Federal Bureau of Prisons dug itself in, slowly fading into the pallor of prison walls and the escalating needs of bureaucracy. But its improvements were to continue for decades.

Lesser was transferred. He was promoted to junior warden's assistant in a federal reformatory camp. He tried to press himself into the system. He wanted to apply what he had been taught and felt to be right, but stubborn reality deepened his bewilderment. It was hard for Lesser to preserve the social distance thought to be required by the custodial system of prison for its efficient operation. Treatment was always secondary. The patient duplicity required of a reformer for survival in the prison system began to worry him.

Early in 1933, he received from Dr. Menninger a cordial letter with the only circulating copy of Panzram's confession.

"We are very interested in it from a psychoanalytic standpoint," Menninger wrote, "because it shows so clearly how hostilities are stimulated in the child and how his desire for revenge works out in antisocial behavior." Lesser put the copy away and saved the letter.

In 1934, he was surprised to receive an inquiry and request for the Panzram confession from Fulton Oursler, the serious-minded editor of *Liberty* magazine. H. L. Mencken, still thinking about Panzram these three winters later, had written to Oursler and urged him to consider publication in some form of Panzram's journal of hate and killing.

Lesser sent the manuscript to Oursler, only to receive it back a month later with Oursler's note of astonishment and regret. The editor saw no way to present such a document to the America of 1934. Lesser saved the letter.

His increasing disillusionment with his prison job sharpened when Lesser learned that his old boss, Washington District Jail Superintendent W. L. Peak, now a colonel, had all but clinched a position as supervisor of the correctional system of the District of Columbia. By one of those ironies so inevitable in penology, Colonel Peak had become head of the Lorton Reformatory in Virginia, the first prison without walls in the United States.[102]

Misfortune befell Colonel Peak, however, in the form of a letter published in the Washington *Daily News* in 1935, signed by one Henry James. James, who had of course revealed his true name to the editor, questioned the colonel's qualifications and gave dates and details of the torture methods under his superintendentship. After a full investigation, the harassed colonel resigned from jail service. He was killed in an automobile crash several years later.

This exposure of his former employer, however gratifying to Lesser as a reformer, did not facilitate his adjustment as a prison staff man. Disillusioned and alone, he resigned from prison service, leaving a secure position to endure six months without work or income, eating from the breadlines still operating side by side with Roosevelt's New Deal, in 1935.

The following year Lesser returned to his old job as a clothing salesman. He was turning thirty-three, and he had begun to accept the shattering of his dreams. Then, at least in his personal life, his luck turned: he fell in love with a very pretty and charming brunette who shared his love of music, good company and social idealism. Two months after he met her, Lesser married Esther Brooks. The next year, Richard, their only child, was born. Now a man with a new family and an "ordinary" job, his prison associations long in the past, Lesser was fast becoming Mr. Everyman.

In 1938, however, when his son Dick was two years old, Lesser was startled to discover in Dr. Karl Menninger's new book, *Man Against Himself*, that the longest and most vivid case history of self-destruction presented was that of Carl Panzram, set forth under the clinical pseudonym of John Smith. The ghost in the closet had come alive again.

Even after he had left prison service, Lesser had become known to some authorities in correctional circles as "the former guard who secured a long murder confession." Already respected as a capable prison man, Lesser gradually discovered that it was the presence in the closet, Carl Panzram, who was helping him. The prisoner's untold life had become Lesser's rock in the dike against engulfing obscurity.

Lesser began attending meetings of penologists and started a correspondence with some of them. It was a pleasant experience for an otherwise obscure clothing man, and in unguarded moments he acknowledged a debt to "My Friend P," whose body lay under Kansas prison grass.

Beyond its value as a conversation piece, however, the dead murderer's confession elicited little interest. In 1939, the world was plunging toward chaos under the swelling destruction of Hitler's Germany and Tojo's Japan. During these years, no one had time for prisons and prisoners. After Pearl Harbor, convicts joined the war effort, displaying their proverbial patriotism, donating blood, striving to enlist in dangerous war assignments and working unaccustomedly hard.

Young Dick heard his father's reminiscences from an early age. He listened to anecdotes about the strange prisoner his father had befriended. It was almost as if there were four of them in the house.

Like many another family, the Lessers moved to California. Henry found a solid berth in a large clothing store in the Wilshire district of Los Angeles. His clothing sales were not phenomenal, but his rating with customers was high. Managers exhorted him to sell more. But this was the dilemma of Everyman: it was living; it was life.

In 1946, Lesser enlisted the interest of Dr. Marcel Frym, a Viennese jurist who worked in the Hacker clinic of

Beverly Hills in matters of forensic interest to psychiatry. Frym proved unable to move Lesser's Panzram project as a book or a film. Lesser took back the confession manuscript which now, like his hair, was becoming a bit gray around the edges. He sighed and placed the typed copy back with the original. He now kept his friend P. in a box. But correspondence about the project had accumulated and had become something alive. It reassured Lesser in bad moments and had begun to generate headway of its own.

In 1951, one of the most astute psychologists in the country wrote a best-selling novel about his tenure of research in Fort Leavenworth military prison. Inevitably, Henry Lesser was on hand a year later, the confession manuscript his letter of introduction, to engage the interest of Dr. Donald Powell Wilson, the author of *My Six Convicts*. Wilson read the Panzram manuscript and plumbed its horror. But Wilson, drawn to many projects and under attack from angry prison authorities over his own book, kept the confession for two years without result. The psychologist was becoming one of the literary casualties strewn across the path of reform in criminology.[103]

At this point in the narrative and at his suggestion, I take leave of my collaborator Jim Long to relate my direct personal experience in closing this history.

In 1956, Dr. Wilson handed the Panzram confession to me. He had been of great assistance during my writing of the life of Robert Stroud.

"Here is the most punished and the most punishing man I have ever known about," Wilson said. "Read it and take it over to Lesser at the clothing store. After two years

I don't want to face him." I finished the manuscript at 5:30 the next morning, and went to bed shaken and distracted.

I saw Lesser. Soon I began the process so many others had begun and still would begin—of walking around the story, looking for some way to fathom and express its smoldering meaning, looking for a way to liberate it and those of us held in its spell. That liberation would come through sharing it with the world.

At that time I met Gerry Frank,[104] who was in Hollywood to work on a major film. He was still on the editorial staff of *Coronet* magazine. He was intrigued by Panzram; he backed an article about him.

Brevity lessens horror; it also minimizes research. I wrote a capsule story about Panzram that appeared in *Coronet* in March 1957. It was widely read and remarked upon.

Before the magazine was two weeks on the stands, a letter arrived, forwarded from the offices of *Coronet* in New York:

> I have just read your article about Carl Panzram in the March *Coronet*. I am a psychiatrist who saw this man, and I too have many notes in my files about him. I have also been trying to locate Mr. Lesser. Do you have any idea where he is? You didn't exaggerate things one bit. In fact, I could have told you quite a bit more. Fine article.
>
> Karl Menninger, M.D.

Panzram had remained alive in the psychiatrist's mind; he and Lesser were soon in correspondence. Lesser learned that Dr. Menninger had assisted a young army lieutenant who wanted to write about Panzram. Later we discovered in prison archives Dr. Menninger's early letters of inquiry. We also noted an inquiry from one Malden Grange Bishop—a name of mystery so beautiful that it was difficult to forget.

Gratified by publication of the Panzram article, in which he shared, Henry Lesser's hopes rose. We discussed problems of research. I wrote an outline and Bertha Klausner, the agent, made many submissions seeking publisher interest.

The result was a stalemate. No one expressed enthusiasm about Carl Panzram. My own efforts bogged down in a mire of postponement. Family obligations, an empty purse and a desire to learn new things on a college campus finally eventuated in a life move. I left Los Angeles to enter the graduate school of the University of Oregon in Eugene. Henry Lesser requested return of the Panzram manuscript, and it was returned to him.

The hopes raised by the *Coronet* article and the subsequent lack of interest in Panzram's confession as a book had a whipsaw effect on Lesser. He watched himself grow older and saw the bright promise of his mission fade into frustration and anger. This was followed by an iron patience, and visits to a psychiatrist.

His son Dick had suddenly reached twenty years. After seven years of practice, he had developed into an excellent clarinetist. His wife Esther had helped support the family, working as a secretary. And the country spun on through recovery from the McCarthy era, seeking balance in the relative calm of the Eisenhower years.

Dick was now giving clarinet lessons, and one of his best students, Tony, was the son of Henry Miller. Henry Lesser found his way to Henry Miller. The writer of the

Tropics—Cancer and Capricorn—was moved by Panzram's story. He read it carefully, but finally decided not to try it.

Lesser took back the manuscript. Later he found a mutual friend who took him to Irving Shulman, the author of *The Amboy Dukes*. Shulman absorbed himself in Panzram's story and in the formidable photostats of importance from men now encrusted with history and empinnacled by fame. H. L. Mencken and Fulton Oursler were dead, but Karl Menninger and Sheldon Glueck, Don Wilson and others, were still researching and writing.

Irving Shulman kept the manuscript for two years and finally decided against it after discouragement from his publisher. Lesser sent Panzram back to me.

It was like the return of an old horror, yet with a strange core of unplumbed warmth at its center. From 1959 through 1962 I made notes for the book, tried to enlist interest, kept up a guilty correspondence with Henry Lesser, finished doctoral studies, watched my daughters grow and my wife go back to college, took time out as technical director for the *Birdman of Alcatraz* film, and continued a campaign on behalf of the aging Robert Stroud (who had been transferred from Alcatraz to the medical facility in Springfield, Missouri).

Lesser had long since become overtalkative. "I suffer from logorrhea," he told me, rolling the word with relish. His eyes showed more white at the top. The Lessers watched their son Dick rise in the musical world and proudly saw him off to become the principal clarinetist of the Israel Philharmonic Orchestra.

In February 1963, Lesser wrote me a letter which was like a hoarse cry of pain: "Tom, I will be sixty-one if I am alive next October. I want to bring to completion the Panzram project during my lifetime. I need your help."

I renewed my effort to resurrect Panzram and to secure publisher interest, but it was halfhearted. I felt that the living were more important than the dead; but how could anyone give such an answer to Henry Lesser, who was as alive as any of us? I had become buried in a demanding position in a small college, with the added worry of an unfinished doctoral dissertation.

A month after Henry Lesser turned sixty-one, Robert Stroud died in prison of a heart attack. His death, after a life spent in prison since 1909, drew banner headlines in the London papers. But the entire world press was to reach for larger type within hours. Stroud's death was washed into oblivion by the assassination early the next day of President John F. Kennedy, whose brains were blown out by Lee Harvey Oswald, himself killed during that terrible week.

Three months later, watching the country turn its shocked attention to the psychopathic killer and the acting-out of hate, I wrote to Lesser that publishers were bound to be interested now, my dissertation was finished, and I was starting an all-out effort to do the Panzram book.

But Lesser, inexorable as fate, had made his own decision. He ordered Panzram's confession returned to him again. He had received a glimmer of hope from a story about Panzram in a Los Angeles newspaper, and he had secured the interest of a television producer. But nothing happened.

The effect on me of being forced, just at a moment of total commitment, to turn away from Panzram is hard to describe. The strange killer had become a part of me. I had faced this puzzling man, and his story that had to be told and yet which had defied so many in the telling, for years. I felt hurt, torn. A deep anger with Henry Lesser burned in me. The anger was irrational. Lesser had waited a long, long time. Lesser was through with me.

Fiction is pleasant, reality is distressingly complex. It would be pleasant to characterize Henry Lesser as a man with a single motive concerning the Panzram story. But underneath all the words and the patient incense-burning by Henry Lesser in the worlds of writing and corrections, his mission was a study in complexity. In a strange way, he was not carrying Panzram, but Panzram was carrying him—and had done so for years. The killer's story lived in many famous minds. In a matter of this kind, who is carrying?

Lesser's motivation included the sense of an urgent mission impelled by a command from the dead; a certain feeling of guilt; the knowledge that he held a key to certain professional circles, and thus a hedge against obscurity; a genuine interest in prison research; and always, and increasingly as his life dwindled, a hope for some money. Lesser had become penology's most enduring Ancient Mariner of this era. The mariner was bittter, but he was still mighty in faith.

Through Bertha Klausner, Lesser now secured the firm interest of Edward D. Radin, an extraordinarily well informed writer on crime who had just completed a book on miscarriages of justice, *The Innocents.*[105]

Radin wrote an excellent résumé for a receptive publisher. He was preparing for a total effort to materialize Panzram when he became seriously ill and shortly thereafter died.

With him, the hopes of Henry Lesser died as well. He grew despondent. His wife, Esther, worried and talked to him brightly about a possible trip to Israel. They would seek Dick and hear the great symphony in the new country. But Henry became an automaton, going through the motions of living, selling suits, eating when called to the table.

One day, he went to the closet and opened the box which held the archives of his long-dead friend. He read, not the convict's words, but the letters of his great men and their reaction to Panzram's confession. Most of all he read and heard in his mind Dr. Karl Menninger's statement: that Carl Panzram was one of the most extraordinary men, criminal or non-criminal, that he had ever met.

Surely, the bewildered Lesser thought, such men as these cannot be wrong. And if they are right—should not, *must* not, Panzram's story be told?

Lesser had hardly emerged from his depression when Bertha Klausner told him she had engaged the interest of a brilliant young editor, Richard Marek. Marek was interested in the project provided that I undertake to write it under contract. Grimly, Henry Lesser agreed.

"It is *bashert,*" he kept saying, "fated to be."

After the contract was drawn, I received Panzram's venerable confession again. It was like meeting a sinister old friend. I exhumed old notes and a journal, and started work.

Henry and Esther Lesser made their dream trip to Israel.

In the meantime, I had agreed to organize and direct a government educational prison project with a high-risk quotient, dealing with convicts, all of whom were multiple felons, in Panzram's old prison, Oregon State Penitentiary. Being there would simplify research problems for part of the book, and a new scrutiny of prison would, I thought, facilitate the writing. I soon discovered the depth of my mistake.

It proved almost impossible to write and also to administrate an innovative prison project. Now the quick and the dead, prisoners all, came into flat conflict. The living, struggling convicts in this hard prison engaged my life in ways beyond imagining, and Carl Panzram faded into the background. I found valuable data about the dead convict, but the reality of the situation was that past and present made a poor mix.

Editor Richard Marek, far away in New York, was a model of patience and careful concern. After repeated efforts to get through the overwhelming research problem in checking out the seven institutions where Panzram had spent time decades ago, I began to look for help.

Then on March 9, 1968, a mutiny-riot broke out in the Oregon prison. Convicts seized the control center, marched off guard hostages and set fire to prison buildings. No one was killed, but the property damage was the greatest in Oregon history, estimated at nearly two million dollars. Such property destruction without bloodletting was soon to arouse unprecedented public fury.

As the convict riot committee at 2:00 A.M. pushed its futile bargain with temporarily receptive state officials, it suddenly occurred to me that the big, young, hardhitting newsman I had driven to the burning prison with might be interested in Carl Panzram.

Eight hours later, as we were driving weary and red-eyed from prison smoke on the sixty-mile road back to Portland, I studied Jim Long.

"How would you like," I asked him, "to collaborate on a book about a former inmate here? He was a murdering, overpunished bear of a man. He still owes this prison fourteen years. He was executed in Kansas long ago. If he'd served his full terms in these prisons, he would have come out of Oregon prison two years ago, at the age of seventy-seven."

"I've heard you talk about him for two years," Jim said. "Frankly, I was wondering when you might get around to asking me."

Jim began an incredibly patient inquiry into the background of the confession. He soon experienced the depth of the challenge. Hundreds of letters were sent, trips were made, telephone calls initiated, structure groped for, drafts written and discarded. We both realized that nothing else would be written by either of us until we could bring this to an end. We became a strange team of the living and the dead—two living writers and a dead convict—all, in a sense, compulsively pulling the wagon of the indefatigable Henry Lesser.

Thus it developed that an executed murderer in his unnamed grave in the federal prison ground of Kansas' Leavenworth penitentiary carried on his dead back the guard Henry Lesser, the unending concern of a psychiatric giant in the modern world, Karl Menninger, the bright wild hope of a young writer, Jim Long, and my ordained enactment of a mission. My feeling is strong as this book closes that truly we are actors, playing our destined roles, clattering down the calendar in some blind design we cannot fathom—and yet, here at least, the design is filled in: the years-muted outcry of a strange man has been heard, his killer's cause presented.

NOTES

1. Taken from the writings of Carl Panzram.

2. Menninger presented a brief case history of Carl Panzram in *Man Against Himself* (New York: Harcourt, Brace & World, Harvest Books, 1938), pp. 179–181, using "John Smith" as a pseudonym for his subject. This paragraph, inserted here by the authors, appeared in that work, p. 180.

3. Thomas E. Gaddis, "The Man Who Lived and Died for Hate," *Coronet,* March 1957.

4. Records, Minnesota State Training School, Red Wing, Minnesota.

5. As a small boy Panzram underwent a serious mastoid operation which took place in the home under primitive conditions. The infection continued, he was removed to a hospital and a second operation was performed. Whether any brain damage resulted and was a factor in his later life must remain a complex speculation for medical authorities.

6. "The notion of punishment meant just that and was not the momentary correction of a smack across the face. Generally the 'spankings' were rather formal, cold and not very emotional." Letter from Orville B. Pung, Assistant Superintendent, Minnesota State Training School, Red Wing, Minnesota, May 15, 1968.

Whipping of runaway boys was routine until at least 1947, according to interviews with former MSTS inmate Leonard Thompson.

The momentum of cruelty in training schools seems to have been offset by the determined and intelligent adaptation of the "Highfields" type of progressive, group-oriented treatment of delinquents (developed at the Highfields, New Jersey, training school). This system of group interaction is in use at Carl Panzram's old school in Red Wing. Under the recent administration of Milton Olsen and Orville Pung, a new philosophy of treatment has emerged.

Dante Andreotti, a San Francisco policeman specializing in community relations, expresed most succinctly the problem of early violence: "Social-cultural felonies committed in the past are resulting in criminal felonies of today," Portland *Oregonian,* February 28, 1969.

7. Sadism of this type was common in training schools at that time, and it continues in decreasing physical but increasing psychological form in most training schools today. Behind the expressionless faces of local staffs lies the knowledge of what has occurred in these schools over decades of time. Boys are still whipped and paddled on their hands and feet; staffs are still underpaid, undertrained and overworked. This subculture of violence has become part of the world of the "disadvantaged," and creates a gulf of difficulty in attempts to "rehabilitate" the sons and daughters of former victims who survived.

Howard James, Midwest bureau chief of the *Christian Science Monitor* after twelve years of study and travel around the United States, testified as follows before the United States Senate Subcommittee to Investigate Juvenile Delinquency in 1969: "I found extreme and inhuman use of solitary confinement and other cruel practices in every state in the nation from California to New England and from Florida to Washington and Oregon. Mistreatment of children, some as young as seven or eight years old, is common in institutions across the nation. . . . I can tell you about brutality, about inhuman treatment all over the United States. Where would you like to begin?"

8. A fire of unknown origin occurred at the school on the evening of July 2, 1905, destroying a warehouse containing winter clothing and heavily damaging the blacksmith shop. Shortly before the fire, young Panzram had been informed of the drowning of his older brother

Louis in a logging accident on the Red Lake River. Judge Sullivan had written a letter to Superintendent Whittier on June 25 endorsing Lizzie Panzram's request that Carl be released to help support her. Whittier refused the request, noting that the boy had made little progress since coming to the school. Whether Carl was told of the effort to release him at this time is unknown.

9. Panzram's furlough agreement reflected the stern Calvinist morals of the ruling establishment of the time. It required him to "lead a steady industrious life, obedient to those in authority," unless he wished to return to the reform school. It also warned him to avoid "all idle and evil companions, and all places where such resort; all saloons, public billiard or pool rooms or bowling alleys, all dances where liquor is sold and all public dances generally. Should the world prove a harsh taskmaster, should misfortune, poverty or despair overtake you, it is the wish of the management of the School that you shall regard the School as a refuge and a home. . . . With such a provision against an unkind fate . . . trust in God whose blessing is invoked on you as you leave the safe shelter of the Training School to begin your journey in the great world without." Records, Minnesota State Training School, 1904.

10. Immanuel Lutheran Church was established in 1902 as part of the strict Missouri Synod. The school operated in the basement of the small frame church. From 1902 to 1908, the pastor was the Reverend A. F. Parge. Carl Panzram's sister, Louise, three years older than Carl, was confirmed in the church in 1902, and his mother was a charter member. There is no evidence of church affiliation or activity by any of the Panzram men. Carl's brief stay is documented only by his words, since the school records have been destroyed.

11. Jack London rode the blinds for hundreds of miles, defeating train crews' efforts to dislodge him. See his *The Road* (New York: Macmillan Co., 1907); available as "Tramp Days," in Philip S. Foner, *Jack London: American Rebel* (New York: Citadel Press, 1947), pp. 325–339.

12. Jim Tully, *Beggars of Life: A Hobo Autobiography* (New York: Albert and Charles Boni, 1924); Bertha Thompson, as told to Ben L. Reitman, *Sister of the Road: The Autobiography of Box-Car Bertha*

(New York: Macaulay Co., 1937); Robert Stroud in "A Voice from the Grave," *Looking Outward* (unpublished manuscript, Stroud estate), 2:60.

13. The I.W.W. (Industrial Workers of the World) probably was the most feared radical labor movement in American history. Launched by breakaway unionists in 1905, the "Wobblies" gained adherents among the unorganized, ruthlesslessly exploited loggers, miners and farm workers of the Far West. This was an era of wage cuts, child labor and literal starvation for the families of workingmen killed or maimed in industrial accidents. The Wobblies preached utopian anarchy, and they were not pacifists. Industrial sabotage was recommended as a means of toppling all government, which the Wobblies saw as corrupt, dictatorial and inextricably linked with the rule of business. Accordingly, they also disdained labor contracts because, they believed, the workingman had nothing in common with his employer. This kind of talk, in an era when even mere union membership was not looked on with favor, touched off a retaliatory explosion. The business and political establishment of the day used police and military power to suppress the Wobblies, and any laborer caught with a red I.W.W. card in his pocket was likely to be beaten, run out of town or even killed. Armed goon squads searched trains for suspected Wobblies at the height of the I.W.W. panic following World War I. At its flood tide in 1923, the I.W.W. had an estimated 110,000 members—including 8,000 in prison. The movement gradually died out as other unions became more militant, included more workers and resisted Wobbly efforts to merge their organizations into "one big union."

14. The terror of anal rape is described with the force of a poet writing prose in James Dickey's novel, *Deliverance* (Boston: Houghton Mifflin Co., 1970).

A landmark work on sex in prison is George Sylvester Viereck's *Men into Beasts* (New York: Fawcett World Library, Gold Medal Books, 1952). Much of his account is based upon experience in the Washington District Jail.

15. Panzram used the word *sodomy* to refer specifically to anal male copulation. The term has changed in usage and meaning since Panzram's day, although his use of the word is in line with half of Krafft-Ebing's definition and also is correct in terms of the biblical sense of

the word in Genesis 19. For a brief discussion and references see Harry Elmer Barnes and Negley K. Teeters, *New Horizons of Criminology,* 3d ed. (Englewood Cliffs, New Jersey: Prentice-Hall, 1959), p. 100.

Pederasty is the "normal" abnormal sex practice in prison (aside from masturbation). It simulates male–female relations, and it carries complex meanings that go beyond sexual gratification: for example, Stroud and other convict writers make it clear that pederasty roles can be important in determining a prisoner's social status. The "active" pederast—the "jocker" who assumes the male role—is considered socially superior to the "passive" pederast or "punk." However, the passive partner who remains circumspect about his activities and who remains "married" more or less permanently to one, or relatively few, successive active pederasts is considered socially superior to the promiscuous "prison prostitute." Somewhere near the bottom of the social scale is the active fellatioist who, in some southern prisons, is required to drink from a separate cup in the fields and is subjected to other forms of ostracism. On the other hand, the "jocker" suffers no social penalties and is often a high-status convict in the warped, monosexual prison environment; furthermore, his relationship with his "punk" usually demands that he be able and willing to provide protection and favors in return. Rivalry between status-conscious jockers, and even between punks, can be keen, and it is said by many prisoner-observers that sex-based conflicts are at the root of most prison violence.

Official reticence, convict reticence and the revulsion of most persons from the discussion of abnormal sex practices does not make these any less relevant to an understanding of prison sociology. Few academic criminologists know much about the subject, as their writings reveal, and a survey of medical and psychiatric literature indicates an almost total lack of inquiry.

Stroud, one of the few scientific minds to focus seriously on prison sex, theorized that passive pederasts receive a distinctly "female" erotic reward owing to the nerve linkage between sexual organs and the rectum. He pointed out that the rectum appears first in the development of the human fetus and is supplied by nerves which, later, merely send out branches to serve the developing sexual organs (see Stroud, *Looking Outward,* 4:57–59).

One of the more arresting clues to the socio-biological derivations of pederasty is hinted in a study of monosexual groups of young male rhesus monkeys in Chile. The researchers noted that the more dominant males mounted submissive ones under a variety of stimuli including "active play, an aggressive approach by another of the young males, general excitement—for example the stimulation of a nearby fight—or the close approach of an observer. . . . As in female–male relations, attacks may be foiled when the object of the attack suddenly presents and thus diverts the aggressor from attacking and stimulates him to mount instead."

The researchers observed that "young males who are gradually becoming more closely associated with heterosexual grouping seem to gain the tolerance of subordinate males at first, among other things, by submitting to being mounted. Subordinate males who stay close together and fight cooperatively against attackers frequently mount each other during the excitement of aggressive action. The tension and emotional excitement which persistently characterize these subordinate animals with *insecure social status* seem to be important factors in provoking homosexual mountings." Among the conclusions of the investigators was the assertion that pederasty among rhesus monkeys "seems to be an outlet, at times, for aroused but displaced instigation for fighting." C. R. Carpenter, *Naturalistic Behavior of Non-Human Primates* (University Park, Pa.: Pennsylvania State University Press, 1964), pp. 327–329.

Despite the awkward embarrassment this subject usually causes, pederasty has been rather widespread throughout human history and, in some cultures, was institutionalized. It was part of public education among the ancient Dorians and in Crete and Sparta (see Albert Ellis and Albert Abarbanel, eds., *The Encyclopedia of Sexual Behavior* [New York: Hawthorn Books, 1967], p. 631). Later, the North American Indians shocked Christian European explorers by some of their habits, which were similar to those practiced by some Siberian peoples (including the Chukchees, who condoned marriage between two men) (see C. S. Ford and Frank A. Beach, *Patterns of Sexual Behavior* [New York: Harper & Brothers, 1951], p. 131.)

In Western Christian civilization, pederasty traditionally has been condemned as "sodomy" and regarded as one of the worst of sins.

Under old English law, pederasty was referred to simply as "the horrible crime not to be named among Christians." Later, under the term *buggery,* it became a capital crime which called for burial alive or burning at the stake. By the nineteenth century England had softened its law to provide a simple hanging (see William Blackstone, *Commentaries on the Laws of England* [Philadelphia: Rees Welsh & Co., 1902], 4:215–216). In most jurisdictions of the United States, sodomy still is severely punished as a felony and, if death results during its commission, elevates homicide to first-degree murder in Maryland, New Jersey, North Dakota and in all federal and military courts (see Hugo A. Bedau, *The Death Penalty in America* [Garden City, N.Y., Doubleday & Co., 1964], p. 41.)

16. Actually, Taft did not approve Panzram's three-year sentence, since, according to law, this was done by President Theodore Roosevelt. Taft signed Special Orders No. 30 on February 5, 1908, authorizing a general court martial at Fort William Henry Harrison "as soon as practicable."

17. The official reason for reopening the military prison was the contention by William Howard Taft, Secretary of War, that discipline in the services was suffering because guardhouse punishment was not severe enough. In his Report to Congress on Prisons, 1908, Taft said that the prison's reopening "made it possible to resume the practice of sending long-term military convicts to undergo their terms of confinemen at hard labor. . . . Undoubtedly the knowledge that the convicted deserters will be compelled to undergo the rigors of prison discipline and to suffer the stigma of prison confinement instead of being permitted to serve their terms with more comfort, less disrepute, and greater chance for escape . . . in more congenial surroundings at military posts, has deterred many would-be deserters from taking the step that they would have been ready to take if they had seen no severer punishment before them in the event of their capture than a comparatively short term of confinement at some military post."

18. Young's Report to the War Department, 1907 stated: "This prison lacks at present almost everything needed by a modern institution of this kind. There is a constant and increasing danger from fire, which is a source of great and continual anxiety. . . . As in all old

buildings of inferior construction, the ventilation and sanitary arrangements are a source of constant trouble. The lighting and heating systems are also in poor condition."

19. A fire of "unknown origin" destroyed the prison shoe shop in 1919. Elvid Hunt and Walter E. Lorence, *History of Fort Leavenworth, 1827-1937* (Fort Leavenworth, Kansas: General Staff School Press, 1937), app. U.

20. Third-grade prisoners had their choice of hard labor or being handcuffed to a cell door during the workday. The intense vermin problem and the possibility of being chained up backwards in a dark cell—excruciating punishment—made most incorrigibles choose the rockpile. See Winthrop Lane, "Fort Leavenworth," *Survey,* July 5, 1919, pp. 531–536.

21. The Snorting Pole and other physical tortures are described by Panzram on pp. 73–78.

22. A raging fire destroyed a large part of Houston on Wednesday, February 21, 1912.

23. Records in the Wasco County, Oregon, sheriff's office indicate that one Jack Allen was booked into jail on September 4, 1912, on a charge of "assault with a dangerous weapon" and was bound over to the grand jury. "Allen" escaped, according to these records, on October 27, 1912.

24. Deer Lodge Prison in Montana was apparently little changed as late as 1968. On October 31, 1966, one Larry Cheadle died, allegedly in the Hole (officially known as detention cells). The three cells in the Hole were placed underground with steam pipes running through them and no light. Furnishings included a mattress and a bucket. Prisoners sat in darkness and were fed bread and water daily and a meal every three days. The cells were characterized as "unbearably hot and moist." Officials stopped using the dungeon after Cheadle died in it. Associated Press, by Wick Temple, February 4, 1968.

25. Montana State Penitentiary records indicate that Panzram was sentenced to one year at hard labor for burglary of a dentist's office in Chinook. He was delivered to the prison on April 27, 1913, escaped the following November 3 and was caught the next day burglarizing

a house in Three Forks where he stole a suit and coat. On November 20 he arrived back at the prison under the name "Jefferson Rhoades." He served sixteen months under this new alias.

26. Conley was accused of converting $300,000 in state funds by using convicts as slave labor on his ranch and misappropriating prison supplies. However, like most men of power and property, Conley did not have to face a criminal proceeding. The state named the former warden as defendant in a civil suit in 1922 and eventually lost the case. Conley went on to serve a term as chairman of the state highway commission and died in a Butte hospital at the age of seventy-five on March 5, 1939.

27. This "double crossing" of Panzram was not unusual in the courts of this country in 1914, nor is it unusual today. Such bargaining is a habitual part of our judicial process in practice. A plea of guilty has financial and other value to lawyers and crowded court calendars. The affluent defendant, however, is rarely under pressure to plead guilty because he can pay his attorney. For the strange ways of prosecutors, see Roscoe Pound, *Criminal Justice in America* (New York: Henry Holt & Co., 1929); Sheldon Glueck, *Crime and Justice* (Boston: Little, Brown & Co., 1936); Sol Rubin, "Developments in Correctional Law," *Crime and Delinquency* 16, no. 2, 185–197.

28. Panzram's description of this incident hardly appears exaggerated. A report from District Attorney Mullins to the warden of Oregon State Penitentiary stated: "This defendant was the source of more trouble while he was in jail here than any other prisoner we have had for many years. After he was sentenced he broke various articles of furniture of the jail, started fires in the blankets and mattresses and committed every act of depredation that he possibly could." Archives, State of Oregon, Jefferson Baldwin 7390 [Carl Panzram].

29. J. S. Murray, clerk of Oregon State Penitentiary for fifty years, began his career as a guard in the notorious Yuma Territorial Prison. He stated flatly in an interview that Yuma hardly compared with Oregon State Penitentiary for the severity of its punishments and discipline. Personal interview, 1969.

30. This lashing was done in the lobby of the administration building after "lights out." Cooper's "cat" was described by a former staff

man as consisting of several strands of waxed rawhide fastened to a wooden handle. Several accounts of floggings are contained in a privately published booklet by former inmate Joseph "Bunko" Kelley.

31. A commission appointed to investigate the prison recommended on January 26, 1917, that inmates without funds be furnished with toothbrushes and properly fitted dentures and eyeglasses. Regarding food, the commission found "that about two-thirds of the beans and hominy placed on the tables was not eaten and went to the hogs." Archives, State of Oregon, Report of Commission to Investigate Oregon State Penitentiary, January 26, 1917, p. 54.

32. Accounts of Hooker's escape are found in the Portland *Oregon Journal* and Portland *Oregonian,* September 21–30, 1915.

33. The man killed earlier, Joseph Kocor, was one of a group of Austrian-born citizens attacked by some Portlanders caught up in the patriotic fever of World War I. Patrolman A. L. Long said the victim had tried to strike him with a board. The explanation was accepted. Long was commended by Portland's chief of police. Portland *Oregon Journal,* September 29, 1915.

34. A fire on May 26, 1916, destroyed part of the penitentiary flax mill and gutted three nearby shops. The loss was valued at $25,000. Portland *Oregonian,* May 27, 1916.

35. Also known as the Gardiner shackle, the Oregon boot is a steel anklet weighing from five to twenty-eight pounds, supported partially by a steel brace fitted like a stirrup under the arch of the foot. Conceded to be one of the cruelest punishments devised in an American prison, the Oregon boot was patented by Oregon State Penitentiary Warden J. C. Gardiner in 1866 as a device to keep prisoners from escaping. He attempted to collect royalties for its use. He had the boots manufactured in the prison shops, and during early regimes each inmate of Oregon State Penitentiary was required to wear one during his term of confinement. (According to State of Oregon Archives, in 1873 Superintendent William Watkinds protested to the governor against this barbaric practice, pointing out that "there are prisoners who have worn this instrument of torture, known inside the prison as a man-killer, until they are broken down in health and constitution. Young and strong men, with this continuous and steady weight, which

pulls all day on their loins, yield after a few years, leaving the prisoner broken down physically, not from overwork or underfeeding, but simply from lugging a lot of iron to keep them from scaling the fences. Men lay in the hospital for weeks from wearing these things, suffering great pain and begging to be relieved from the load. . . . The Oregon Penitentiary is the only prison in the United States where this mode of murdering men by inches is practiced. It is murder, and of the worst type.") The boot was declared illegal as a form of punishment after 1913, but its use was reported in the transport of prisoners as late as 1939. Personal interviews with J. S. Murray, former clerk of Oregon State Penitentiary, 1967–1968.

36. Portland *Oregonian,* November 19, 1916.

37. Warden Murphy hated to lose ball games, and he was desperate when the parole board released his star pitcher just before a much-touted meeting with Willamette University. According to a local legend, Murphy slipped $20 to a traveling professional southpaw who donned a prison uniform and won the game 3–0, striking out seventeen men.

38. The "barracks parole" concept was developed at Fort Leavenworth Military Prison. Inmates without specific trusty duties were allowed to spend some time outside the walls each evening. See Lane, "Fort Leavenworth"; note 20.

39. "Jocker" is the prison term for the aggressive male sex partner. The passive partner is known as the "punk." In prison there is a saying that "he who catches can later pitch"; and another, "sometimes the jocker is a punk looking for revenge." No one would be more amazed than the participants themselves in these relationships to hear such behavior termed "homosexual." To convicts, the word "homosexual" is the generic label applied to a basic sexual orientation; sociologists, of course, are using the word as an operational term describing the nature of specific behavior under specific circumstances.

Among the more grotesque prison reports on this subject is one made in Oregon in 1917. The Commission to Investigate Oregon State Penitentiary, shocked by the prevalence of what it referred to as "vice," suggested castrating the penitentiary's homosexuals. "In cases of congenital homo-sexuality in the penitentiary, ordinary punishment is of no avail," concluded the gentlemen of the commission. "In such cases and in cases of incest and in all cases where sex abnormality has manifested itself in criminal tendency we recommend a well-guarded law providing for castration. . . . [Mere] sterilization does not deprive the individual of his desire for congressus nor the ability to perform the same, nor the faculty of experiencing libido. Hence the murderous and erotically degenerated criminal classes will remain a menace to society until they are deprived, not only of the potency of procreation but also the potency *concarnationis* and of experiencing libido. The method of castration, therefore, should be reserved as a penalty for the outspoken, habitual, brutal criminal, the rapist, the incorrigible burglar or gunman, the gibbering idiot, or imbecile cretin with inherited tendency to crime, and the unstable erotopath." Archives, State of Oregon, Report of Commission to Investigate Oregon State Penitentiary, January 26, 1917, p. 75.

40. All letters quoted in the Oregon section of this book are from Archives, State of Oregon, Jefferson Baldwin 7390 [Carl Panzram].

41. Warden Murphy was quietly replaced in the autumn of 1918, and his brief regime became a memory. A new governor was elected on a Ku Klux Klan ticket.

42. Panzram's choice of names plainly had symbolic meaning for him. An earlier alias, "Jeff Davis," was, of course, the name of the president of the rebellious Confederacy. "Jeff Baldwin" may well have been taken from the name of the most famous United States manufacturer of steam locomotives—an apparatus which Panzram knew, used and admired. "John O'Leary" happened to be the name of a man accused of treason at the time Panzram escaped from Oregon State Penitentiary.

43. This act of arson was to be confirmed by Harry F. Sinclair, chairman of Sinclair Consolidated Oil Corporation, whose involvement in the Teapot Dome scandal and subsequent imprisonment eventually was to bring him across Panzram's path. See Chapter XX.

44. According to the National Archives, a forty-one-foot motor vessel of this name and number was registered to John O'Leary, New York City, on September 21, 1920.

45. The victim was Henry McMahon, twelve, beaten to death with a rock on July 18, 1922. See Boston *Globe,* July 19, 1922.

46. American Bar Association records confirm that an attorney, D. J. Cashin, was practicing in Yonkers, New York, at this time.

47. The identity of this victim was never definitely established. The New Haven police department reported that on August 10, 1923, one William F. Berger, no age listed, was found dead in West Haven. Also, one David Daily, forty-five, was killed in Plainville. Panzram was not officially connected with either murder.

48. After transfer to Dannemora, Panzram asked for and received a release on the Oregon "hold." According to Murray, the real reason Oregon did not insist on returning Panzram to Oregon State Penitentiary was that not enough money was available to send a deputy to get him.

49. See Lewis E. Lawes, *Twenty Thousand Years in Sing Sing,* (New York: R. Long and R. R. Smith, 1932).

50. The innocuous-sounding canes were standard equipment in many federal and state prisons at this time. Perhaps the most complete description of this instrument is found in the vast prison manuscript of Robert F. Stroud, who lived in maximum-security institutions from 1909 until his death in 1963: "They were not ordinary walking sticks, but one of the most dangerous and deadly hand weapons ever invented. The canes were made of turned and steamed hickory rods about one inch in diameter at the thickest point, where the hand grasped the handle, which was bent in the form of a shepherd's crook. The shaft of the cane tapered slightly to a point about ten inches from the [tip]. That last ten inches was a heavy, tapering steel ferrule that was not over one-half an inch in diameter at the end, and that end was neatly rounded. When new, the canes were painted black, but in use the paint soon wore off. It was the theory that guards could use the crook end to separate fighting men without danger of being struck. In practice, it was much easier to knock a man down than to struggle with him. The steel ferrule would spit a man's scalp. That there were many guards who accepted this view was evidenced by the number of white turbans always to be seen in that sea of heads in the big dining room.

The canes were even more dangerous when used for thrusting. The small end concentrated the blow into such a small area that even a moderately hard thrust was sure to produce deep-seated injury." Stroud, *Looking Outward,* 1:261–262. Corroborated by former inmate Leonard Thompson in personal interviews.

51. This peculiar situation, with its inbred subculture of punishment, was looked on with disfavor in the *Handbook of American Prisons, 1925,* prepared by the National Society for Penal Information, ed. Austin H. MacCormick and Paul W. Garrett (New York and London: G. P. Putnam's Sons, 1926), p. 221: "Such a condition of living," noted the *Handbook,* "tends, in the course of time, to develop an official personnel interrelated by birth and marriage. This undesirable result has long been apparent at Clinton."

52. The claustrophobic feeling experienced by new prisoners in a Dannemora cell was aggravated by the extremely close spacing of bars in the cell gate: they were too narrow to allow the man to grip them, or even see out very clearly. Adolph Lewisohn's Prison Survey Committee at this time (1929) called Dannemora's cell blocks "barbarous and atrocious for fifty years." It added: "No one can see [the cells] without realizing what prison punishment means in one of its most brutal and degrading forms."

53. A few months before Panzram arrived, a prisoner named Moreatis was transferred to Bellevue Hospital, where he was found to be suffering from leprosy. For an excellent description of Dannemora as experienced by other transferees from Sing Sing see Frank Canizio, as told to Robert Markel, *A Man Against Fate* (New York: Frederick Fell, 1958), pp. 158 ff., and John Resko, *Reprieve: The Testament of John Resko* (Garden City, N.Y.: Doubleday & Co., 1956); Carmelo Sorci, *The Convict and the Stained-Glass Windows* (New York: John Day Co., 1961).

54. An unattractive picture of Dannemora State Hospital was given during this period by George W. Alder, a prison inspector. Although Alder discounted stories of gross mistreatment and even murder of patients there, he described one ward as being filled with "creeping, shaking, palsied imbeciles . . . a human Sargasso Sea filled with hulks . . . a living graveyard." Although some patients complained about

being kept long past their prison release dates, others were only too happy to remain in the hospital. These included one elderly Jewish man who had gone mad in the death house at Sing Sing, Alder noted.

55. New York prison officials react in about the same way as any others when asked for details on this or other local punishment practices, whether these consist of dark "strip cells" or something more exotic, such as Tucker Prison Farm's scrotal torture. John R. Cain, deputy commissioner of the New York Department of Correction, responded to a query about Dannemora: "I am unable to give you a description of 'the hole' and I do not believe there was any such facility in Clinton Prison during O'Leary's [Panzram's] time there. . . . At that time, there was a segregation building in Clinton Prison and the inmates might have referred to the cells in that building as 'the hole,' or they might have used this terminology in describing a small facility adjacent to the Guard Room, where inmates were placed for keep-lock for an hour or for several days while awaiting action of the Disciplinary Court. Nowhere, however, was there any cell or other place of confinement that could be classified as being 'the hole.'" (Letters from John R. Cain to James O. Long, April 24, July 30, August 13, 1968.)

56. According to Dannemora records, Panzram tried to escape on July 25, 1924. Cain recalled that Panzram "sustained some temporary injury to his feet and legs; nothing as spectacular as breaking both legs and rupturing himself. . . . With reference to the removal of a testicle, this was done for medical reasons at his own request on August 7, 1925, and had no connection with any of his misbehaviors at the institution." Cain correspondence.

57. Probably Elizabeth Novell, secretary of the Arctic Club in Seattle, who had taken an interest in Panzram's case in Montana and Oregon. See pp. 102–103.

58. *The New York Times* blamed a tightening of paroles by Parole Chairman George Benham and Commissioner Alexander Konta of the parole board for causing even more atrocious conditions in the New York prisons. The Baumes Laws, named for State Senator Caleb H. Baumes of Newburgh, chairman of the New York State Crime Commission, required judges to sentence second offenders to at least the

longest term provided for a first offense and a maximum of twice as long. A life sentence was mandatory on fourth conviction for a felony. The Baumes Laws also cut in half the "good time" a prisoner could earn. Hence this legislation was known as the "Bum's Law" among prisoners. Under the new law, for example, the earliest release under a twenty-year sentence was sixteen years, eight months.

59. Despite the overcrowding, virtually the only construction money doled out by the New York legislature at this time was $300,000 for a new electric chair and death cells at Sing Sing. Warden Lawes reported that 700 persons applied for the job of executioner, some offering to do the work free. Others asked to be executed instead of the condemned. See Lewis E. Lawes, *Life and Death in Sing Sing* (Garden City, N.Y.: Doubleday, Doran & Co., 1928).

60. After the abortive gun-smuggling plot, a bloody riot broke out in Dannemora on July 22, 1929, in which several hundred inmates set fire to buildings and tried to rush the walls armed with rocks and chunks of iron. Three were shot and killed and twenty others were wounded.

61. Panzram's murder plan may have derived from the details of the dynamite murder of four trainmen in an Oregon mountain tunnel by the three D'Autremont brothers on October 11, 1923. The brothers escaped and were not apprehended until 1927. The case was attracting national headline attention during the time Panzram was in Dannemora. Perhaps the greatest sociological crime story in the history of the Northwest, the D'Autremont story has never been told in book form. The D'Autremonts served decades in Oregon State Pentitentiary. One is still serving time after forty-two years, having been turned into a vegetable by a lobotomy performed in the prison ward of the state hospital. See files of the *Oregon Statesman* and *Capital Journal* (Salem, Oregon); Archives, State of Oregon.

62. Bizarre as it sounds, researchers who examined secret British cabinet papers a few years ago turned up the fact that Britain in 1927 was planning for the possibility of a war with the United States if the two nations failed to reach agreement at a Geneva conference on naval disarmament. Associated Press, December 30, 1967.

63. Panzram's gruesome fantasy later was echoed in Antofagasta, Chile, where unintentional homicide charges were brought against a number of utility officials after twenty children died due to a spillage of arsenic into the city's water supply. Associated Press, July 5, 1968.

64. Reported by Henry Lesser. All material concerning Panzram during his imprisonment in the District Jail is from Lesser's extensive notes and recollections, and from corroborated news stories.

65. Official federal records indicate that Panzram had a five-pointed star tattooed on his left shoulder and an anchor on the left forearm. On his right forearm was a rose, eagle and anchor with the head of a Chinese mandarin. On his chest was a double eagle, a five-pointed star and the words "Liberty—Justice."

66. During Lesser's tenure at the jail, a young addict was allowed to die in the toilet-like atmosphere of a cellblock while a wealthy industrialist, who was not sick, occupied two private rooms of the institution's hospital. The superintendent's later explanation for the addict's unattended death was "lack of room" in the hospital.

67. As a group, physicians have been throughout history notorious laggards in reform or social change; an impartial history of medicine would show a barren waste in this area. Innovations generally came from outside the medical profession, and their originators usually suffered at the hands of organized medicine. Prison doctors are generally disliked by inmates, although there are many individual exceptions. The increasing power and wealth of the medical doctor and his organized pressure groups in this country today have become a cause of grave concern to students of this trend. The Medicare scandal is the current example of an increasingly serious situation.

The behavior of physicians during the period of the Third Reich in Germany was truly frightening. They were the only group in society who moved even further into the realm of pain and experimental death than Hitler had ordered. Nothing is more repugnant than the infliction of death at the hands of a doctor.

For details of this little-discussed area, see Frederic Wertham, M.D., *A Sign for Cain* (New York, Macmillan Co., 1966), pp. 153–191.

68. Usual public indignation centers on those who live from crime.

The prisoner's bitterness, of which Panzram's is representative and traditional, concerns those who live from criminals, i.e., those who in any way profit or even earn employment from the imprisonment of others.

The special rancor of inmates is reserved for the white-collar and professional level of workers: sociology professors, criminologists, writers, prosecuting attorneys, scholars, researchers—i.e., anyone who "uses" the prisoners as objects of comment or of study. The prisoners reason this way: if *we* weren't in this prison, *they* would be out of a job, out of a research grant, out of a book, etc. Inmates sense that their existence in prison advances goals which may be neither theirs nor even society's, but merely the survival-needs of the institution or of various career professionals. Some more educated convicts realize that they are being used to reinforce the norms of society as living examples of the slogan that crime doesn't pay. They resent this. Hard-line prisoners also sense a greater ego-threat in the soft liberal approach; they prefer hard wardens. They react violently to the insecurity that comes from having been done favors. An educated inmate expressed the position this way:

> There appears to be an inverse correlation between the amount of delinquency research and delinquency reduction. Or as Lopez-Rey put it, the higher the standard of living the more crime and delinquency; or . . . the more money spent to understand and prevent, the more of the same. Perhaps if these experts stopped telling us about causes and cures, the kids themselves would have a better chance to escape into normality. The tragedy of all this frenetic commotion is that the solid knowledge we now have . . . has been completely ignored as bright young men persist in rediscovering the obvious and of course getting well paid for it. And, my brethren, I don't need any foundation money to see as far thru a brick wall as all the eager, hypertensive scholars and research experts who have to be subsidized to do a job they proclaim needs to be done by interested and competent observers, always if the price is right. A dedicated scholar is a guy who knows somebody who will pay him handsomely for doing what he claims he is the only person trained to do. I wonder whatever became of the scholars who investigated and learned for the simple purpose of learning, without having to

fight their way out of a sackful of C notes. "The Cockleburr," *American Journal of Correction,* November–December 1960, p. 32.

69. Robert F. Stroud gives a description of the Moundsville march as related to him by an alleged survivor, J. S. "Heck" Wallace, whom he had known for years in Leavenworth and later in Alcatraz. According to Stroud, the Moundsville prisoners were called up before daybreak and herded into the prison yard, where a blacksmith had set up his anvil next to a pile of shackles with extra-long chains. Each man, in an operation reminiscent of the branding of cattle, was riveted into a set of shackles. Then he was given a string with which to fasten the middle of the shackle-chain to his belt, making it possible for him to walk without tripping. The convicts were paired and handcuffed along fifty-foot chains and began their march behind a chuckwagon driven by trustees wearing Oregon boots. The guards rode behind with firearms. Meals along the way were mostly cornpone and pork fat, eaten out of hand or on the ground. Each man was outfitted in a new pair of cowhide army marching shoes, but no socks. Straggling, regardless of the reason, was not permitted because it slowed up the entire formation. Stroud, *Looking Outward,* 1: 177–185.

Moundsville penitentiary officials acknowledge that federal prisoners once were "boarded" there, but are unable to confirm the march because "these earlier records were ordered destroyed by a former warden." Letter from E. E. Godfrey, a prison official at West Virginia State Penitentiary, October 20, 1969.

70. That cruelty breeds corruption is almost axiomatic in prison lore. Prisoners with money or "clout" in Leavenworth usually did not endure strict privation of good food, liquor or even women. An underpaid, undermanned staff helped to assure many irregular arrangements. The most fantastic lapse in Leavenworth in the 1920s was revealed with the discovery of a counterfeiting ring operating in one of the prison shops. See *Handbook of American Prisons, 1926;* John Bartlow Martin, ed., *My Life in Crime: The Autobiography of a Professional Criminal* (New York: Harper & Bros., 1952).

71. This rule was common, in varying form, in many United States prisons and seems to have arisen in Leavenworth from the chain-gang conditions which existed prior to completion of the huge wall. But,

like other prison rules, it persisted long after its reason for being had disappeared. See *Prison Rules,* McNeil Island (prison publication, 1912).

72. Thomas E. Gaddis, *Birdman of Alcatraz* (New York: Random House, 1955; New American Library, Signet Books, 1958). Stroud was originally known as the "Bird Doctor of Leavenworth."

73. Carl Panzram's name is still misspelled in Leavenworth records, in many newspaper accounts and even on his death certificate, despite extensive records at hand from five prisons and two training schools. We have corrected the name on his death certificate, which appears on page 327.

74. An inmate with enough "reputation" and influence over guards could obtain a sexual partner of his choosing by the simple expedient of writing out a transfer request and signing the victim's name to it. It was dangerous for the victim, usually youthful, to refuse. Stroud tells of knifings and even murders between rivals disputing a transfer. Interestingly, some of the violent "transfer" episodes seemed to have more to do with strivings for status than with sexual desire, as such. Stroud, "Administration at Leavenworth," *Looking Outward;* see also note 15.

The feeling of prisons and what takes place in them is almost impossible to convey, even by prisoners themselves when they are out of the institution. This is especially true concerning ego and sexual relationships, which are so altered in confinement. For perhaps the best work of narrative fiction of modern prison environment, see Malcolm Braly's *On the Yard* (Boston: Little, Brown & Co., 1967; Fawcett World Library, Crest Books, 1968).

75. Panzram's hatred of police and their ways requires that his admiration for one policeman be noted. The officer named Allen is mentioned more than once in his letters. Panzram wrote the following about Allen in 1928:

> Right here and now in this city there is a man on the police force by the name of Allen. I don't know him personally. Never saw him and never spoke to him. Still I know that he is a college graduate, he is a clear and clean-minded man. He has both brains and a high

moral mind with good principles. He is physically fit or he wouldn't be on the police force. He has brains enough to see right and he has the moral courage to stick by his principles. There are very few like him on any police force. Any man like this guy is, should be a welcome addition to any law-abiding community or police force. . . . And what is the result? The result is that the big majority of his companions and fellow officers are all out to sink him. They are watching every move he makes and at the same time they are trying to trip him up and prefer charges against him. They don't want him on the police force. Why? Simply because he is clean and they are dirty. Even a skunk like me can respect a guy like that man Allen. People want everyone to have respect for the law but how the hell is anyone going to have any respect for the law and order when the law doesn't respect itself?

76. Harry F. Sinclair, probably the richest American to serve a prison term, must defer to Alfried Krupp von Bohlen for the world title. Krupp was sentenced to twelve years as a Nazi war criminal in the Nuremberg trials. He was worth a quarter of a billion dollars, including profits from slave labor he employed to furbish Hitler's war machine. The Krupp family owned 138 private concentration camps, some of which worked children to death.

Krupp, like Panzram, refused to take the stand in his own behalf. Unlike Panzram, he spoke through thirty-three lawyers who protested his "unfair treatment."

Krupp served thirty months of the twelve-year sentence. As the Cold War heated up, his property was restored in a move described by United States High Commissioner John J. McCloy as "the moral and American thing to do." By the 1960s, Krupp had rolled up a personal fortune of $1.1 billion, a sum far greater than what he had made under Hitler. See William Manchester, *The Arms of Krupp* (Boston: Little Brown & Co., 1968).

American runner-up to Sinclair was probably financier Louis Wolfson. He was worth $100 million in the shrunken dollars of 1969, some of it stock paper, when sentenced to a year in federal prison after conviction for stock mail fraud. He served nine months and emerged critical of the prison system.

James R. Hoffa, the $100,000-a-year president of the International Brotherhood of Teamsters in the United States, was sentenced to an eight-year term in 1967 for jury-tampering. His treatment did not parallel the exotic jail life of Sinclair. The Federal Bureau of Prisons fired an employee who reportedly let Hoffa enjoy a steak in a restaurant.

Among the jailed wealthy in modern times, General Electric vice presidents William Ginn, Lewis Burger, George Burens and Edward Jung served thirty days each for their roles in an $88-billion price-fixing conspiracy involving nineteen companies.

Billy Sol Estes, Texas boy-wonder millionaire, and Anthony DeAngelis, former New Jersey salad-oil king, were tried and sentenced to prison for swindling fellow financiers on loans backed by nonexistent products in warehouses or tanks. DeAngelis invoked loses around $190 million and collapsed fifteen unwary companies. At last report both were in prison; treatment reports were unavailable.

History is studded with a few millionaires, such as utility mogul Sam Insull and former stock wizard Richard Whitney, whose empires collapsed before they went to prison. Few individuals have entered prison with great wealth.

This limited compendium should not exclude, for contrast, mention of America's leading ex-convict, the late Charles A. Ward. Ward became cellmate of a millionaire named Bigelow who was convicted of income tax evasion in the twenties and was serving time in the Leavenworth penitentiary. When Bigelow was freed he facilitated Ward's release and made Ward an executive in Brown and Bigelow, the largest calendar house in the world. Ward became the multimillionaire president of the company. He led the United States in employment of ex-convicts and was proud of his life and record. Ward contributed to the late Robert F. Stroud's campaign for release and similar causes.

77. The federal trial and court ruling were unusual. Harry F. Sinclair and Albert Fall were tried on charges of conspiracy to defraud the government. During the trial, Sinclair hired Burns detectives to follow jurors. The United States attorney asked for a mistrial, which was granted. After an eleven-week hearing on a charge of contempt, Judge Frederick L. Siddons of the Washington, D. C., Supreme Court ruled that having jurors shadowed constituted contempt of court even

though no contact was made. Sinclair appealed from the ruling and lost. He was sentenced to a total of nine months: six months for contempt of court and three months for contempt of the Senate. Few United States attorneys today are aware of the Siddons ruling and indeed have ever heard of "shadowing" a jury.

Sinclair's comment on the jury charge was that "observation of a jury only became contempt of court when I engaged in it. I only did what I did because of the conviction that attempts would be made to influence the jury against me and felt justified in so doing because of the knowledge that the same identical practice had been indulged in by the government so frequently that it had become a common occurrence." Associated Press Biographical Service, 3313, November 13, 1947.

78. In convict language, "Sinclair clammed up and beat a big rap." With former Secretary of the Navy Albert B. Fall, Sinclair was tried for conspiracy to defraud the government in the leasing of Teapot Dome oil lands in 1922. In 1927, amid public uproar, the United States Supreme Court invalidated the lease and Sinclair was called before a United States Senate oil committee to answer questions regarding bribery and conspiracy. Sinclair refused. Meanwhile, the conspiracy trial took place and Sinclair was acquitted. Albert Fall was sentenced to a year in prison and served nine months in the New Mexico state penitentiary.

Harry Sinclair, before his prison sentence a millionaire oil king at thirty-three, bounced back into domination of the Sinclair oil empire in 1930. He arranged a merger of Sinclair Consolidated with the Rockefeller-controlled Prairie Oil Company. The righteous John D. Rockefeller, Jr., agreed to the merger only on conditions that Sinclair's name be stricken from the company title. But in 1943 the company was renamed Sinclair Oil Corporation. In 1954, when Harry Ford Sinclair stepped down as chairman of the board, Sinclair Oil Corporation was worth $1.2 billion. Sinclair died in Pasadena, California, two years later, at the age of eighty.

79. In the *Saturday Evening Post* of January 26, 1924, is a picture captioned "Natives Hauling American Material and Machinery for the Angola Oil Fields, West Africa." The white man in the picture is probably Carl Panzram. The series of articles by Isaac Marcosson includes a

discussion of Sinclair Consolidated's penetration of Angola, Portuguese West Africa, a concession of 60,000 square miles, much of it on the coast.

80. At this time, the Hole was easier to endure than earlier models, which were abolished in 1916. Triangular in shape, these six "dark holes" were located on the second floor of the Isolation building. They were deliberately dark and uncomfortable because they were designed for punishment. The prisoner, after being tried and found guilty by the deputy warden, was stripped of his regular clothes and handed a set of ragged cotton longjohns and cloth slippers. A guard escorted him to a vacant dungeon, shutting him inside by padlocking a heavy wooden door made of several thicknesses of flooring material. The only furnishing was a sanitary bucket and a tin cup. During working hours, a man on punishment was handcuffed to the door. At noon he was let down long enough to eat some small pieces of bread. The cells were not completely dark during the day because of a small amount of light and air entering an iron mesh near the ceiling. Radiators were affixed to this ceiling, and Stroud ("A Voice from the Grave," *Looking Outward*, pp. 244–247) reports that some guards turned the steam up or down, depending on the season, to punish men in the Hole who made a disturbance. At night, according to Stroud, dungeon prisoners were given a small piece of blanket which was too small for adequate cover. The peculiar shape of the cell made it impossible for the prisoner to stretch out comfortably, and sleeping or resting has to be done with one's feet on the wall, or the body curled up in fetal position, convicts reported.

81. It was accepted by many experienced Leavenworth inmates that the only way to get out of third grade was to commit an offense serious enough to be placed in Isolation. This was so because, they said, the more vengeful guards in third grade would sometimes wait until a man was due to be released from this low status before writing a report which would send him back to start over again. Many convicts reportedly owed several years in third grade at the time of discharge.

82. The question of "face" was reflected to some degree in the *de facto* gradation of offenses which could be committed by a convict. Stroud noted, for instance, that hitting a guard during an escape attempt was not considered very serious unless the guard were need-

lessly injured. However, striking a guard in a fit of anger, even if it resulted in no injury, was looked on as a grave matter. In addition to the question of "face" was the universal staff fear of any kind of action which could lead to riot.

The status system in prison is of profound importance and has received growing attention from sociologists (see Gresham Sykes, *Society of Captives: A Study of a Maximum Security Prison* [Princeton, N.J.: Princeton University Press, 1958].) Outsiders are likely to make dangerous mistakes and false inferences concerning what are the important values in a prison society.

83. What factors operate in the ability of a prisoner under solitary confinement to endure, stay sane and to accomplish?

Panzram probably spent a total of four years in one or another kind of solitary. The longest period was in Dannemora, where he was segregated from other men for two and a half years.

In 1874 Jesse Pomeroy was sentenced in Massachusetts at the age of fourteen to "life in solitary confinement." He served thirty-eight years alone, some of it under heavy restrictions in a "coke oven" type of cell. See "The Life and Crimes of Jesse Harding Pomeroy," *Journal of Maine Medical Association* 39, no. 4 (April 1948).

Joe Redenbaugh served several years of tough isolation in the Stillwater, Minnesota, prison as a result of murder convictions in 1917. He was a teenager at the time, and served in prison for forty-five years. He became well-educated. He was freed in the spring of 1962 and is now working in an electronic firm. See Giles Playfair and Derrick Sington, *The Offenders* (New York: Simon and Schuster, 1957).

Probably the longest term in isolation was served by Robert F. Stroud in the Leavenworth and Alcatraz federal prisons from 1916 to 1959, when he was released from isolation at the age of seventy. A comparison of the two longest solitary confinement terms in modern history—those of Stroud and Pomeroy, appears in a doctoral dissertation by Thomas E. Gaddis, "The Evolution of Personality under Correctional Stress" (University of Oregon, 1963).

84. Professor Sheldon Glueck is one of the handful of researchers concerned with crime as early as 1928 who survives to this day (April 1970). A naturalized United States citizen born in Warsaw, he has been

for decades a research associate in criminology at Harvard University. He was a consultant in the Nuremberg war crimes trials and has served on committees for the United States Supreme Court. Among his many works is a little-remembered but important introduction to a reprint of a book by John Augustus of Boston, who originated one of the few American innovations in criminal justice: the probation system (*John Augustus, First Probation Officer: Reprint of the Original Report of John Augustus, Published in Boston in 1852, with an introduction by Sheldon Glueck* [New York: National Probation Association, 1939].)

Professor Glueck and his wife, Eleanor, have become noted in recent years for a decade-long, complex and controversial study of predelinquent patterns of reaction, with a view to treatment and control *before* offenses are committed, a concept condemned by libertarians.

85. Aside from considerations of its sheer size, the evolution of the Federal Bureau of Prisons into an effective model for reform has been impeded historically by an anachronism of governmental structure. The F.B.P. remains in the Department of Justice, the prosecuting arm of the government. Since improvement and reformation are not part of prosecution, many state governments have long since divorced their prison systems from their attorney general's domain.

Conditions in federal prisons today have come far since the twenties. Some of the improvements in federal institutions are the most advanced in the country. But however paternalistic and well subsidized, prisons are traditionally confused and usually hostile to the consideration of the rights of inmates to create, to be heard and to have their legal rights defined. A number of book manuscripts are buried in federal-prison files; see Paul W. Tappan, "The Legal Rights of Prisoners," *Annals of the American Academy of Political and Social Science* 293 (May 1954): 99–111. For a more recent summary of legal decisions in this field, see Rubin, "Developments in Correctional Law."

Increased protection of the rights of individuals, especially of defendants and prisoners, was provided by United States Supreme Court decisions in the fifties and sixties. These decisions (the *Gideon* decision in particular) are partially indebted for a "corpus of precedents" to the work of probably the most astute "con lawyer" of modern times, an Irishman who served a six-year sentence in a New York state prison during the forties. Patrick O'Rafferty, a self-educated man, had conceived a deep respect for the United States Constitution, which he had first encountered during his legal readings in the Dublin library at the time of the Irish "Troubles."

Using for a desk an orange crate in his cell, O'Rafferty wrote brilliant legal briefs for a series of precedent-making appeals to higher courts. He established the "writ of error coram nobis," derived from the English common law, in this country (See *Canizio* v. *New York,* 327 U.S. 82; *Lyons* v. *Goldstein,* 219 N.Y. 19; *Betts* v. *Brady,* 316 U.S. 455). Twenty years later, the United States Supreme Court overruled the adverse decision in this last case, in *Gideon* v. *Wainwright,* 372 U.S. 335, in 1963. O'Rafferty's successful appeal to the United States Supreme Court in the Canizio case and successful reversals in the New York State higher courts reduced some of the vicious practices of state attorneys and other prosecutors, as well as judges, in their interpretation of law with respect to prior felony convictions, perjury knowingly used by a prosecutor, denial of counsel, and similar violations of individual rights.

Prison censorship is a little-researched area. Many state prisons are superior to federal prisons in recognizing the individual's right to create and to communicate. Instructive contrast in the study of federal prison censorship is afforded by the cases of Robert F. Stroud and of Joseph Valachi, the Cosa Nostra gangster. The Justice Department encouraged publication of Valachi's confession, ignoring federal prison rules, only to reverse its decision under pressure from Italian-American groups who resented the ethnocentric implications of high visibility for the Mafia. The result was an action by the United States Attorney General, the first of its kind in history, to ban a book. After a face-saving compromise, the substance of the Valachi revelations and some documentation were published in an appalling account, *The Valachi Papers,* by Peter Maas (New York: G. P. Putnam's Sons, 1968).

In contrast, Robert Stroud fought without success for twenty years to get his manuscripts out of prison. Civil action in a federal court after his death finally caused the government to back down and release his historical manuscripts, mooting the legal issue before a precedent could be set. See Thomas E. Gaddis "The Civil Litigation of R. F. Stroud," *Criminologica* 3, no. 4 (February 1966).

86. The existence of this will was revealed in a letter dated September 12, 1930 from Dr. Van Horn to the superintendent of the Minnesota State Training School. Van Horn evidently was trying to research a paper on Panzram, and he obtained from the school the only existing copy of the municipal court record under which Panzram was remanded in 1903. There is no clue that Van Horn ever published this paper, and all efforts to locate the documents have failed. The Federal Bureau of Prisons says it does not have possession of the will, nor the confiscated Panzram manuscript.

87. The Little Blue Books of the Haldeman-Julius Company sold for five cents each and were the precursors of the paperback industry in the United States. Parallel publications, for comparatively more money, were the Tauchnitz editions in Europe. Such editions were the poor man's avenue to classical literature. Blue books were not allowed in federal prisons in Panzram's day.

88. Panzram's concern for Lesser and the guard's possible work in a boys' training school stimulated the prisoner to outline his thoughts about how to conduct such a school:

> If you are going to get a job in that boys' training school, and if you intend to make a study and a life work of the delinquency and the rehabilitation of young boys, then this won't do any harm, and may be of some benefit, not only to yourself in your work, but also the youngsters that you will have to teach and guard; that's why I am offering you these few ideas and suggestions.
>
> You know that I spent several years in one of those places when I was a boy and the so-called training that I received while there is mainly the cause of my being the degenerate beast that I am today. I have thought about that system of training young boys for all of my life and I know that the whole system is wrong. That system, of beating goodness religion and Jesus into boys in 99 times out of 100 has the direct opposite effect of taking all of the goodness, kindness and love out of them and then replacing those feelings

with hate, envy, deceit, tyranny and every other kind of meanness there is. If you are really sincere in wanting to teach those boys how to grow up to be good men, then you will have to go at it far differently than the way I was taught. If you should be appointed the commander of one of the companies of boys, you will find when you start out that by far the largest majority of them are already in such a frame of mind that they will be suspicious of you and your methods in handling them.

You will find that their minds are already poisoned and twisted into believing the worst of everybody and you especially. You will never be able to accomplish much with any of them until you first gain their good will and confidence. You can never gain either until you absolutely assure them that you're not a liar or a hypocrite. This you will have to prove by word and deed to them.

Once you are able to convince them that you yourself are a good, clean honorable man, and that you mean only good to them, then they will listen and believe you.

When you get there, you will find that they are all being taught a lot of bull by a lot of lying hypocrites just the same as I was taught when I was a boy, with just about the same results. I know now that if I had it all to do over again and if I had any choice in what subjects I should be instructed, then my real choice should be to disregard all hypocrisy and foolish impractical things such as are taught today in the name of religion. That's the bunk. The Golden Rule is religion enough to teach any boy. Teach them the meaning of such things as truth, lie; honest, thief; honor, dishonor; bravery, cowardice; clean, dirty; love, hate.

For each lesson just take one word. For instance, take the word truth. Teach them the full meaning of that one word in all its tenses. Then teach them how to spell it, pronounce it, and speak and write it in every day usage. Teach them what it really means to be truthful, how they will be respected by all others and how they will respect themselves by being truthful. Teach them by example, word and deed until they throughly know that one word Truth.

The next day for the next lesson, take the antonym of truth, the word lie or liar. Teach that word until it is thoroughly understood, and what a despicable thing a real liar is. Show them the harm it does, show them that it does no good and only harm to lie. How a liar loses his own self-respect and the respect of all others and then on the other hand show them what a mean thing a liar is.

After these two lessons are over, let each boy write out a short composition of what he has learned and his belief and theories of same. Keep all of each boys' records on file. Keep track of each time he tells the truth or lies. Keep a separate record of each boy's conduct. Give him credits for his truthfulness, and punish him for lying. Let these records be the real standard to judge the boy by as to the fitness or unfitness for release from the institution. Don't judge the boy because he learns or does not learn his Sunday school lessons or because he is mischievous and misbehaves by having a fight with another boy or breaking something or because he does not do his work, or some of the other standards they use today in judging of boys' fitness or his unfitness. Only a fool will judge another person for what he does. They should be judged not for what they do but for *how they do it and why they do it.*

One or two words like these each day will do more to make better men out of young boys than all the long-haired wind bags and all the Bibles in the world.

You will find that the boys will all be interested. Their new words will be in their vocabularies in every day usage. They will believe in these lessons because they will be true and something they can see, feel, taste, or wear or keep always, and not merely a piece of paper full of hot air that they have no real belief in.

You will find that when you go to that place to work, they will have some sort of a credit system that they use to judge boys by. So many credits for each day's good behavior. When a boy has earned a certain amount, he is elegible for parole.

The boys who get their credits the soonest are usually the most despicable ones of the lot. They are the clever liars, the hypocrites and the stool pigeons. But they sure do learn their Sunday school lessons, all right. And they know how to be very polite stool pigeons by saying Yes sir, No sir, and please sir, good morning sir and how do you do, sir. But all these are merely surface feelings, and their real feelings are hidden out of sight where you will have a hard time discovering them.

If you have a list of synonyms and antonyms, you just get it out some time and make out a long list of words much as I have written down and then you study each one and teach what you have learned to those boys. When you get that job, you will find out that there are several hours each day when the boys have nothing to do except to plan mischief. Those hours you could take and put to good use. You could accomplish more if you should follow my suggestions than all of the rest put together.

Teach them how to be gentlemen; teach them the first rule of conduct of a gentleman is to have consideration for the other fellow.

Such things as these you can easily teach them. Let others if they will, teach them how to learn Sunday school lessons, scrub floors, work and be hypocrites, liars and rogues, as I was taught when I was a boy.

89. Johnny Wren, an ex-boxer who was placed in Isolation for knifing and disfiguring a young convict in a jealous rage. A notorious bully and gang rapist, Wren was ostracized in Isolation, where he slowly went insane, writing threatening letters to Warden White and repeatedly being thrown into the Hole for doing so. He later died in a federal institution for the criminally insane.

90. Panzram's notions anticipated the mass industrial growth of dried foods processing. Drum, spray and now foam-mat food-drying have begun to return to low levels of heat—under 135 degrees Fahrenheit—to preserve vitamins and to avoid flavor and color deterioration. Data supplied by Don O'Neill, Foamat Foods Corporation, Corvallis, Oregon.

91. See *Handbook of American Prisons, 1926.*

Despite obstacles of many kinds, however, the Federal Bureau of Prisons managed to institute a series of improvements in federal institutions. Prison industries, improved education, more adequate physical conditions of confinement and better-trained personnel were important developments. Unfortunately, and possibly inevitably, the system became bureaucratized and came to wield great power, with institutions that included anachronisms like Alcatraz and, upon its abandonment, a super-Alcatraz built and now functioning in Marion, Illinois. It was built over the objections of the best criminologists and its existence is clouded in supersecrecy that makes it virtually unknown outside of custody circles.

For a discussion of what the authors term "the frenzy for security and custody," see Barnes and Teeters, *New Horizons in Criminology,* pp. 440–464.

92. At this writing Professor Austin MacCormick is seventy-seven years old and still going strong. MacCormick, one of the best-informed men in the world on prisons, has combined political acumen and writing talent into a raft for survival in the tossing waters of corrections work since 1917. A crusading reformer in the steps of the pioneer Thomas Mott Osborne, MacCormick was one of the architects of the Federal Bureau of Prisons, where he served as assistant director from 1929 to 1933. Later he became professor of criminology at the University of California at Berkeley. He was called often as an impartial investigator of prison conditions.

In the twenties MacCormick edited the annual Handbooks of American Prisons, financed by the Osborne Society (also known as the National Society for Penal Information). This series was virtually the only authoritative investigation of prisons during the twenties. In fact, no survey comparable has been made since, especially of the federal prison system. Correctional moguls have things self-contained except, in Negley Teeter's phrase, for "an occasional will o' the wisp" which sheds a faint light into their hidden domains.

MacCormick's later investigation reports drew criticism from reformers as "too political." Dr. Vernon Fox in the 1952 Michigan prison riot investigation and more recently Dr. Tom Murton in the attempted reform of the notorious Tucker and Cummins prisons in Arkansas, registered complaints. See Vernon Fox, *Violence Behind Bars* (New York: Vantage Press, 1959); *Accomplices to the Crime* by Tom Murton and Joseph Hyams (New York: Grove Press, 1969).

93. Prison literature is one of the most grossly undervalued founts of human insight and social change in history. The following names and titles constitute a cursory overview of prisoner contributions,

offered without evaluation, but with the suggestion that the hiding, suppression or withholding of conceptual works of prisoners, regardless of offense, should itself be made a federal crime: Caryl Chessman, John Cleland, Eamon De Valera, John Bunyan, Martin Dies, Milovan Djilas, Fyodor Dostoevski, Mohandas K. Gandhi, Adolf Hitler, Sir Thomas Malory, Jawaharlal Nehru, Ezra Pound, Robert F. Stroud, Joe Valachi, Oscar Wilde.

94. The protagonist-killers of Truman Capote's *In Cold Blood* (New York: Random House, 1966; New American Library, Signet Books, 1967), Richard E. Hickok and Perry E. Smith, were hanged in Kansas in 1965 for the murder of the Clutter family.

The abolition of the death penalty and its restoration in various states forms a fascinating if somewhat macabre study. In 1872, Kansas passed the so-called "Maine Law," which allowed no execution of any defendant until a year after his conviction. Then, in 1907, Kansas abolished capital punishment, only to bring it back in 1935.

> Between the peak of the Progressive Era and the years when women got the vote and whiskey got the gate, no less than eight states. . . . abolished the death penalty for murder and for most other crimes. In only a few states did the reform last, however. By 1921, Tennessee, Arizona, Washington, Oregon and Missouri had reinstated it. During the Prohibition Era, when law enforcement often verged on total collapse, the abolitionists were nearly routed in several states. Had it not been for the persuasive voices of Clarence Darrow, the great "attorney for the damned," and of Lewis E. Lawes, the renowned warden of Sing Sing Prison, and the organization in 1927 of the American League to Abolish Capital Punishment, the lawless era of the twenties might have seen the death penalty reintroduced in every state in the Union," Hugo A. Bedau, *The Death Penalty in America,* rev. ed. (New York: Doubleday & Co., Anchor Books, 1967), 10.

The Bedau book is an absorbing and authoritative study of the death penalty. With respect to the federal government, the author points out that in the 1880s Congress reduced the dozens of capital crimes to three: murder, treason and rape. More than thirty crimes are still punishable by death in various states, but most of them are legal curiosities and are not operational. By 1970, more than fifteen states had again abolished the death penalty and actual executions in the United States had become a rarity, although prisoners in Death Rows throughout the country were piling up.

President Nixon, an asserted Quaker (the Society of Friends opposes capital punishment), requested the death penalty for homicide by bombing in 1970.

95. This test of criminal responsibility, fundamental in English and American jurisprudence, holds that an offender pleading guilty by reason of insanity must be subject to some mental disease or disorder, and that this mental impairment prevents him from knowing that his act was wrong. The formula was established following the case of Daniel McNaughton in 1843. McNaughton was a paranoid who believed he was being persecuted by Peel, the prime minister of England. He intended to kill Peel, but in error shot and killed the prime minister's secretary. McNaughton was tried, and the jury found him not guilty by reason of insanity. The verdict was debated in the House of Lords, which appealed to the fifteen judges of England to make a determination of the question of criminal responsibility in such cases. The judges' response was the rule stated above: briefly, that the accused must lack the knowledge and ability to distinguish between right and wrong if he is to be excused from criminal liability.

The McNaughton rule has come under professional attack for years. For a spirited defense of the rule against the stream of attack, see Wertham, *Cain,* pp. 246–259.

In 1970, the McNaughton rule was discarded by the United States Ninth Circuit Court of Appeals with the statement that "knowing right from wrong" is not enough. "It fails to attack the problem where the accused may have understood his actions, but was incapable of controlling his actions," according to Circuit Judge Walter Ely. "The new rule holds that a person is not responsible if, as a result of mental disease or defect, he lacks substantial capacity either to appreciate the criminality of his conduct, or to conform his conduct to the requirements of law."

The 127-year-old McNaughton rule was last upheld by the United States Supreme Court in 1897. Only one federal appeals court, the

First Circuit in Boston, still adheres to it. Gene Blake, Los Angeles *Times*, April 1970.

96. Panzram's defense of himself in favor of his own death raises a host of issues.

Attempted suicide had been a felony in Kansas since 1925. To aid another to commit suicide is manslaughter in many states. Panzram made his desire to die abundantly clear; anyone who facilitated his death would be committing a crime. The prisoner who helped a fellow convict cheat the executioner would be guilty of a felony. Then what about a jury, or a judge, whose decision results in the death of someone who is trying to commit suicide?

In the current age, where death is both more immediate (in television in the living room, and everywhere on the highway), and more remote (the lengthening of senescence by medical means), the taking of one's life has now surfaced as a discussible subject. The treatment of suicidogenic individuals has reached the agency stage in prevention centers and has stimulated a large and expanding literature. But a different climate prevailed in 1930. Frank discussion of suicide was subtly taboo even in professional circles until Menninger, Durkheim and others "legitimized" the subject as a public matter for discussion outside of the context of suicide as a sin.

Suicide is regarded by some as the last, deepest, and most inalienable right of man. The Eastern and the Western cultures differ on these matters; and in the West, respect for the individual enters into the matter with impact as our technology depersonalizes us.

In penology, there is an especially little-known side to suicide: the right to fast was once respected as a decision of the individual. Terence MacSwiney, the jailed mayor of Cork in Ireland, fasted to death for his principles. Gandhi's fasts altered history. Today, any federal convict who elects to fast is seized, spread-eagled and tube-fed, whether sane or insane, sick or well. The rights of the free individual come into sharper focus when we look at the rights of the institutionalized individual. Both are shrinking.

The increasing numbers of people in the world invite more open discussions of these matters. Suicide ceased to be a crime in New York in 1919, in England, in 1961.

There are too many varieties of suicide for discussion here, except that the Panzram situation might be termed by some a "balance suicide" (Joost A. M. Meerloo, *Suicide and Mass Suicide* [New York and London, Grune & Stratton, 1962], p. 15), that is, on balance, the factors involved in further living made life no longer feasible for Carl Panzram.

Compare "alimentary rape" by tube-feeding of convicts who hunger-strike with the prolongation of life of the old and the terminally afflicted. "In our mechanized era," Meerloo states, "people have lost the right to die their own death" (p. 101). Against this rises the specter of euthanasia and death in the doctor's hypodermic. And more frightening still is the disenchantment of some biologists with the results of humanism in the perpetuation of the defective. See Robert Ardrey, *The Social Contract* (New York: Atheneum, forthcoming 1970; excerpted in *Life* magazine, February 20, 1970, pp. 48ff.)

For a fascinating and authoritative discussion of these subjects from a unique vantage point, read the arguments for and against capital punishment in Bedau, *Death Penalty,* in particular the discussion of the prisoner's right to die, pp. 217-220.

97. The first three paragraphs are taken from letter of Karl Menninger to James O. Long, June 13, 1968; the fourth paragraph, from his *Man Against Himself*.

98. Topeka *State Journal,* April 16, 1930.

99. "This difference is in my favor." By this, of course, Panzram meant that the trial furthered his desire to die. He was making use of the retributory quality of criminal law. "Criminal law is really a legitimate way of hating," according to Professor Caleb Foote, University of California Law School. Peter Tugman, Portland *Oregonian,* March 2, 1969.

Panzram goes on to say, "I was not only given what the people wanted to give me, but what I also wanted them to give me." The defendant thus destroys the punitive power, even of a death sentence, by identifying with death.

"Self-destruction is the last image of power; it is the last means of maintaining a feeling of being valuable and potent." Meerloo, *Suicide,* p. 74.

100. Details of hangings and the literature of the gallows, including gallows humor, have been covered by writers interested in the subject. For an introduction to this macabre lore, see August Mencken, ed., *By the Neck: A Book of Hangings* (New York: Hastings House, 1942); the ironic classic by Charles Duff, *A New Handbook on Hanging* (London: Andrew Melrose, 1954; there have been four editions since the book was written in 1928); Arthur Koestler, *Reflections on Hanging* (New York: Macmillan Co., 1957); and more recently for the United States, Negley K. Teeters and Jack Hedblom, *Hang by the Neck* (Springfield, Ill.: Charles Thomas Co., 1967).

101. The same public which gives its heart to good causes can be manipulated by ruthless officials to express its mob denominator. Prisoners are among the most helpless of minority victims, and the swings between decency and brutal repression are wilder in institutions than in the world outside.

As William Alanson White pointed out years ago, we toil in prison work to give the underdog a better kennel rather than to make a basic change.

The 1970s are ushered in by a crisis in the United States of such unprecedented depth that the prison problem is dwarfed in importance. Yet crime in the United States is now the worst in the civilized world, according to the National Commission on the Causes and Prevention of Violence. How much of felony crime is related to seven generations of prison policy is a speculation for sociologists.

102. Barnes and Teeters, *New Horizons in Criminology*, p. 442.

103. Wilson's book *My Six Convicts: A Psychologist's Three Years in Fort Leavenworth* (New York: Rinehart & Co., 1951) became the most widely read bestseller about prison life since World War II. Its romanticized anecdotes drew violent criticism from the fossilized prison establishment. Wilson did not push back, and and as a result, *My Six Convicts* was officially condemned by the American Prison Association. This affected Wilson's professional standing and morale. But Chapters 9 and 17 of his book, covering punishment and narcotics, are landmark pieces of concentrated writing in this field. Wilson collaborated with Dr. Harry Elmer Barnes in an article on drugs for *Life*

magazine in the middle fifties. Their approach to the drug problem was so advanced that *Life* refused to print it without changes. Wilson refused to weaken the piece, which still remains in the magazine's files, an unprinted classic.

104. Gerold Frank later abandoned ghostwriting for actresses to write the chilling *The Boston Strangler* (New York: New American Library, Signet Books, 1967).

105. Books about miscarriages of justice are rare. In addition to Edward D. Radin, *The Innocents* (New York: William Morrow and Co., 1964), see Edwin M. Borchard, *Convicting the Innocent* (New Haven, Conn.: Yale University Press, 1932) and Erle S. Gardner, *Court of Last Resort* (Clifton, N. J.: William Sloane Associates, 1952).

INDEX

POST OFFICE BOX 7

31614.

Leavenworth, Kansas April 1. 1929.

Mr. Henry James.
% Miss Elanor Trott.
The Lenmar. Apt 47.
2100. N. St. N. W.
Washington.
D. C.

Mr. James:

Your letter of March 30th was handed to me this evening and I am answering at once to thank you for it and its enclosure of one dollar. Your letter was quite short but straight to the point as usual. I enjoyed reading it and I expect to enjoy the spending of your dollar. I never got the post card which you sent me.

This is my first letter since I have been here. I shall be glad to hear from you at any time you care to drop me a line. You can write to me without sending me any money. I'll be glad to hear from you just the same and I'll allways answer you.

There is very little news that I can give you because there is none to give so far as I know. I have been here 2 months today. Nothing very unusual has happened to me so far. I have been treated just the same as every-body else here. I have no complaints of any kind. What the future may have in store for me I dont know or very much care. Your postscript in regards to Allen was the natural result to be expected considering the conditions and circumstances in which he was situated. He will be the gainer in the long run. That sort of a man will allways be up in front sooner or later.

I believe you know the regulations about my privilage in letter writing. So please dont ever send me any thing unless your sure I'll get it. I dont need anything. I can manage all rights. My wants are very little and I think